CW01662997

Young Women, Work, and Family in England 1918–1950

Young Women, Work, and Family in England 1918–1950

SELINA TODD

OXFORD
UNIVERSITY PRESS

This book has been printed digitally and produced in a standard specification in order to ensure its continuing availability

OXFORD
UNIVERSITY PRESS

Great Clarendon Street, Oxford OX2 6DP

Oxford University Press is a department of the University of Oxford.
It furthers the University's objective of excellence in research, scholarship,
and education by publishing worldwide in

Oxford New York

Auckland Cape Town Dar es Salaam Hong Kong Karachi
Kuala Lumpur Madrid Melbourne Mexico City Nairobi
New Delhi Shanghai Taipei Toronto
With offices in
Argentina Austria Brazil Chile Czech Republic France Greece
Guatemala Hungary Italy Japan South Korea Poland Portugal
Singapore Switzerland Thailand Turkey Ukraine Vietnam

Oxford is a registered trade mark of Oxford University Press
in the UK and in certain other countries

Published in the United States
by Oxford University Press Inc., New York

© Selina Todd 2005

The moral rights of the author have been asserted

Database right Oxford University Press (maker)

Reprinted 2009

All rights reserved. No part of this publication may be reproduced,
stored in a retrieval system, or transmitted, in any form or by any means,
without the prior permission in writing of Oxford University Press,
or as expressly permitted by law, or under terms agreed with the appropriate
reprographics rights organization. Enquiries concerning reproduction
outside the scope of the above should be sent to the Rights Department,
Oxford University Press, at the address above

You must not circulate this book in any other binding or cover
And you must impose this same condition on any acquirer

ISBN 978-0-19-928275-3

For
Ruth Todd
and
Nigel Todd

Acknowledgements

My apprehension that this would prove too solitary a project for sanity was proved wrong by the support of many people, only a few of whom can be thanked by name here. The project began as a doctoral thesis and my thanks must go first to my D.Phil. supervisors, Pat Thane and Ian Gazeley—truly 'without whoms'. My D.Phil. examiners, Paul Johnson and Claire Langhamer, offered excellent advice that helped this book to find a publisher. Thanks are due to Anne Gelling, my editor at OUP, whose efficiency and advice immeasurably aided the process of turning the original manuscript into a publication. Numerous people have offered invaluable comments and criticisms, among them members of research seminars at the Universities of Cambridge, London, and Warwick, and graduate and faculty members of the University of Sussex's lively and supportive History Department, where Carol Dyhouse, Alun Howkins, and Ben Jones deserve special mention.

For their assistance and expertise, I thank the staff of the various libraries and archives consulted. I was kindly permitted to use archived oral history interviews by Professor Richard Brown; Mrs Josie Castle; Miss E. M. Rodger; the Imperial War Museum Sound Archive; the North-West Sound Archive; Nottingham City Council, Leisure and Community Services, Local Studies Library; Reading Museum Service; and Tameside Local Studies Library.

I could not have undertaken this project without an ESRC D.Phil. Studentship, while its completion was greatly assisted by a Scouloudi Fellowship at the Institute of Historical Research; an ESRC Postdoctoral Fellowship at the Centre for Contemporary British History, University of London; and, latterly, a Research Fellowship at Girton College, Cambridge. That I was able to reach graduate-level study was largely due to being an undergraduate in the era before the abolition of state maintenance grants and the levying of tuition fees, and to a fully comprehensive schooling, where John Bell was an outstanding history teacher.

The friendship, hospitality, discussion, and distraction offered by, among others, Lucy Robinson, Liz Allen, Manus and Joseph Doherty,

Daniel Cuzner, Jane Greening, Lin Harwood, Toby Harrison, Tara Kielmann, Alex Shepard, and Lesley Whitworth have been greatly appreciated, as has Andy Davies's intellectual and emotional support. Finally, the book is dedicated to Ruth and Nigel Todd, who survived tripartite education and the youth labour market to fight against the injustices experienced there, but have still found time to be the most supportive of parents.

Contents

List of Figures

List of Tables

Abbreviations

AEU	Amalgamated Engineering Union
ASE	Amalgamated Society of Engineers
ATS	Auxiliary Territorial Service
AWCS	Association of Women Clerks and Secretaries
CCWTE	Central Committee for Women's Training and Employment
CPGB	Communist Party of Great Britain
GMWU	General and Municipal Workers' Union
HP	Hire purchase
JEB	Juvenile Employment Bureau
JEE	Juvenile Employment Exchange
JIC	Juvenile Instruction Centre
JUC	Juvenile Unemployment Centre
LEA	Local Education Authority
LHU	Leicestershire Hosiery Union
NFWW	National Federation of Women Workers
NUC	National Union of Clerks
NUDAW	National Union of Distributive and Allied Workers
NUGW	National Union of General Workers
NUWM	National Unemployed Workers' Movement
PAB	Public Assistance Board
PEP	Political and Economic Planning
TGWU	Transport and General Workers' Union
TUC	Trades Union Congress
TUCGC	Trades Union Congress General Council
UCWU	United Clothing Workers' Union
WAAF	Women's Auxiliary Air Force
WRNS	Women's Royal Naval Service
WTUL	Women's Trade Union League
WU	Workers' Union
YES	Youth Employment Service
YWCA	Young Women's Christian Association

Money

s	Shillings
d	Pence

Where calculations involving money are presented, money is presented in decimal form; thus, 3d becomes 0.25s.

Abbreviations of archives are noted in the Bibliography.

Introduction

Between the end of the First World War and the late 1940s, young women workers served as motifs of social, economic, and cultural continuity and change. The figurative 'clumping of the mill-girls' clogs down the cobbled street'[1] in Orwell's *Road to Wigan Pier* spoke evocatively of depressed, interwar northern England, while the combined optimism and disquiet caused by the development of new industries and mass consumerism was embodied in the young factory workers 'with lipstick copied from actresses'.[2] Young women between the school-leaving age—12 prior to 1921, 14 from 1921 until 1947, 15 thereafter—and 24 years of age constituted a significant proportion of the labour force, accounting for over 45 per cent of the female workforce throughout this period. The average age of first marriage among women never fell below 24 between 1918 and 1950—the reason it forms the upper age limit of this study—and consequently paid work was a distinguishing characteristic of youth for many women. Work dominated their daily lives and shaped their social and domestic responsibilities and relationships.

This book is concerned with the dramatic changes in young women's employment opportunities that occurred during this period, and with the way in which these shaped the growth of youth culture, young women's familial relationships and friendship networks, and their role as agents of change within working class households and communities, as well as within workplaces. At the end of the First World War, residential domestic service was the largest employer of young women, most of whom began working between the ages of 12 and 14, primarily due to familial need. By 1950, with the school-leaving age raised to 15, many expected to enter relatively lucrative retail or clerical jobs, and their social and financial independence was increasing.

[1] G. Orwell, *The Road to Wigan Pier* (Harmondsworth: Penguin, 1962), 5.

[2] J. B. Priestley, *English Journey* (London: Heinemann, 1934), 212.

In examining these changes, this study illuminates the English experience of a wider trend that has been traced across Western Europe and North America. Soland has shown that young women were increasingly prominent as wage-earners and as leisure consumers by the late 1920s in northern Europe, and that these trends were central to their representation as 'modern'.[3] In North America, young working women were at the forefront of shaping new lifestyles and identities for immigrant groups between the 1900s and the 1940s.[4] Such studies demonstrate that the 'modern' young working class woman identified by contemporaries was distinguished from her predecessors primarily in her employment and earning patterns, and by the consequences of this for her family relations and social independence. Studying young women's employment, then, offers insights not only into significant social, economic, and cultural developments in young women's lives, but also into the ways in which their actions and aspirations brought about wider changes within the workplace and within working class families and communities.

Despite the centrality of England's young woman worker to contemporary literature, social investigations, and the press, her expanding employment opportunities and social independence frequently cited as symbols of modernity,[5] this book is the first to bring her into the historical limelight. She has previously fallen between two historiographical stools: the study of paid work, which has focused on married women and on men, and the study of women's and young people's social and domestic lives. Although a body of important research on paid employment has developed over the past four decades, much of it has been concerned with adult men.[6] Since the early 1990s an increasing degree of interest has been paid to younger male workers, but most of the limited literature concentrates on the decades prior to 1914, when a

[3] B. Soland, *Becoming Modern: Young Women and the Reconstruction of Womanhood in the 1920s* (Princeton, N.J.: Princeton University Press, 2000). See also C. Benninghaus, 'Mothers' Toil and Daughters' Leisure: Working Class Girls and Time in 1920s Germany', *History Workshop Journal*, 50 (2000), 45–72.

[4] S. Glenn, *Daughters of the Schtetl: Life and Labor in the Immigrant Generation* (Ithaca, N.Y.: Cornell University Press, 1990); M. Cohen, *Workshop to Office: Two Generations of Italian Women in New York City* (Ithaca, NY: Cornell University Press, 1992).

[5] A. Bingham, *Gender, Modernity, and the Popular Press in Inter-War Britain* (Oxford: Oxford University Press, 2004), 96.

[6] See, for example, E. J. Hobsbawm, *Labouring Men* (London: Weidenfeld and Nicolson, 1964); id., *Worlds of Labour* (London: Weidenfeld and Nicolson, 1984); G. S. Jones, *Outcast London: A Study in the Relationships between Classes in Victorian London* (Oxford: Clarendon Press, 1971).

political debate over the concentration of 'boy labour' in unskilled work emerged. The lack of a similar debate over young women—the reasons for which are explored in chapter 1—is partially responsible for the exclusively male focus of such studies. Nevertheless, the gap in the literature is surprising, since, as the opening of this Introduction indicates, young women's work profoundly structured contemporary representations of them and was central to debates over the political and social status of young people and women in society.

Increasing attention has been paid to women's work since the 1980s, but many studies have concentrated narrowly upon women's participation in the expansion of light manufacturing and service sector employment over the twentieth century.[7] This overlooks the slow decline of older forms of employment, like domestic service, and the emergence of clerical and retail work as major employers. It has also fuelled a largely ahistorical debate about the potential role of women as a 'reserve army of labour', a Marxian term meant to refer to a specific group of workers defined by their labour rooted in a specific time and place (the original example being nineteenth-century agricultural labourers), rather than to a group defined by social or biological characteristics (such as women).[8] The notion that married women constituted a reserve army of labour has been used sensitively by historians like Humphries, who has used it to explain convincingly aspects of married women's changing employment patterns in twentieth-century England.[9] This book argues that when applied to specific historical contexts, the reserve army of labour hypothesis has great strength as an explanation of rural young women's increasing migration into urban areas, and in illuminating the significant shift that

[7] Among those most relevant to this study are V. Beechey, 'Some Notes on Female Wage Labour in Capitalist Production', *Capital and Class*, 3 (1977); I. Bruegel, 'Women as a Reserve Army of Labour: A Note on Recent British Experience', *Feminist Review*, 3 (1979); M. Glucksmann, *Women Assemble: Women Workers in the New Industries of Inter-war Britain* (London: Routledge, 1990); A. Amsden (ed.), *The Economics of Women and Work* (Harmondworth: Penguin, 1980). Notable historical studies that do not take this approach include L. Tilly and J. Scott, *Women, Work and Family* (London: Holt, Rinehart and Winston, 1978); J. Lewis, *Women in England 1870–1950: Sexual Divisions and Social Change* (Brighton: Harvester Wheatsheaf, 1984); E. Roberts, *Women's Work 1840–1940* (Cambridge: Cambridge University Press, 1988); P. Hudson and W. R. Lee (eds.), *Women's Work and the Family Economy in Historical Perspective* (Manchester: Manchester University Press, 1990).

[8] See, for example, V. Beechey, 'The Sexual Division of Labour and the Labour Process: A Critical Assessment of Braverman', in S. Wood (ed.), *The Degradation of Work?: Skill, Deskilling and the Labour Process* (London: Hutchinson, 1982).

[9] J. Humphries, 'The "Emancipation" of Women in the 1970s and 1980s: From the Latent to the Floating', *Capital and Class*, 20 (1983); J. Rubery, 'Structured Labour Markets, Worker Organization and Low Pay', in Amsden (ed.), *Women and Work*.

young women workers experienced from non-industrialized domestic service to industrialized employment between 1918 and 1950. In doing so, however, this study also illuminates that women workers cannot be treated as a homogeneous 'army', with significant differences being apparent between the employment patterns of married women and those of younger, single women. Moreover, it moves away from the rather narrow focus of existing studies of women's work upon their relationship to the labour process, by considering the effect of young women's employment on family and community roles and relationships. The interaction between women's domestic and workplace responsibilities has been central to historical studies of women's war work, but, again, these have been primarily concerned with married women, whose labour force participation increased dramatically in the 1940s.[10] Only a very limited number of regional case studies, the most valuable being those of Alexander,[11] Roberts,[12] and Sarsby,[13] have reflected on the interaction of youth with gender and social class in constructing women's working lives. This book draws on the methodology and findings of such studies, but offers a national perspective.

The national focus of the book, nuanced by consideration of regional variation, enables questions to be asked about the relative homeogeneity of youth, young womanhood, and the working class across this period. Social histories of the late nineteenth and twentieth centuries have demonstrated that local studies can offer a rich sense of place, and point up the continuation of important regional socio-economic, political, and cultural variation into the late 1940s.[14] However, the coverage offered by existing studies is patchy, confined largely to London, Manchester, and the Lancashire textile towns. This is largely due to the rich data they offer, the former as centres of industrial and commercial innovation, the latter as a depressed region characterized by an unusually high degree of female labour force and trade union participation. They were not, however,

[10] P. Summerfield, *Women Workers in the Second World War: Production and Patriarchy in Conflict* (London: Croom Helm, 1984); G. Braybon and P. Summerfield, *Out of the Cage: Women's Experiences in Two World Wars* (London: Pandora, 1987).

[11] S. Alexander, 'Becoming a Woman in London in the 1920s and 1930s', in ead. (ed.), *Becoming a Woman: Essays in 19th and 20th Century Feminist History* (London: Virago, 1994).

[12] E. Roberts, *A Woman's Place* (Oxford: Blackwell, 1984), 39–80.

[13] J. Sarsby, *Missuses and Mouldrunners: An Oral History of Women Pottery-Workers at Work and Home* (Milton Keynes: Open University Press, 1988).

[14] For example, Roberts, *Woman's Place*; J. White, *The Worst Street in North London: Campbell Bunk, Islington, Between the Wars* (London: Routledge, 1986); A. Davies, *Leisure, Gender and Poverty: Manchester and Salford 1900–1939* (Buckingham: Open University Press, 1992).

typical of other regions. The national coverage of this book enables an assessment of the relationship between local particularities in a range of urban and—often overlooked in existing studies—rural communities and national economic and social developments. It allows consideration of how far apparently uniform practices, such as the contribution of a worker's earnings to the household economy, were forged by localized employment patterns, thus shedding more light on the relationship between employment and social and emotional relations, and the extent of homogeneity within the English working class. This enables the argument to be made that sufficient similarities were evident in people's social and economic circumstances, and in their expectations and aspirations, to enable the identification of a specifically working class culture.

The book therefore argues that strong links existed between paid work and other aspects of people's lives, and that, consequently, employment deserves a far more central place in social history than it has recently been allotted. A growing number of extremely valuable studies of working class social life in the first half of the twentieth century have focused attention upon changes in young people's lives between the 1920s and 1950s, demonstrating that young women were increasingly distinguished from their parents by their leisure activities, appearance, and political enfranchisement. Social historians have demonstrated that youth became a distinct period of working class life much earlier than the 1950s, when most sociologists date the genesis of youth culture,[15] and have persuasively argued that young women were at least as important as young men in this development.[16] However, these studies have focused on leisure rather than on the world of work. This book demonstrates that young women's role as workers, wage-earners, and labour activists was as important as their leisure consumption in distinguishing them from earlier generations, as well as being largely responsible for their growing degree of financial and social independence.

In bridging these two largely discrete bodies of research, the book fills a gap in the broader historical studies of women's lives that have appeared over the past fifteen years and have highlighted the significance of social, economic, political, and cultural developments during this period for

15 White, *Worst Street*; Davies, *Leisure*; D. Fowler, *The First Teenagers: The Lifestyles of Young Wage-Earners in Interwar Britain* (London: Woburn Press, 1995); C. Langhamer, *Women's Leisure in England, 1920–1960* (Manchester: Manchester University Press, 2000).

16 White, *Worst Street*, 188–90; Langhamer, *Women's Leisure*, 53–60; K. Milcoy, 'Between Image and Reality: Working Class Teenage Girls' Leisure in Bermondsey during the Interwar Years', D.Phil. thesis (Sussex, 2001).

women. The location of domesticity and motherhood in contemporary political, social, and literary discourse has received attention;[17] the strengthening connection between women's leisure and consumerism has been analysed;[18] the development of women's citizenship in peace and war has been traced;[19] and the importance of suburbanization and social welfare in shaping the strategies of post-1918 feminist organizations and the lifestyles of working class women has been examined.[20] Yet although many of these studies emphasize the importance of the life cycle in shaping women's experiences, the focus is predominantly on adult women; young women are often absent, or portrayed primarily as consumers.

The centrality of paid work to young women's lives indicates that the construction of femininity was not solely centred on domestic life, as much existing research implies. The prevailing concentration on social and domestic life has failed to entirely undermine the older judgement that femininity was strongly correlated with domesticity during the interwar and post-Second World War years. Beddoe's notion that women returned to 'home and duty' following the First and Second World Wars, and that press, politicians, and feminists alike championed housewifery as women's primary profession throughout the interwar and post-1945 years[21] is, as Bingham has pointed out, not supported by the plethora of representations of women available within contemporary gender discourse.[22] The chronology of this book, and the material presented, makes

[17] B. Melman, *Women and the Popular Imagination in the Twenties: Flappers and Nymphs* (Basingstoke: Macmillan, 1988); A. Light, *Forever England: Feminism, Literature and Conservatism between the Wars* (London: Routledge, 1991).

[18] D. Beddoe, *Back to Home and Duty* (London: Pandora, 1989), 114–31; J. Giles, *Women, Identity and Private Life in Britain, 1900–1950* (Basingstoke: Macmillan, 1995); L. Whitworth, 'Men, Women, Shops and "Little Shiny Homes": The Consuming of Coventry, 1930–1939', Ph.D. thesis (Warwick, 1997).

[19] A. Bingham, ' "Stop the Flapper Vote Folly": Lord Rothermere, the Daily Mail, and the Equalization of the Franchise 1927–28', *Twentieth-Century British History*, 13:1 (2002); P. Graves, *Labour Women: Women in British Working Class Politics 1918–39* (Cambridge: Cambridge University Press, 1994); C. Law, *Suffrage and Power: The Women's Movement, 1918–1928* (London: I. B. Tauris, 1997); S. Rose, *Which People's War?: National Identity and Citizenship in Britain 1939–1945* (Oxford: Oxford University Press, 2003); P. Thane, 'What Difference did the Vote Make? Women and British Politics since 1918', in A. Vickery (ed.), *Women, Privilege and Power: British Politics 1750 to the Present* (Palo Alto, Calif. Stanford University Press, 2001).

[20] P. Thane, 'Visions of Gender in the Making of the British Welfare State: the Case of Women in the British Labour Party and Social Policy, 1906–1945', in G. Bock and Thane (eds.), *Maternity and Gender Policies: Women and the Rise of the European Welfare States 1880s–1950s* (London: Routledge, 1991); M. Pugh, *Women and the Women's Movement 1914–59* (Basingstoke: Macmillan, 1992).

[21] Beddoe, *Home and Duty*; Melman, *Popular Imagination*.

[22] Bingham, 'Flapper Vote'.

clear that both World Wars had lasting social and economic effects on young women's lives, but that cultural constructions of femininity were never as one-dimensional as existing studies imply. Domesticity was not nearly as central to young women workers' lives as paid employment, and their widespread desire to leave the workforce for marriage and domesticity in adulthood did not prevent employment affecting their lifestyles, relationships, and aspirations.

A note about terminology regarding age should be made here. Phraseology changed between 1918 and 1950, signifying wider changes in the social, political, and economic status of young people. 'Juvenile' was widely used to refer to young people between the school-leaving age and 17 until the late 1940s, when it was widely abandoned in government literature; a 'Youth' Employment Service was established in 1948. This was partly due to the raising of the school-leaving age to 15 in 1947 and points to the growing social and economic independence of youthful workers. 'Young people' was the phrase used by contemporaries to describe anyone in their teens and twenties who was unmarried. These definitions are used whenever possible in this study, with due consideration being given to the changes in these definitions that have been wrought by subsequent academic investigations. The concentration on males in existing studies of young people, for example, means that 'youth' and particularly 'youths' have become terms heavy with masculine connotations. Although the former is used pragmatically here to describe the period of life between the early teens and the mid-twenties, the latter is not. 'Teenager' is also avoided as it is an a-historical term that dates from the 1950s, and because it neglects the experiences of the considerable number of single women in their early twenties. A more appropriate general description, common to contemporary discourse, is the 'young wage-earner', emphasizing the importance of employment in the construction of young people's identities and representations of them. None of these terms, however, adequately express gendered distinctions between young people, nor heterogeneity among 'young women', the term used here to describe those aged between the school-leaving age and 24 (their male counterparts being described as 'young men'). This book shows that significant differences existed between the lifestyles of 14 to 17 year olds (defined as juvenile girls or boys) and those of 18 to 24 year olds (defined as young adult women or men). Such distinctions suggest that although 21 was an increasingly important age in political citizenship after the enfranchisement of all adult women in 1928, it had less social and economic significance.

The consideration given to the life cycle in this book questions the primacy accorded to gender dichotomy within many social histories. Young women's employment patterns, and their reactions to change within the workplace, for example, were in some important ways very similar to young men's. Arguments for the regulation of young women's employment by interwar politicians, trade unionists, and feminists, moreover, were inspired by growing concern to protect the welfare of young people, or by a desire to direct the juvenile labour supply to demand, rather than being rooted in gendered anxieties over women's 'proper' role.

The focus on age as well as gender does not, however, undermine the relevance of social class in shaping people's experience, and as a tool of historical analysis. Rather, consideration of gender and age offers a new dimension to our understanding of class relations. In doing so, this book engages with the ongoing debate over working class formation and culture. Older studies of working class life represented the period from 1880 to 1950 as one of class homogeneity, within communities defined by strong occupational continuity and political, economic, and social association, centred around trade union, Labour Party, and Co-operative Society.[23] From the late 1970s historians began to point up the marginalization of women within such studies, tracing their role in more informal social neighbourhood and kinship networks.[24] This did not explicitly challenge the existence of working class identity and community; sociological studies of the 1950s had in fact previously suggested that kinship and home cemented class and community ties.[25] However, recognition of the significance of gender and age in differentiating experience within working class communities fuelled intense debate over the relevance of class to historical analysis and to people's lives. A shift away from a Marxist emphasis on the importance of people's relationship to the means of production in the creation of a class identity occurred.[26] Greater

[23] See, for example, R. Johnson, 'Three Problematics: Elements of a Theory of Working Class Culture', in J. Clarke, C. Critcher, and R. Johnson (eds.), *Working Class Culture: Studies in History and Theory* (London: Hutchinson, 1979); Hobsbawm, *Labouring Men*, chs. 10 and 11.

[24] Two of the most notable studies are Roberts, *Woman's Place*; and E. Ross, 'Survival Networks: Women's Neighbourhood Sharing in London before World War I', *History Workshop Journal*, 15 (1983).

[25] M. Young and P. Wilmott, *Family and Kinship in East London* (Harmondsworth: Penguin, 1957); P. Townsend, *The Family Life of Old People* (Harmondsworth: Penguin, 1957).

[26] P. Joyce, *Visions of the People: Industrial England and the Question of Class 1848–1914* (Cambridge: Cambridge University Press, 1991) is one of the most comprehensive contributions to this approach.

attention began to be paid to regional identities; to the role played by consumption, which Hilton argues has 'eclipsed other social, culture and economic identities, particularly those of a productivist mentality';[27] and to the importance of gendered and generational divisions, rather than simply those of social class.[28]

Yet it has proved difficult to greatly diminish the significance of class in social historical research. The most careful and incisive histories that consider gender and life cycle in modern England, such as those undertaken by Davies and Langhamer, do not argue against the use of social class as an analytical tool; rather, in drawing heavily upon oral testimony, they have found that, as Whitworth writes, 'conventionalised motifs of poverty'[29] signified a shared experience among working class respondents, although one fractured by gender and generation. They rely, as I do, upon the Thompsonian understanding of class as a social, economic, and political relationship, which arises out of shared experience forged by productive relations.[30] Thus Davies draws on Roberts's definition of 'working class', one that I also find helpful:

> Men and women believed themselves to be working class because they worked with their hands, were employees and not employers, and, in comparison with the latter, were poor and lacked material goods: even the better-paid workers had comparatively few consumer goods and little surplus income.[31]

As this suggests, class, and particularly class consciousness—'the way in which these experiences are handled in cultural terms'[32]—cannot simply be defined by a person's occupational status. Chapter 1 points out that definitions of skilled, semiskilled, and unskilled work were contested and subjective throughout our period. No 'objective' measure of class can be given by occupational status alone. Young women's lives demonstrate the importance of the interaction between occupation and family circumstances in forging a person's class status and shaping their life experience. I have chosen to classify young women clerical workers as working class when they come from households headed by manual workers. The social class of young workers derived from parental occupations as well as their

[27] M. Hilton, 'The Fable of the Sheep, or, Private Virtues, Public Vices: The Consumer Revolution of the Twentieth Century', *Past and Present*, 176/1 (2002), 224.

[28] J. Bourke, *Working Class Cultures in Britain, 1890–1960: Gender, Class and Ethnicity* (London: Routledge, 1994); Davies, *Leisure*.

[29] Whitworth, 'Coventry', 7.

[30] E. P. Thompson, *The Making of the English Working Class*, 2nd edn. (Harmondsworth: Penguin, 1968), 8–9.

[31] Roberts, *Woman's Place*, 3–4.

[32] Thompson, *Making*, 9.

own, because the pooling of income into the family economy meant that collective household earnings defined individuals' own standard of living.[33] In addition, as chapters 4 and 7 show, young clerks from working class backgrounds, like manual workers, tended to define themselves against more affluent middle class young women.

As the example of young clerical workers suggests, social class identity and experience was defined and shaped by individuals within specific historical contexts. Individuals consciously defined their class identity through their relations with different socio-economic groups, highlighting a degree of negotiation and fluidity. However, the class experience was also shaped by factors beyond their control, like the need to pool incomes in working class households, examined in chapter 2, or the prejudice shown by teachers or employers towards children from poorer neighbourhoods, highlighted by chapter 3. This book argues, then, that young women made their own history, but not in circumstances of their own choosing.

This approach resolves a paradox that has characterized recent histories of working class life. Their prevailing focus on leisure and consumption implies that, as Joyce has argued, workplace identities and relations had little relevance for other aspects of people's lives.[34] Yet as is made clear earlier, these studies have not produced any adequate alternative to the definition of class as forged largely by a person's relationship to production. Their research supports the notion that a working class culture existed, albeit one less rigidly determined by occupational status than Hobsbawm's 'aristocracy of labour' thesis suggested.[35] It is argued in this book that this reflects a close relationship between what Lawrence calls ' "class as culture" and "class as economic role" ',[36] which can only be fully understood by examining the connections between working life and family and social life. Although Lawrence and Davies are sceptical about such links, few existing studies have attempted an extensive examination of them, instead focusing on leisure or work in isolation. This has led to conclusions that simply posit age or gender as fixed social categories rather than class. The preferential treatment that many sons received in the allocation of leisure and spending money, for example, has frequently been attributed to gender inequality, with no interrogation of the reasons for this.[37] As chapter 7 shows, such treatment

[33] E. W. Bakke, *The Unemployed Man: A Social Study* (London: Nisbet, 1932).

[34] Joyce, *Visions*, 3–8 and ch. 14.

[35] Hobsbawm, *Labouring Men*, ch. 11.

[36] J. Lawrence, 'The British Sense of Class', *Journal of Contemporary History*, 35/2 (2000), 315.

[37] Davies, *Leisure*, 88; Langhamer, *Women's Leisure*, 103.

was often shaped by the different economic and social roles that individuals played within their household. Such an approach thus allows greater analysis of the historical construction of age and gender, as well as class.

A focus on the years between 1918 and 1951 is crucial in this respect. It is a cliché to claim one's period of study as of special historical significance, and one of the aims of this book is to examine continuity over time as well as change. Moreover, it is important to avoid a Whiggish account of the development of youth culture and service sector employment that overlooks groups who, while they may have constituted the 1950s equivalent of 'the "obsolete" hand-loom weaver',[38] were extremely significant in the 1920s: chief among these are domestic servants, who remained the largest group of working women until the 1940s; others include those semiskilled workers who fought against the introduction of the mass production line.

Nevertheless, as well as witnessing some genuinely profound changes in young women's lifestyles, this period is important in the development of the working class. Despite this, it remains greatly neglected. Prior to the 1980s, the periodization of working class history was greatly influenced by Hobsbawm's argument that working class formation was largely complete by 1914,[39] whereas empirical sociological investigations of twentieth-century British society have been confined to the post-1950 period. The years between were subject to generalizations: the interwar period often viewed as one of stasis[40] or, in the popular view, of bleak depression,[41] followed by the 'People's War' defined as an important, almost complete, break with the past;[42] the late 1940s almost entirely ignored in favour of studies of the 'post-war' years, which commenced in the 1950s and emphasized political and class consensus.[43] Over the past two decades this view has been revised. Social and economic change, in the form of increasing suburbanization, the expansion of light manufacture, and a rising standard of living, have been highlighted.[44] The period has become

[38] Thompson, *Making*, 12.

[39] Hobsbawm, *Labouring Men*, ch. 11.

[40] R. Graves and A. Hodge, *The Long Weekend: A Social History of Great Britain, 1918–1939* (London: Faber, 1940).

[41] On this see Stevenson and Cook, *Britain in the Depression: Society and Politics 1929–39*, 2nd edn. (London: Longman, 1994), 3–4.

[42] A. Calder, *The People's War: Britain, 1939–1945* (London: Jonathan Cape, 1969); A. Marwick, *Britain in the Century of Total War: War, Peace and Social Change, 1900–1967* (London: Bodley Head, 1968).

[43] A. Sked and C. Cook, *Post-war Britain: A Political History* (Harmondworth: Penguin, 1993).

[44] Stevenson and Cook, *Britain in the Depression*, 15–39.

viewed as demonstrating working class heterogeneity, rather than homogeneity.[45] Studies of women in wartime challenged the consensus emphasized by the 'People's War' thesis.[46] The rise of the 'affluent worker' in the 1950s has questioned the strength of working class identity.[47] Yet although developments between 1918 and 1950 are crucial to this wider debate, only McKibbin has produced a comprehensive social history of this chronological span.[48] His work highlights the value of considering this period as a whole, but does not engage with debates over change within class, gender, and generational relations and experiences over these years.

Young women's work and family lives offer a valuable prism for this analysis, not only because they have been neglected by historians and are worthy for study in their own right, but also because, as White argues, they were agents of change in working class communities during these years.[49] The chapters that follow are concerned with three related subjects: young women's employment and earning patterns; the effect of their employment on gender-, generational-, and age-specific roles within workplaces, households, and communities; and the importance of young women's working lives to social, economic, and political change. The centrality of paid work to their lives, and the expansion in their employment opportunities following the First World War, accelerated further during the 1930s and particularly by the Second World War, is the subject of chapter 1. Young women's continued value as household breadwinners, and the importance of the family economy in shaping their lives, is examined in chapter 2. This theme is continued in chapter 3, which demonstrates that while young women's job opportunities expanded significantly, social background remained highly influential in structuring and constraining their limited employment choices.

While the first three chapters are primarily concerned with the ways in which employers, family, and the state shaped young women's lives, the latter four focus on young women's own choices, aspirations, and ability to act autonomously. Chapter 4 highlights that although young women's social mobility remained limited, their occupational mobility grew

[45] Baines and Johnson, 'Occupational Continuity'; M. Savage and A. Miles, *The Remaking of the British Working Class, 1840–1940* (London: Routledge, 1994), 48–55. See also T. Griffiths, *The Lancashire Working Classes c. 1880–1930* (Oxford: Clarendon Press, 2001), 1–55.

[46] P. Summerfield, *Women Workers.*

[47] J. H. Goldthorpe et al., *The Affluent Worker in the Class Structure* (London: Cambridge University Press, 1969).

[48] R. McKibbin, *Classes and Cultures in England, 1918–1951* (Oxford: Oxford University Press, 1998).

[49] White, *Worst Street*, 188–91.

dramatically. Migration and mobility patterns were shaped primarily by economic necessity but also, increasingly, by aspirations for social independence and financial security. Chapter 5 examines the culture of the workplace. Recent leisure historiography has moved away from the emphasis placed by Hobsbawm[50] and Stedman Jones[51] upon the links between social and political association among male workers. Chapter 5 challenges this marginalization, analysing relations between workmates to argue that the collective experience of work forged a collective, social identity formed partially in opposition to employers' demands. Chapter 6 examines young women workers' labour relations and activism, but moves beyond the traditional confines of labour history by outlining how the work culture developed by young women provided a means of developing militant resistance to employers' aims. This indicates that young women were not the 'passive' workers that contemporary representations, upheld by the subsequent historiography, often suggested. These chapters thus argue that the experience of work shaped a sense of identity, grounded in class but mediated by gender and age, that encompassed a desire for social change. Yet, as Lawrence has noted, social context can produce different types of class relations, and consequently 'A polarized view of class relations may be embraced at the workplace, but not extended to wider social relationships'.[52] The final chapter examines whether this was so by focusing on young women's lives beyond the workplace: on their increasing importance as leisure consumers, and on their courtship aspirations and experiences. Young women's understanding of their value as wage-earners, breadwinners, and workers fuelled their claims to economic independence as well as political citizenship. They thus played a pivotal role in constructing new definitions of working class femininity and in the emergence of the affluent 'teenager'.

Finally, in conclusion, some general themes are drawn out. This points up the fact that while the chapter structure is shaped by analytical convenience, workplace and household; family, individual, and community; and class, gender, and life cycle are tightly interconnected elements of life that cannot be understood in isolation.

The role of the household is central to this examination. Care is taken throughout the book to distinguish between the household and the

[50] Hobsbawm, *Labouring Men*, 187–92.

[51] G. S. Jones, *Languages of Class: Studies in English Working Class History, 1832–1982* (Cambridge: Cambridge University Press, 1983), ch. 4.

[52] Lawrence, 'British Sense of Class', 311.

family where necessary. Discussion is, however, generally confined to co-residing kin—siblings, parents, and children—since these relationships appear in social surveys and oral testimonies to have been most influential in shaping the family economy and young women's educational, working, domestic, and social lives. Whereas Humphries and most labour historians have argued that the household's survival was important to working class interests,[53] feminists have rightly pointed out that conflict over saving and spending could be central to many working class households. The male head of the household, as prime wage-earner, often operated a degree of individual control over his wage as well as over household decisions more generally.[54] This book argues that the household, like the workplace, was an arena of struggle that cannot be viewed as exclusively serving the interests of a single class or group. The first two chapters indicate that workers as well as employers had a vested interest in the survival of the familial household throughout this period, largely because the persistence of poverty and financial insecurity sustained mutual economic dependence between household members. This stresses the wider historical significance of the subject under study: young women's wage-earning affected lifestyles other than their own because of their financial and domestic responsibilities, and their own employment and leisure experiences were in turn affected by the family economy. The book makes clear that relations between wage-earning daughters and their parents were frequently characterized by economic and emotional reciprocity, challenging the emphasis placed on generational conflict in existing studies of youth in Britain, such as Fowler's examination of interwar teenagers.[55] However, as Blaikie cautions, ' "family strategies" and "household strategies" evoke consensual behaviour', which can overlook tensions between different household members and their needs.[56] Such 'strategies' are therefore at times better characterized as pragmatic solutions to immediate problems rather than as long-term investments.

One potential problem of household-centred history is that it can imply a wide separation between the co-residing family and the wider

[53] J. Humphries, 'Class Struggle and the Persistence of the Working Class Family', *Cambridge Journal of Economics*, 1/3 (1977); S. Blackburn, 'Gender, Work and Labour History: A Response to Carol Morgan', *Women's History Review*, 10/1 (2001).

[54] See, for example, S. Alexander, 'Men's Fears and Women's Work: Responses to Unemployment in London between the Wars', *Gender and History*, 12/2 (2000), 413.

[55] Fowler, *First Teenagers*.

[56] A. Blaikie, 'Problems with "Strategy" in Micro-social History: Families and Narratives, Sources and Methods', *Family and Community History*, 4/2 (2001), 95.

community. Recent studies have critically scrutinized older representations of working class solidarity, forged through kinship, occupation, and neighbourhood networks. Bourke has argued that neighbourhood ties were forged largely through necessity, their significance limited to mitigating short-term economic need, and diminishing as living standards rose between the late 1930s and the 1950s.[57] However, the social surveys and personal testimonies drawn on in this book strongly suggest that kin, neighbours, and friends all helped to shape employment patterns, living standards, and values. Friends became increasingly important to young women over this period as a source of information, advice, and support, as their employment and educational opportunities began to differ from those of which their parents had any experience. Such friendship networks need to be given a more central place in historical studies of class and community, just as older women's neighbourhood networks have recently begun to receive their due attention.

This book's attempt to illuminate and examine people's experiences, shaped within a dynamic social and economic context, draws upon a range of rich source material. The sources used overcome the long-standing division between social and economic historical research that has often prevented historians from adequately examining the connections between social, economic, cultural, and political life. The *Census of England and Wales*, recorded in 1921, 1931, and 1951, provides valuable demographic and occupational data. Previous researchers have pointed to the limitations of this source.[58] As a snapshot of the population on a particular day its representativeness is restricted. The interwar census years, particularly 1931, were characterized by high unemployment. It is likely, as is made clear in chapter 1, that depression led to the emergence of some short-term employment trends, which partially disguise longer term developments in young women's employment patterns. No census was taken in 1941, constraining attempts to date changes in employment and migration patterns between 1931 and 1951, although Ministry of Labour data help to fill this gap. In addition, significant revisions to occupational classifications render some comparisons difficult, particularly between 1931 and 1951. Despite this, the census remains an extremely rich

[57] Bourke, *Cultures*, 148–9.

[58] S. Alexander, 'Women's Work in Nineteenth-Century London', in ead. (ed.), *Becoming*, 7–8; E. Higgs, 'Women, Occupations and Work in the Nineteenth-Century Censuses', *History Workshop Journal*, 23 (1986); Roberts, *Work*, 19. Although the main focus of these studies is the nineteenth century they all point up more general points about ambiguities in the enumeration of women's work in nineteenth- and twentieth-century censuses.

dataset. Hatton and Bailey have convincingly argued that women workers in full-time employment (such as the majority of unmarried young working class women) were not undercounted in the censuses studied here, although part-time workers may well have been.[59] Moreover, Fowler's claim that the interwar censuses provide only condensed and generalized lists of juvenile workers[60] is erroneous, since these workers were also recorded within the main, more detailed and accurate, census occupation tables, together with young adults. Most importantly, the census, unlike the Ministry of Labour's records of insured workers, enumerates servants, shop assistants, casual workers, and juveniles aged under 16.

Also of importance are contemporary social surveys, government records, and those of trade unions and employers. Social surveys include large-scale investigations undertaken in various interwar communities and smaller studies undertaken in the 1940s, many focusing specifically on young people because of concern over high juvenile wages, maternal employment, and the importance of the younger generation in post-war reconstruction plans. These are used in conjunction with surveys of attitudes to employment and leisure compiled throughout the late 1930s and the 1940s by Mass-Observation and the Wartime Social Survey. Also of importance are the print media, which offer contemporary representations of young women and information on their participation in workplace disputes.

Central to the book are the oral testimonies of eighty-one women who were themselves young workers in England during this period, and the published autobiographies of many more. These illuminate the individual experiences of workers who can so easily become buried in the statistics, and also offer an alternative to some of the assumptions and crude stereotypes that proliferate in the contemporary press, government reports, and social investigations. My selection of oral testimonies was based upon the construction of a sample that covered a variety of regional labour markets and that had been collated with a high degree of professionalism. These were drawn from a large number of underexploited oral and life history collections, held in archives across England, which are listed in the Bibliography. They offer a breadth of material, and many benefit from having been recorded by interviewers with a sound knowledge of the local area.

[59] T. J. Hatton and R. E. Bailey, 'Women's Work in Census and Survey, 1911–1931', *Economic History Review*, 54/1 (2001), 87–107.

[60] Fowler, *First Teenagers*, 10.

Savage and Miles have cast doubt on the reliability of working class autobiography, 'frequently written by academics from working class backgrounds who possibly romanticised working class life and solidarity',[61] emphasizing consensus and homeogeneity. However, women's life histories tend not to adopt the strong narrative characteristic of much male working class autobiography, in part because women reflect more upon ambivalent relationships with family members and the wider community,[62] and also because working class women's autobiography is not as well established a genre as men's, meaning that women interviewees and writers cannot draw as easily upon a range of existing, strong literary devices and narrative structures that can conceal ambivalence and ambiguity.[63] The historian must of course engage as critically with oral and life history as with other source material, paying close attention to silences,[64] as well as to the language used, to the way that retrospective, adult judgements shape the reconstruction of youthful experiences, and to the role of the interviewer in the process where one is present. Conclusions presented here are never exclusively based upon oral testimonies and autobiographies, but they are nevertheless extremely valuable, not only in the vivid recollections of youthful experience that they offer, but also because they demonstrate that for many women, paid work retrospectively appeared central to their life experience. That this theme emerged from interviews and reminiscence workshops, the majority of which were led by researchers conducting life-history research, rather than specific projects on employment, makes its prominence all the more significant. Information on the respondents is provided in the Appendix.

Despite my attempt to provide a comprehensive study of young women's employment in interwar England, some significant omissions remain, due to constraints of time and space, and to the limitations of the source material. Casual workers were probably under-recorded by the Census: young women like Rose Gamble's sister Luli, who worked as a part-time cleaner, spending the rest of her time caring for younger siblings.[65] Those who worked partially or entirely outside the law were

[61] Savage and Miles, *Remaking*, p. 4.

[62] C. Steedman, *Past Tenses: Essays on Writing, Autobiography and History* (London: Rivers Oram, 1992), 41–50.

[63] L. Stanley, *The Autobiographical I* (Manchester: Manchester University Press, 1992), 12–13, 242–3.

[64] On silence in working class and women's autobiographical writing see Stanley, *Autobiographical I*, 13; Steedman, *Past Tenses*, 46.

[65] R. Gamble, *Chelsea Child* (London: British Broadcasting Corporation, 1979), 124.

certainly not captured by the sources relied on here. Existing studies convincingly suggest that young men were more likely to be delinquents than young women,[66] but the neglect of prostitution and theft as ways of making ends meet in this study testifies to the under-representation of some sections of the working class both in official records and in existing oral histories and autobiographies. Also missing in this regard are travellers of all kinds, who included a range of seasonal workers. Migrant workers are also under-represented. Contemporary social surveys provide brief, tantalizing glimpses of the employment patterns and lifestyles that distinguished groups of migrants from England's depressed areas who moved to obtain work in large cities such as London or Birmingham in the 1930s. It remains, however, difficult to trace the influence of regional custom upon migrant workers' employment patterns and lifestyles. Moreover, very little information is forthcoming from surveys or autobiographical material on immigrant workers, such as Irish women who were employed in England as residential servants. Despite these gaps, it is hoped that the approach and content of this book will help to broaden the remit of existing research and thus aid historians' ongoing attempts to discover more about the lives of neglected social groups, like young working class women, whose history, even in the recent past, is still so much a matter for conjecture.

[66] Davies, *Leisure*, 99–102; A. E. Morgan, *The Needs of Youth: A Report Made to King George's Jubilee Trust Fund* (London: Oxford University Press, 1939), ch. 9; White, *Worst Street*, 176–8.

1

Young Women and Work

Entering paid employment was a fact of life for most young women reaching the end of their compulsory schooling between 1918 and 1950. Winifred Foley's fourteenth birthday approached in 1928 'like the sword of Damocles'. She had grown up with the knowledge that leaving home to enter domestic service was 'the common lot of every girl in our mining village. . . . Now the time had come, I found it hard to bear'.[1] This transition from elementary school to full-time employment was experienced by 86 per cent of girls and 84 per cent of boys in 1926. In 1951 just 33 per cent of 15-year-old girls and the same proportion of boys were at school, 62 per cent of girls and 64 per cent of boys being in full-time work.[2] The youth of these school leavers—the school-leaving age was 12 in the earliest part of our period, and 14 from 1921 until 1947, when it was raised to 15—greatly affected their experience of this transition. Nellie Oldroyd was one of the many women who felt no regret at leaving school but who still, when engaged in her first factory job, 'longed to go back and play in the fields and the park again.'[3]

For women in most communities, full-time paid work distinguished youth from adult life. Young women (under the age of 25) constituted almost 50 per cent of the female workforce in interwar England, and although this figure fell slightly in the 1940s, this was due to a rise in married women's work rather than a decline in young women's labour force participation. As Table 1 shows, the proportion of young women in the workforce actually increased, from 63 per cent in 1921 to 72 per cent in 1951.[4] This figure was

[1] W. Foley, 'General Maid', in J. Burnett (ed.), *Useful Toil: Autobiographies of Working People from the 1820s to the 1920s* (Harmondsworth: Penguin, 1977), 227.

[2] Report of the Board of Education for the year 1926–7, ix (PP 1928), Cd. 3091, 121; *Census of England and Wales, 1951: Occupation Tables* (London: HMSO, 1954).

[3] N. Oldroyd, 'Sweetmaking', in R. Van Riel (ed.), *All in a Day's Work* (Pontefract: Yorkshire Art Circus, 1982), 9.

[4] See Table 1. Although 12 and 13 year olds could undertake full-time paid employment in 1921, they are excluded from this analysis because relatively few of them were recorded as doing so by the 1921 Census.

TABLE 1. Proportion of Young and Adult Women Occupied in Paid Employment, 1921, 1931, and 1951

Year	Young women[a]			Adult women[b]		
	Total	Occupied	% Occupied	Total	Occupied	% Occupied
1921	3,841,480	2,425,218	63	11,117,802	2,611,509	23
1931	3,823,570	2,621,440	69	12,587,324	2,984,603	24
1951	2,869,406	2,059,859	72	15,129,887	4,213,017	28

[a] Aged between 15 and 24 years of age. [b]Aged over 24 years of age.

Source: *Census of England and Wales, 1921: Occupation Tables* (London: HMSO, 1924), Table 4; *Census of England and Wales, 1931: Occupation Tables* (London: HMSO, 1934), Table 3; *Census of England and Wales, 1951: Occupation Tables* (London: HMSO, 1954), Table 3.

even higher during the Second World War; high labour demand and conscription meant that 90 per cent of single women under 30 were in paid work by the end of 1943.[5] Neither men nor married women experienced such dramatic changes in their employment patterns. Less than 30 per cent of women over the age of 24 were recorded in paid work over this period.

Despite the fact that the vast majority of young women could expect to experience about a decade of full-time paid employment prior to marriage, their working lives have been neglected by the limited existing historiography on women during this period. Research has been confined to valuable but localized studies of women's work, most of which focus on textile communities, characterized by high labour force participation among married women;[6] on the growth industries,[7] such as light metals manufacture and food processing, which did not become significant employers of women until the later 1930s; or on women's war work.[8] Most studies of women's lives concentrate not on their employment but on leisure, courtship, and domestic life. The focus of this book highlights the importance of the labour market in shaping the transition from girlhood

[5] H. M. D. Parker, *Manpower: A Study of War-Time Policy and Administration* (London: HMSO, 1957), 291.

[6] E. Roberts, *A Woman's Place: An Oral History of Working Class Women 1890–1940* (Oxford: Blackwell, 1984). See also J. Sarsby, *Missuses and Mouldrunners: An Oral History of Women Pottery-Workers at Work and Home* (Milton Keynes: Open University Press, 1988).

[7] M. Glucksmann, *Women Assemble: Women Workers in the New Industries of Inter-war Britain* (London: Routledge, 1990).

[8] P. Summerfield, *Women Workers in the Second World War* (London: Croom Helm, 1984).

to adulthood for the majority of women between the end of the First World War and the early 1950s.

This chapter is concerned with young women's employment and earning patterns and the factors that shaped these. A highly significant shift occurred in young women's employment between 1918 and 1950, as they became an increasingly attractive source of cheap labour for employers in the expanding retail, clerical, and industrial sectors. Existing explanations of changes in women's employment patterns do not adequately account for this development. Both the argument that employers preferred to use young women for 'feminine' tasks, accepted almost unquestioningly by many social historians,[9] and Braverman's rather rigid interpretation of the Marxist notion that women constituted a 'reserve army of labour', brought into the industrial workforce as demand for unskilled and semi-skilled workers grew,[10] suggest that it was exclusively their gender that defined the work that women were employed to do.

The evidence presented here demonstrates the need for a more historically specific approach. The first two sections of this chapter trace young women's employment and earning patterns, highlighting that young people, particularly juvenile girls and boys, constituted a source of labour for poorly paid and often insecure jobs, but that young women were rarely employed in the same occupations as young men. Age emerges as an important factor in structuring labour demand. Adult women earned significantly more than younger women, and were frequently employed on different kinds of work, often of a casual or part-time nature. The third section of the chapter examines young women's working conditions across the major occupational sectors. This section highlights that young women's actions and desires interacted with wider social and economic developments to shape and change the English labour market. An examination of unemployment, which demonstrates that age was as important as gender in determining a worker's likelihood of being out of work, follows and highlights that this was an extremely common experience in the youth labour market. Finally, the ways that age and gender shaped young women's employment and earning patterns are considered. Political and popular interest in young women's paid work grew over this period, but no debate over young women's work comparable to that over the 'boy labour problem'

[9] D. Beddoe, *Back to Home and Duty* (London: Pandora, 1989), 67; J. Giles, *Women, Identity and Private Life in Britain, 1900–50* (Basingstoke: Macmillan, 1995), 132–51; Glucksmann, *Women Assemble*, 16 and 198–9.

[10] H. Braverman, *Labor and Monopoly Capital: The Degradation of Work in the Twentieth Century* (New York: Monthly Review Press, 1974), 385–7.

emerged. This points to significant differences in the role of paid work in the lives of men and women, but the nature of the boy labour debate also glossed over important similarities in the working patterns of young people of either sex. Yet a sexual division of labour was also evident: young women and young men were used for different types of work, in a labour market that remained highly segregated by gender. An evaluation is thus made of the factors that accounted for young women's attraction for employers vis-à-vis the other major sources of cheap labour, to explain their concentration in a range of gender- and age-segregated jobs.

Employment Patterns

In 1921 domestic service was young women's largest employer, occupying 552,337 of them; by 1951, it occupied only 5 per cent of the young female workforce, whereas clerical work, in which only 12 per cent of young women workers had been engaged twenty years earlier, accounted for the single largest group within the young female workforce. Table 2 shows that the numbers of young women who worked in industry and, to a lesser extent, retail, also increased significantly. As this suggests, the short-term effects of the First World War on young women's employment were limited, but important, long-term trends were accelerated by it, the effects of which only became fully apparent from the later 1930s. Braybon and Wollacott have rightly pointed out that the First World War dramatically increased young women's prominence as workers and expanded their employment opportunities.[11] Young women's labour force participation rose from 47 per cent in 1911 to 63 per cent ten years later, while adult women's remained fixed at 23 per cent.[12] Moreover, the increase in young women's industrial, retail, and clerical employment between 1914 and 1918 raised the employment expectations of those who entered work in the immediate aftermath of war. Mrs Cleary, who grew up on the outskirts of Manchester, and began work as a confectioner in 1922, felt that the war

> made all the difference in the world—you see there was nothing much for girls before—girls of my class I mean—girls—country girls like that, there was nothing for them except service.[13]

[11] G. Braybon, *Women Workers in the First World War*, 2nd ed. (London: Routledge, 1989); A. Woollacott, *On Her Their Lives Depend: Munitions Workers in the Great War* (Berkeley, Calif.: University of California, 1994), 89–113.

[12] *Census of England and Wales, 1911: Occupation Tables* (London: HMSO, 1914).

[13] Tameside Local Studies Library (TLSL), Manchester Studies tapes, tape 28, interview with Mrs E. Cleary.

TABLE 2. Major Occupations of Young Women in England, 1921, 1931, and 1951

Occupation	No. young women employed			% young female workforce			% change	
	1921	1931	1951	1921	1931	1951	1921–31	1931–51
Metals	73,782	61,658	55,082	3	2	3	−1	1
Textiles	305,494	228,449	99,374	13	9	5	−4	−4
Textile goods	274,089	273,417	176,692	11	10	9	−1	−1
Shop assistants	211,167	258,497	251,583	9	10	12	1	2
Professions	87,737	94,112	150,167	4	4	7	0	3
Domestic service	552,337	639,057	108,919	23	24	5	1	−19
Other personal service	111,773	169,911	125,264	5	6	6	1	0
Clerks and typists	295,269	426,436	627,981	12	12	30	0	18
Warehousemen and packers	91,249	108,845	65,892	4	4	3	0	−1
Undefined unskilled	N/A[a]	151,404	134,966	N/A	6	7	N/A	1

[a] This category first appeared in the 1931 *Census*.

Source: *Census, 1921: Occupation Tables*, Table 4; *Census, 1931: Occupation Tables*, Table 3; *Census, 1951: Occupation Tables*, Table 3.

Robert Roberts's memories of Salford concurred with this; he noted that after the Armistice, 'English working class girls preferred any kind of job in mill or factory, or even a place with rock-bottom wages at Woolworth's, and freedom . . . to the best that domestic service could offer'.[14] Elizabeth Roberts rightly claims that the most significant long-term effects of the First World War for women's employment was its acceleration of the growth in retail and clerical job opportunities.[15]

These effects were not, however, immediately apparent outside England's largest and most economically buoyant cities. Domestic service and the textile industry retained their importance as young women's major employers. Alternative employment opportunities contracted in the early 1920s due to economic depression; continuing insecurity meant that retail, clerical, and light manufacturing work did not begin to expand rapidly once again until the mid-1930s. As a consequence, domestic service continued to be young women's largest employer until the Second World War. Mrs Cleary, quoted earlier, lost her first job at the age of 15 and was forced to enter domestic service due to the lack of alternative occupations. The residential nature, low wages, and long hours worked meant that the large proportion of young women who entered domestic service experienced a form of work—and a daily lifestyle—quite different to that in which their peers who worked in offices, shops, or factories were engaged. It was not until wartime labour demand rose in the industrial and clerical sectors from 1940 that the sector declined as a major employer of this group, with the consequent erosion of some of the social and economic distinctions within the youthful workforce that it had perpetuated.

While industrial employment expanded, its nature changed. The textile industry, one of the few sectors that offered women skilled work, never recovered from the adverse effects of the First World War on trade, and its decline was exacerbated by the slump of 1929–32. Its share of the young female workforce fell from 13 to 9 per cent between the interwar censuses, and dropped to just 5 per cent by 1951. Textile goods manufacture was young women's largest industrial employer by 1951, but other industries also began to employ them in larger numbers, as Glucksmann's analysis of the expansion of 'new' industries, such as light metal manufacture, highlights.[16] Seven per cent of young women were employed as 'undefined

[14] R. Roberts, *The Classic Slum* (Harmondsworth: Penguin, 1974), 222.

[15] E. Roberts, *Women's Work, 1840–1940* (Cambridge: Cambridge University Press, 1988), 28–9.

[16] Glucksmann, *Women Assemble*, 41 and 259.

unskilled workers' in 1951, a census classification that highlighted their attraction as cheap, unskilled, industrial labour.

The rate of industrial expansion prior to the 1950s must not be overemphasized. Only 2 per cent of young women were employed in metal manufacture in 1931 and 10 per cent in textile goods production. Of greater significance was the increase in retail and clerical employment. Employment for women in these sectors, already rising slowly prior to 1914, increased dramatically during the First World War, a trend that continued in the following three decades. Here, as in industrial work, the greatest increase was in the employment of younger women. By 1951 12 per cent of young women were employed as shop assistants. Most notable, though, was the expansion of clerical work for this group: 30 per cent were recorded as clerks by the 1951 Census. Between the end of the First World War and the beginning of the 1950s, then, non-manual employment became a realistic aspiration for young working class women, while manual labour moved from private households to industrial workplaces.

This expansion of employment opportunities, significant though it was, occurred within junior, lower grade, or unskilled occupations. Historians and social scientists have often cited this period as one of widespread 'deskilling' and 'feminization' of the workforce, suggesting that employers replaced expensive skilled men with unskilled and semiskilled women. Braverman argues that technological change in the mid-twentieth century facilitated this strategy.[17] Summerfield has highlighted the importance of the Second World War in the process, as skilled adult men's tasks were subdivided and given to unskilled females.[18] However, a closer look at young women's changing employment patterns challenges this as a wholly adequate explanation of change. Young women constituted 14 per cent of England's workers in 1921 and 10 per cent in 1951: clearly, no significant shift in the gender composition of the workforce was apparent. There was no widespread displacement of male workers by young women. In the clerical sector, for example, the numbers of both men and women increased, but the latter group increased at a faster rate as unskilled and semiskilled jobs proliferated.

This supports Hakim's contention that vertical gender segregation remained characteristic of most occupational sectors.[19] This gender hierarchy was challenged by the Second World War, when some women

[17] Braverman, *Labor*, 385–8. [18] Summerfield, *Women Workers*, 10–11 and 53.

[19] C. Hakim, *Occupational Segregation: A Comparative Study of the Degree and Pattern of the Differentiation between Men and Women's Work in Britain, the United States and Other Countries*, Research Paper 9 (London: Dept. of Employment, 1979), 22–34.

benefited from the absence of male workers and were able to gain promotion. Mrs Andrews 'rose to the dizzy heights of Corporal' in the Auxiliary Territorial Service (ATS), benefiting from the expansion in promotion opportunities available in the Army due to a lack of 'A1' men.[20] Florence Rosenblatt, a former shop assistant, became a factory forewoman: 'some of the women used to say "we can do the work same as"—well it was true! We done the work as well as the men'.[21] Summerfield's study provides similar examples.[22] In the longer term, the Second World War prompted the abolition of the marriage bar in most occupations, both manual and white-collar. Yet this was the most permanent of the changes wrought. Women who did obtain skilled or supervisory positions in wartime were particularly likely to feel that 'we were there to do a job, until the men came back'.[23] As Hakim has shown, women who remained in clerical or factory jobs into adulthood and marriage after 1945 were unlikely to progress beyond the typing or semiskilled grades. Married women were used in increasing numbers as part-time factory, shop, and office workers in the late 1940s, while full-time younger women workers also remained concentrated in unskilled and semiskilled work.[24] The expansion of these types of jobs, as the use of mass production techniques, including conveyor belts in factories and typing pools in offices, grew, rather than the 'deskilling' of existing skilled jobs undertaken by men, was largely responsible for the increasing employment of young women across a range of occupational sectors. The reasons young women constituted a source of cheap labour for such jobs will be examined more closely in the final section of this chapter.

Wages and Working Hours

Historians have noted that the years between 1918 and 1950 witnessed the emergence of the prominent, young female leisure consumer, but the reasons for this have not been extensively analysed. Significant in explaining this crucial social, economic, and cultural development was the rise in young women's earnings, both in real terms and relative to other groups

20 TLSL, Manchester Studies, 8, interview with Mrs Andrews.

21 Lancashire Records Office (LRO), North West Sound Archive (NWSA), tape ref. 2002.0531a, interview with Florence Rosenblatt.

22 P. Summerfield, *Reconstructing Women's Wartime Lives* (Manchester: Manchester University Press, 1998), 121–3; 209–16.

23 TLSL, Manchester Studies, 77, interview with L. Baker.

24 Hakim, *Occupational Segregation*.

of workers.[25] This was partly as a result of changes in their occupational distribution and partly also due to a general rise in pay. Young women's wages and earnings followed the wider trend, increasing between 1914 and 1920, falling between 1920 and 1923, after which they stabilized until 1938, before rising significantly during the 1940s.[26] The discussion here will be confined to juvenile girls' earnings, partly because the Ministry of Labour's 'Average Hours and Earnings Enquiries' provide age-disaggregated data for this group from 1938 onwards, but not for older women. Comparisons are drawn with adult women's and men's earnings, but comparisons with boys' earnings are more tentative, because of differences between the definition of youths and boys (aged between 14 and 21) and that of girls (aged between 14 and 17) employed by the Enquiries. The discussion is divided into two chronological sections, in order to highlight the often-overlooked significance of the Second World War and its aftermath in increasing young women's pay.

1918–38

Historians of women's work have emphasized inequality between male and female earnings, but in fact juveniles' income was characterized by a striking level of gender parity. The gender differential in wage rates, so significant at adult level, did not begin to affect young women until their late teens; in some cases, in fact, girls' earnings exceeded those of boys, as Figure 1 shows. This was largely due to the concentration of male school leavers in poorly paid apprenticeships—metal apprentices' starting wage averaged 10s per week in 1925,[27] when a 14-year-old girl's average weekly wage was approximately 13s—while girls benefited from the increase in better paid factory and office jobs. As such job opportunities expanded, so girls' economic status was heightened.

Gender alone did not shape young women's value as workers; juveniles of either sex were cheaper than adult women. Roberts and Lewis have shown that adult women were more likely to be employed in casual work or, increasingly by the late 1940s, in part-time jobs.[28] They were thus

[25] As the gap between earnings and wages was negligible for these workers over these years, earnings data are considered to be representative of wage rates here, and vice versa.

[26] S. N. Broadberry, *The British Economy between the Wars: A Macroeconomic Survey* (Oxford: Blackwell, 1986), 81–3.

[27] Ministry of Labour, *Report of an Enquiry into Apprenticeship and Training for the Skilled Occupations in Great Britain and Northern Ireland, 1925–26*, 7 (London: HMSO, 1928), 187–9.

[28] E. Roberts, *Women's Work*, 35–45; J. Lewis, *Women in England, 1870–1950* (Brighton: Harvester Wheatsheaf, 1984), 218–19.

FIGURE 1. Mean weekly wage (shillings) of juveniles across various trades, by age and gender, 1929

Source: Ministry of Labour, *Standard Time Rates of Wages and Hours of Labour in Great Britain and Northern Ireland at 31st August 1929* (London: HMSO, 1929).

unlikely to find themselves in direct competition for jobs with cheaper, girl labour. However, unmarried young adult women could find their employment prospects threatened by younger girls, a trend discussed in an examination of their unemployment later in this chapter.

Although gender parity was notable in juveniles' earnings, young women were, overall, the cheapest section of the workforce. In 1938, girls' mean hourly earnings averaged 0.41s, 28 per cent of adult men's, while boys' earnings averaged 39 per cent, and women's 52 per cent. Figure 1 shows that from the age of 16, gender inequality in earnings significantly increased. This was partly due to young men's transition into skilled employment while young women remained in unskilled or semiskilled jobs. Also of importance was a gender difference in the attainment of adult wage rates; young women were defined as adults at 18 in most industrial and clerical jobs, whereas young men, who qualified for a youth wage rate at 18, received the adult rate at 21. This was maintained in agreements between employers and trade unions, in recognition of the higher status afforded young men who had undertaken apprenticeships; though in practice it was extended to most young male workers.[29]

[29] P. Scott, 'Women, Other "Fresh" Workers, and the New Manufacturing Workforce of Interwar Britain', *International Review of Social History*, 45/3 (2000), 465–6.

Consequently, young men benefited from larger age-specific increments than young women did for a crucial four-year period between the ages of 18 and 21.

Although gender fractured earning potential from the late teens, the relatively rapid wage rise experienced by both young men and young women through their youth meant that this life stage, particularly the late teenage years and early twenties, was characterized by a temporarily large degree of financial and social independence, as Davies has identified.[30] Clearly, young workers themselves were not an entirely homogeneous group, with a significant earnings differential existing between juvenile and young adult workers. Yet equally important was the lack of a notable gender earnings differential among young workers, particularly juveniles. Age interacted with gender to shape young women's earning potential and, as subsequent chapters will show, their family relationships and leisure consumption.

Young women benefited not only from a rise in earnings but also from reductions in working hours. In 1918 and 1919 the forty-eight-hour week was widely implemented across industry and was extended to cover all juvenile and women factory workers by the 1920 Employment of Women and Young Persons Act. No further dramatic decreases in working hours occurred until 1946, but a decline was evident in the later 1930s, partly as a result of trade union agitation, which helped to bring about the Factories Acts of 1937 and 1938. These limited juvenile employment to nine hours per day, and reduced the maximum weekly working hours of workers aged between 14 and 16 to forty-four across a range of trades. The 1938 'Enquiry' recorded average working hours as forty-four per normal working week. It is, however, important to note that this investigation, together with most other official enquiries, excluded domestic servants, the largest single group of young working women prior to the Second World War, and the section of the workforce that worked the longest hours for the lowest pay. Moreover, the rate of change should not be exaggerated. In 1938 juvenile girls in these jobs still experienced, on average, a working day of over eight hours, five days per week, and four hours on a Saturday. They were paid less than half the adult male hourly rate and significantly less than adult women. Mrs Johnson, for example, recalled that as a young chargehand in a Coventry factory during the 1930s she had no tea break and an unpaid half-hour for lunch.[31] Work continued to occupy an extremely large portion of young women's daily lives.

[30] A. Davies, *Leisure, Gender and Poverty in Manchester and Salford, 1900–1939* (Buckingham: Open University Press, 1992), 83–7.

[31] Modern Records Centre, University of Warwick (MRC), Coventry Women's Work Collection, MSS 266/6/4, interview with Mrs E. Johnson.

1939–50

The Second World War and the years immediately following it witnessed more conspicuous changes in young women's earnings and working hours. In particular, the significant earnings differential between young and adult workers was slightly reduced, with young women's earnings rising significantly. The findings presented here conflict with the emphasis that recent social histories have placed on the limited effect of the Second World War on women's earnings. This conclusion has been largely based on the failure of the Equal Pay Campaign, a major issue for women that was a cause of numerous wartime workplace disputes.[32] A closer look at earnings differentials indicates that despite this, the earnings gap between males and females narrowed during the war, and, in particular, the relative value of juvenile girls' earnings substantially increased.

In common with other groups of workers, girls experienced a substantial rise in earnings during the first years of the war, as Table 3 shows. In the case of adults and young men, part of this rise was accounted for by an increase in working hours, but juvenile girls' working hours rose less than those of other groups, averaging forty-five in 1943, compared with 44.6 in 1938. Their comparatively short working week was not due simply to their gender. Differences in the age ranges of girls and young men in the Enquiries make comparisons between girls' and boys' working hours difficult, but since the working hours of adult men and women were longer than those of youths it seems likely that boys also experienced only a limited increase in working time.

The relative advantage experienced by juveniles should not be overemphasized. Within days of war breaking out, employers sought the relaxation of restrictions on young people's working hours; by the beginning of 1940 they were able to obtain government orders allowing them to employ women over 16 for more than forty-eight hours per week; most orders permitted a fifty-seven hour week.[33] This was despite the fact that the number of unemployed adults still stood at over a million, and, as Price points out, there was no convincing case for altering regulations at this early stage.[34] Employers' demands were prompted by the cheaper cost of younger workers. The state registration of 16 and 17 year olds from December 1941 revealed some cases of extremely long working

[32] Summerfield, *Women Workers*, 151–84; H. L. Smith, 'The Effect of the War on the Status of Women', in id. (ed.), *War and Social Change* (Manchester: Manchester University Press, 1986).

[33] *Ministry of Labour Gazette*, 48/2 (1940), 77.

[34] J. Price, *Organised Labour in the War* (Harmondsworth: Allen Lane, 1940), 77.

TABLE 3. Girls' Mean Earnings per Hour (shillings), 1938–49[a]

Industry	Year			
	1938 Earns/hr	% change 1938–43	% change 1938–45	% change 1938–49
Metal, engineering, and shipbuilding	0.45	188	195	272
Textiles	0.43	179	202	316
Clothing	0.41	166	186	291
Food, drink, tobacco	0.41	166	189	274
Woodworking	0.39	196	216	291
Paper, printing, etc.	0.38	168	182	305
Chemicals, etc.	0.41	176	191	303
Brick, pottery, glass	0.34	194	204	N/A
Leather	0.38	182	194	300
Miscellaneous manufacturing	0.41	195	204	303
Non-metalliferous mining products	0.40	207	190	300
Public utilities	0.49	182	189	N/A
All above	0.41	183	197	297

[a] These means were calculated by weighting results by the number of workers in each occupation and sector.

Source: Ministry of Labour, 'Average Hours and Earnings Enquiry', October 1938, July 1943, July 1945, and October 1949, *Ministry of Labour Gazette*, various volumes.

hours: of the 2,659 juveniles interviewed in Coventry for this purpose, 64 per cent of boys and 43 per cent of girls worked for more than fifty hours per week.[35] For the first time, many of the workers not enumerated by the Ministry of Labour's 'Enquiries' came under regular state scrutiny, bringing to light many cases of teenage shop assistants and servants working in excess of fifty-five hours per week.[36] Many employers used the excuse of war to maintain or extend long working days.

Nevertheless, from the mid-1940s, young women's working hours were significantly reduced. As Tinkler has pointed out, the exigencies of war heightened concern over the effect of long working days on juveniles, fuelling concern not only to curtail excessive wartime working hours, but

[35] The National Archives (TNA), ED 124/48, MS: 'Particulars of Long Hours Worked in Industry as Disclosed by the Spring 1942 Registration', 1942.

[36] TNA, ED 124/48, 'Long Hours Worked in Industry'.

also to reduce the peacetime maximum.[37] The deleterious effect of long hours on young women's health and morale was felt by many workers. Edna Delves, a factory worker, realized the extent of her own fatigue when, one morning late in 1940, 'I got to our factory, the roof had all been blown off. I didn't think, "am I out of a job?" I thought, "Good. I can go back home and have a sleep." '[38] Investigators conducting a survey of young people in Bristol in 1943 'commented in a number of cases on the paleness and physical apathy of the young people', thought to have been caused by lengthy working days.[39] Mass-Observation studies demonstrated that longer working hours did not necessarily increase productivity and could have a deleterious effect on morale.[40] Such findings, together with Ernest Bevin's influence as Minister of Labour, led to a reduction in working hours after 1943 that significantly affected the youngest workers. The Ministry of Labour recorded girls' average weekly working hours as 43.5 in 1945, lower than the 1938 average of 44.

Whereas Summerfield and Smith have argued that the wartime erosion of gender and age earnings differentials was partial and temporary,[41] the data presented in Tables 3 and 4 add strong support to the argument of some economic historians, notably Seers, that the narrowing of gendered earnings differentials lasted into the post-war years.[42] The same was also true of the age-specific pay differential. Girls' hourly earnings increased by 83 per cent between 1938 and 1943. This was smaller than the 93 per cent increase in adult women's earnings (who included those aged between 18 and 24), but slightly higher than the 81 per cent experienced by young men, and substantially greater than the increase of 76 per cent in adult men's earnings. However, the most notable rise in girls' earnings came in the immediate post-war years. By 1949, as Table 3 illustrates, their hourly earnings were 297 per cent higher than ten years previously, while adult women's had risen by 242 per cent, young men's by 234 per cent, and

[37] P. Tinkler, 'Girlhood in Transition? Preparing English Girls for Adulthood in a Reconstructed Britain', in C. Duchen and I. Bandhauer-Schoffman (eds.), *When the War Was Over: Women, War and Peace in Europe, 1940–1956* (London: Leicester University Press, 2000), 61.

[38] TLSL, Manchester Studies, 1075, interview with Edna Delves. See also LRO, NWSA, 2002.0531a, interview with Florence Rosenblatt.

[39] B. A. Fletcher et al., *The Welfare of Youth: A City Survey* (Bristol: University of Bristol, 1945), 16.

[40] Mass-Observation, *People in Production* (Harmondsworth: Penguin, 1942), 157–63, 187; Mass-Observation, *War Factory* (London: Gollancz, 1943), 52.

[41] Summerfield, *Women Workers*, 151–84; Smith, 'Status of Women'.

[42] D. Seers, 'The Levelling of Incomes', *Bulletin of the Oxford Institute of Statistics*, 12/10 (October 1950), 290.

TABLE 4. Relative Hourly Earnings (shillings) of Girls, Youths, and Women, 1938–49

Year	Men earns/hr	Girls[a] % male earns	Youths[b] % male earns	Women % male earns
1938	1.5	28	39	52
1943	2.3	33	45	59
1945	2.4	33	41	60
1949	3.0	41	46	63

[a] Girls = 14–18 year olds. [b] Youths = 14–20 year olds.

Source: Ministry of Labour, 'Average Hours and Earnings Enquiries', October 1938, July 1943, July 1945, and October 1949, *Ministry of Labour Gazette*, various volumes.

adult men's by 203 per cent. Although the large rise in girls' earnings was partly attributed to the removal of 14 year olds from the job market in 1948, it had clearly begun prior to that date. As labour demand for women, particularly young women, was sustained and in fact increased in the second half of the 1940s, so their pay rose and in 1949 stood at 41 per cent of adult men's earnings. Moreover, young women's working hours fell proportionately more than adults', being recorded as 42.4 per week in the 1949 'Enquiry'. By this stage, this official statistic covered a section of the workforce larger than that of a decade earlier, since a far smaller proportion of young women were experiencing the long hours and low pay offered by domestic service. Wartime wage increases thus set a standard for post-war pay, fuelled by sustained demand for young, cheap labour, which assisted the emergence of the affluent, teenage consumer.

Occupations and Working Conditions

Domestic Service

Although domestic service was in decline between 1918 and 1950, it continued to be the largest employer of young women in interwar England, a fact overlooked by historians' prevailing concentration on the expansion of light manufacturing industries.[43] The demise of the

[43] J. Stevenson and C. Cook, *Britain in the Depression: Society and Politics, 1929–39* (London: Longman, 1994), 17–23; Glucksmann, *Women Assemble*.

occupation when alternative opportunities arose during the Second World War, and its long-standing importance as an employer of women from rural and depressed industrial areas, indicates that its survival as a major employer into the 1930s was a response to agricultural and industrial depression in the late 1920s.[44] The sizeable proportion of women employed as servants in both interwar censuses may, then, be unrepresentative of the occupation in the early 1920s, as is suggested by middle class concern over the shortage of domestic servants during this period.[45] In 1923 a committee appointed by the Ministry of Labour to investigate whether domestic service could be used to eradicate female unemployment concluded that

> a large number of girls of 14, especially in rural areas, are desirous of taking up domestic service . . . but . . . very few employers are prepared to engage such young, inexperienced girls, with the result that they drift off into other occupations, become accustomed to the conditions of industrial life, and at 16 or 17 it is very difficult to redirect their thoughts to domestic work.[46]

This preference continued to be noted throughout the interwar years, and reflected wider social changes that diminished demand for young servants.[47] By the late 1920s, the decline in large upper- and upper-middle class households, often situated in rural areas, meant that domestic servants were increasingly likely to find employment in small, middle class, urban households, which could afford only one or two maids. As *The New Survey of London* noted in the early 1930s, such households desired capable, older girls, or, increasingly by the mid-1930s, older women who would undertake part-time cleaning jobs.[48] Demand for part-time workers continued to grow during the 1940s, with offices and institutions accounting for an increasing amount of service employment.[49]

[44] P. Ford, *Work and Wealth in a Modern Port: An Economic Survey of Southampton* (London: Allen and Unwin, 1934), 61.

[45] *Women's Leader* (5 March 1924), 6. Bingham's analysis of the press also suggests that the servant crisis was confined to the early and mid-1920s; see A. Bingham, *Gender, Modernity, and the Popular Press in Inter-War Britain* (Oxford: Oxford University Press, 2004), 68–9.

[46] Ministry of Labour, *Report of the Committee Appointed to Enquire into the Present Conditions as to the Supply of Female Domestic Servants* (London: HMSO, 1923), 12.

[47] See, for example, London Advisory Council for Juvenile Employment, *A Guide to Employment for London Boys and Girls* (London: HMSO, 1928), 103; R. Strachey, *Careers and Openings for Women* (London: Faber, 1935), 110.

[48] H. Llewellyn Smith, *The New Survey of London Life and Labour*, 8/2 (London: P. S. King and Son, 1934), 315.

[49] J. Beauchamp, *Working Women in Great Britain* (New York: International Publishers, 1937), 73–6; R. Gamble, *Chelsea Child* (London: British Broadcasting Corporation, 1979), 124; Roberts, *Women's Work*, 21–2.

Demographic changes in domestic service employment are a reminder that age was as significant as gender in shaping shifts in occupational distribution. Married women's employment patterns were clearly structured by changes in younger women's work. Such developments were inspired by young women's own (limited) choices, as well as by changes in labour demand. Decline in demand for full-time servants coincided with the growth in job opportunities for young women in shops, factories, and offices, offering shorter working hours and better pay. This trend was noted as early as 1918, when the War Cabinet Committee on Women in Industry concluded that young women were reluctant to return 'to living-in service, except as a last resort. They want more freedom and limited hours of work.'[50] The Young Women's Christian Association (YWCA), which concerned itself with raising the social status of domestic service, noted that long working hours and limitations to workers' liberty were cited as compelling disadvantages by young women unwilling to enter the occupation.[51] As job opportunities for young women in factories, shops, and offices expanded, some employers sought to make domestic service more attractive. Edith Edwards recalled that in the early 1930s, her employer let her have each evening free because 'times were changing and servants were getting harder to get—because there were more opportunities for women—and so they had to make the job more attractive.'[52] As these younger workers evacuated the sector, so adult women increasingly obtained part-time domestic employment that fitted around their family responsibilities. The 1931 Census recorded 140,146 charwomen; just 6 per cent of them were under 25 years of age. These changes, accelerated by the wartime growth in labour demand in industrial and clerical work, meant that the proportion of domestic servants who were young women fell from 46 per cent in 1921 to 14 per cent in 1951.

Residential domestic servants frequently endured poor pay for long working days, with one half-day off fortnightly or weekly being their only respite. Interwar surveys indicate that the average level of servants' pay ranged between 4s and 8s among juveniles and between 11s and 13s among young adult women.[53] Personal testimonies suggest that the diminishing

[50] Report of the War Cabinet Committee on Women in Industry, PP. 1919, Cmd 135, xxi. 241, 99–100.

[51] YWCA, *Household Employment* (London: YWCA, *c*.1933).

[52] TLSL, Manchester Studies, 36, interview with Edith Edwards.

[53] Labour Party, *What's Wrong with Domestic Service?* (London: Labour Party, 1930); D. Caradog Jones, *Social Survey of Merseyside*, 2 (Liverpool: University of Liverpool, 1934), 311; and Llewellyn Smith, *London*, 2, 468.

minority employed in large, wealthy households tended to earn most. Marion Kent, for example, was paid just under 10s per week as housemaid at a large country house in the mid-1930s,[54] while Mrs Halliday, who took up her first post with a farming family at the same age and time, earned just 5s per week.[55] The decline of employment in larger households thus had a deleterious effect on servants' earnings.

Yet the attractions of domestic service, particularly prior to employment expansion in the mid-1930s, were important. In emphasizing exploitation and servants' limited social independence, historians have often overlooked the fact that wages were supplemented by board and lodging, which made the occupation suitable for young women who had few local employment opportunities. Mrs Cleary pointed out that servants' wages could not easily be compared with those of other workers 'because you had all your keep—and uniform'.[56] For those who came from poor homes and were fortunate in their employers, the food provided was often the highlight of their job: Marion Kent was one of many former servants who vividly recalled daily teas of 'bread and butter and jam and cake' as well as three regular meals.[57] Clothes could be another attraction; Mrs Halliday found the 'beautiful bottle green dresses' with which her employer furnished her the most tolerable aspect of her job in a doctor's household in the mid-1930s.[58]

A grievance among servants greater than levels of pay was their lack of liberty. Most young servants worked in excess of fifty hours per week.[59] Marion Kent worked almost continuously between 6.30am and 10pm every day, with only one afternoon free each week;[60] Lavinia Swainbank collapsed due to similar conditions.[61] The state registration of juvenile girls from 1942 revealed many cases of excessive hours, including a Cumberland girl hotel worker who worked from 7 o'clock in the morning until midnight every day with Sunday afternoon being her only time off, and twenty-nine cases of Devon servants working between fifty and

[54] LRO, NWSA, 1988.0090, interview with Marion Kent.

[55] LRO, NWSA, 1999.0088, interview with Mrs Halliday.

[56] TLSL, Manchester Studies, 28, Mrs E. Cleary.

[57] LRO, NWSA, 1998.0090, interview with Marion Kent. See also E. Balderson with D. Goodlad, *Backstairs Life in a Country House* (Newton Abbott: David and Charles, 1982), 14; J. Rennie, *Every Other Sunday* (London: A. Barker, 1955), 31–2; Nottingham Local Studies Library (NLSL), Making Ends Meet collection, A50/a, interview with Lily.

[58] LRO, NWSA, 1999.0088, interview with Mrs Halliday.

[59] Caradog Jones, *Merseyside*, 2, 316.

[60] LRO, NWSA, 1988.0090, interview with Marion Kent.

[61] L. Swainbank, 'Housemaid', in Burnett (ed.), *Useful Toil*, 221–2.

ninety hours per week.[62] As Winifred Foley, who experienced similar conditions, commented, most employers 'needed a creature that would run on very little fuel and would not question her lot.'[63] Moreover, as other young workers' wages rose, increasing their ability to engage in commercial leisure and buy clothes, the compensations of service, such as board and lodging and clothing, diminished. From the mid-1930s, many more servants resented 'the hated caps and aprons' and lack of liberty,[64] and clearly took advantage of wartime labour demand to escape their employment.

Factory Work

Like domestic service, industry had been a major employer of young women for decades prior to 1914. During the period between 1918 and 1951, however, factory employment expanded and changed. The textile industry had been the largest industrial employer of women prior to the First World War. Young women in those areas where it was concentrated, such as Lancashire, could earn relatively high wages and it was often possible to acquire skilled employment in early adulthood. Between the 1920s and the 1950s, textile employment declined, but other forms of industrial work expanded, across a greater number of regions. Change was slow, however; light manufacture in the metals or electrical goods industries did not begin to employ large numbers of young women until the post-Second World War years, and textile clothing manufacture remained young women's largest industrial employer between 1931 and 1951.

Young women were in demand as unskilled and semiskilled workers. Their work was frequently heavy and unmechanized, demonstrating that the rate of technological change in industrial workplaces should not be overstated. In 1928, the London Advisory Council for Juvenile Employment noted that 'the average factory worker is either a machine minder or feeder or is engaged in parcelling, filling, wrapping or some form or another of packing, and it is mainly in this latter kind of work that women, girls and boys are employed.'[65] In the mid-1930s, Joan Beauchamp found that many industrial workers were still employed in small, cramped, ill-lit workshops, typical of London's East End, or the

[62] TNA, ED 124/49, MS: 'Particulars of Long Hours Worked by Domestic Servants as Disclosed by the Spring 1942 Registration', 1942.

[63] W. Foley, *The Forest Trilogy* (Oxford: Oxford University Press, 1992), 140.

[64] W. Foley, *Child in the Forest* (London: BBC, 1974), 190.

[65] London Advisory Council for Juvenile Employment, *Guide*, 130.

ill-ventilated workplaces characteristic of Birmingham and Manchester, which were furnished with ancient machinery, evaded the detection of the Factory Inspectorate, and were 'a positive menace . . . to the health of the worker'.[66]

Such conditions were frequently young industrial workers' greatest grievance. At the Ferranti factory where Lucy Lees was employed in the late 1920s, the roof was so dilapidated that bird droppings fell on the workers below.[67] Although the Second World War led to the demise of many small workshops, young women conscripts were often horrified at the state of the decrepit workplaces to which they were sent. One personnel manager of an armaments factory noted the reaction of two young female conscripts in 1942: 'They were very disappointed at our shabby factory . . . .[the l]avatory accommodation . . . will revolt them'.[68] The Factory Inspectorate expressed concern in the late 1940s that modernization was still at the 'planning and aspiration' stage in many factories and judged that labour shortage was partly explained by young women's reluctance to work in the dirty, unsanitary conditions that still prevailed at many firms.[69]

The benefits that technological developments brought to workers were limited. While larger, more modern factories frequently had better sanitation and welfare provision, working conditions could be pressurized. Reductions in industrial working hours during the 1930s were offset by the intensification of the working day that mass-production methods, such as the introduction of conveyor belts, facilitated. The *New Survey of London* noted in 1929 that

> A great proportion of the additional labour which has recently entered the metal-working trades, and the larger part especially of female labour, is engaged on what are virtually new industries, rendered possible on a large scale by the invention of mass-production processes and through the use of machinery and female labour.[70]

As this indicates, young women's increased employment was due to the expansion of labour-intensive processes, whether mechanized or not, rather than the direct replacement of adult men by young women. This type of work could be monotonous, but also stressful. Women workers fainted or became ill with the strain of keeping up the required speed on

66 Beauchamp, *Women*, 24.

67 LRO, NWSA, 1999.0335, interview with Lucy Lees.

68 Mass-Observation, *People in Production*, 138.

69 Report of the Chief Inspector of Factories and Workshops for the Year 1947: xvi (1948–9), Cd. 7621, 6–7.

70 Quoted in Beauchamp, *Women*, 25.

conveyor belts or timed piecework.[71] Winifred Cotterill, who worked at a Coventry factory in the 1920s, recalled her fear at being sent to work 'on the big machines', intimidated by the danger that the combination of their size and the speed demanded of machinists posed.[72] One young Birmingham worker at a large industrial firm complained to Joan Beauchamp in the 1930s that

> I started here at 24s a week, day rate, and then was told I must go on the Points system or get the sack. The speed-up is awful. You have to do 116 to 140 P's [points] to the hour to get a decent wage, and then there is all the waste of time in signing on for each job; you often waste 20 minutes in clocking on and finding the foreman to give you your job first thing. . . . The speed did me in, and I've been on the [sick] panel for weeks now.[73]

During the Second World War, pressure to raise productivity led to an increase in accident rates among juvenile workers between 1938 and 1941 of 20 per cent among girls and 21 per cent among boys.[74] Women at Newton Aycliffe Royal Ordinance Factory recalled headaches caused by the noise and working with cordite, regular accidents, and 'terrible' night shifts; 'you felt you were going to fall asleep.'[75] Such testimonies were common, and emphasize that increased productivity was the result of human effort, not simply technological changes. The women quoted here also illustrate that definitions of skill were always subjective; women workers recognized that speed and dexterity were essential skills, although ones undervalued by their employers who classed these workers as semi- or unskilled.

Despite the continuation of poor working conditions and the intensification of the labour process, factory employment became increasingly attractive to young women. From 1941, the reduction of the wage-incentive, due to wartime wage rises, prompted the government and other employers to recognize the potential contribution that welfare measures could make to increasing production, leading to the introduction of wireless music, tea breaks, and canteens,[76] the latter being available to about 50 per cent of industrial workers by 1944.[77] In the post-war years

[71] Glucksmann, *Women Assemble*, 101.

[72] MRC, Coventry Women's Work Collection, MSS 266/6/2, interview with W. Cotterill.

[73] Quoted in Beauchamp, *Women*, 33.

[74] Report of the Chief Inspector of Factories and Workshops for the Year 1941: iv (1941–2), Cd. 6397, 24.

[75] Imperial War Museum Sound Archive (IWM), tape ref. 19699, interview with S.M.

[76] Report of the Chief Inspector of Factories and Workshops for the Year 1941, 10.

[77] P. Inman, *Labour in Munitions* (London: HMSO, 1957), 185; Report of the Chief Inspector of Factories and Workshops for the Year 1944, xii (1945–6), Cd. 6698, 88–9.

working hours were further reduced: from the end of 1946, no industry was allowed to employ juveniles under 16 for more than forty-four hours per week.[78] By the late 1940s, as the social investigator Pearl Jephcott noted in her 1948 study of 103 teenage girls in various regions of England, factory jobs had proliferated and concurrently grown in popularity because of the security and relatively good pay they offered, and the slow improvement in their working conditions.[79]

Shop Work

Retail was already established as a major employer of young women by 1918, since the First World War accelerated a change in the gender composition of the workforce. The nature and status of shop work underwent significant changes during the following three decades. Prior to the 1930s, however, shop work was still stratified by gender as well as by class, with working class young women, particularly young girls, most likely to be occupied in small shops serving working class communities.[80] These could be 'slovenly, dirty, and inefficient',[81] characterized by working weeks of over sixty hours[82] and no promotion prospects.[83] Wages were poor—in 1925 the average earnings of a girl drapery assistant were 11s for a fifty-hour week[84]—and regulation minimal, with employers permitted to employ juveniles up to seventy-four hours per week prior to the 1934 Shops Act.

Much of the interwar increase in retail work was accounted for by the expansion in department and multiple stores. These shops kept production costs and prices low by offering a wide variety of cheap products, and by employing young, female assistants. Department stores, which increased in number from between 175 and 225 in 1914 to between 475 and 525 in 1938,[85] offered higher wages and more fringe benefits than smaller

[78] Report of the Chief Inspector of Factories and Workshops for the Year 1940, iv (1940–1), Cd. 6316, 24.

[79] P. Jephcott, *Rising Twenty: Notes on Some Ordinary Girls* (London: Faber and Faber, 1948), 128–9.

[80] Llewellyn Smith, *New Survey*, 2, 192.

[81] J. B. Priestley, *English Journey* (London: Heinemann, 1934), 17.

[82] Beauchamp, *Women*, 47.

[83] London Advisory Council for Juvenile Employment, *Guide*, 90–1.

[84] Calculated from Ministry of Labour, *Report Upon the Results of an Investigation into the Rates of Wages, the Hours of Employment and the Degree of Industrial Organisation in the Drapery and Allied Trades* (London: HMSO, 1926), 8–12.

[85] J. Jefferys, *Retail Trading in Britain, 1850–1950* (Cambridge: Cambridge University Press, 1954), 59. Jefferys' figures on department stores are approximations; no conclusive data are available.

shops.[86] The Co-operative Movement, the country's largest retailer until the 1950s, was noted as a particularly good employer, offering training, education, subsidized health-care, and, in common with other large retailers such as John Lewis, relatively high wages.[87]

The attractions of such jobs waned in the 1940s. War, and the limited ability of working class families to engage in luxury consumption prior to the late 1950s, restricted labour demand.[88] Moreover, by the mid-1940s pay and conditions compared poorly with those offered by office work or some factories.[89] Although the Shops Act of 1934 established a forty-eight-hour working week from 1937, many employers accepted this only because they were able to circumvent it, as wartime investigations showed,[90] and because of the gradual intensification of the working day, brought about by an emphasis on the sale of cheap goods through clever and efficient marketing. Many workers were paid an incentive bonus for each sale.[91] Long working hours remained common after the Second World War. Grace Wardle, who worked in a baker's shop from the age of 15 in 1948, recalled working from 5 o'clock in the morning until quarter past six in the evening in her teens, and was paid 26s for a working week of between sixty and seventy-two hours.[92] Adult women, who could work part-time, were increasingly preferred by smaller shops, and the growing ratio of (mostly female) shop assistants to (mostly male) managers limited promotion prospects. Nevertheless, shop work was firmly established as a major occupation of young women, particularly of the cheapest younger girls.

Office Work

Clerical occupations offered the highest earnings and shortest hours of all the sectors detailed here, as well as being widely considered clean, safe, and respectable employment for young women. Opportunities for lower-grade, labour-intensive jobs like typing increased significantly while the

86 Llewellyn Smith, *New Survey*, 2, 147–8.

87 A. M. Carr-Saunders et al., *Consumers' Co-operation in Great Britain* (London: Allen and Unwin, 1938), 334–44; B. Lancaster, *The Department Store: A Social History* (Leicester: Leicester University Press, 1995), 85, 98–9.

88 Jeffreys, *Retail*, 102.

89 Jephcott, *Rising Twenty*, 128–9.

90 TNA, ED 124/49, MS: 'Particulars of Long Hours Worked in Shops, Cinemas, etc as Disclosed by the Spring 1942 Registration', 1942.

91 M. Gardiner, *The Other Side of the Counter* (Brighton: Queenspark, 1985), 15, 18; London Advisory Council for Juvenile Employment, *Guide*, 90.

92 TLSL, Tameside tape collection, tape 28, interview with Grace Wardle.

proportion of clerical jobs in higher grades declined.[93] The widespread use of a marriage bar in the sector following the First World War prevented much career progression. Despite this, clerical employees tended to have more education than other groups of workers; the School Certificate was a requirement for many clerical jobs by the late 1940s. As Cohn and Anderson have noted, the 'feminization' of the clerical workforce was due to employers' preference for cheap workers with high levels of literacy and numeracy, and to the expansion of more lucrative and secure employment opportunities, such as school teaching, for young men.[94]

Wages and conditions were relatively good in clerical work, particularly in the public sector. In the late 1920s the *Social Survey of Merseyside* recorded an average weekly wage among women clerks under 20 of just 15s 6d; in London juvenile girl clerks earned on average 17s 6d per week.[95] However, interwar clerical expansion was concentrated in the private sector, characterized by lower wages, poor working conditions, and hours in excess of fifty per week.[96] This led the London Advisory Council for Juvenile Employment to judge in 1929 that 'The prospects of girls in clerical and commercial life are far more restricted [than those of boys]'. It advised that 'Only girls of good education and really suitable for clerical work should be advised to take it up'.[97]

As labour demand increased from the mid-1930s, and the public sector expanded during the 1940s, conditions improved. Young women employed by the Civil Service or local government could expect to work a forty-hour week and higher than average pay, particularly during the 1940s when the earnings of women clerks increased significantly more than those of female semiskilled and unskilled manual workers.[98] Clerical work was thus relatively well paid and secure. Its respectability was heightened by its cleanliness and its tradition of employing middle class women and, in the higher grades, middle class men. This combination of factors was embodied in Nellie Oldroyd's preference for clerical work: 'I did want to be someone and sit in an office in a white blouse and black

[93] G. Anderson (ed.), *The White-Blouse Revolution: Female Office Workers since 1870* (Manchester: Manchester University Press, 1988), 10–13.

[94] S. Cohn, *The Process of Occupational Sex-Typing: The Feminization of Clerical Labor in Great Britain* (Philadelphia: Temple University Press, 1985), 218–25; Anderson, *White-Blouse*, 6–12.

[95] Llewellyn Smith, *London*, 8, 303.

[96] Beauchamp, *Women*, 58.

[97] London Advisory Council for Juvenile Employment, *Guide*, 49.

[98] G. Routh, *Occupation and Pay in Great Britain 1906–79* (London: Macmillan, 1980), 120–1.

skirt.'[99] The degree of social mobility that clerical work offered was, however, restricted, with most young women confined to junior grades and to the growing number of typing pools. Nevertheless, the shift in the composition of the clerical workforce by class, gender, and age was one of the most significant changes in the English labour market during the period between 1918 and 1951, and getting an office job, long an aspiration of working class servants and factory girls, became increasingly realizable.

Unemployment

While employment opportunities expanded over this period, fear of unemployment remained real for many young women, particularly prior to the Second World War. Youth unemployment has been overlooked by many historians, since young women and men, particularly juveniles, experienced much lower levels of unemployment than adults. Unemployment peaked at 7 per cent for 16- and 17-year-old girls in 1931 and 8.3 per cent for boys in 1932, while adult unemployment in the latter year stood at 13.7 and 25.2 per cent for women and men, respectively.[100] Those studies that do exist concentrate on young men, implying that they were more likely to experience unemployment.[101] Yet, as these statistics suggest, it was not until the late teens that men's likelihood of experiencing unemployment rose significantly above women's. Moreover, the short duration of juvenile unemployment indicates that, as Beveridge found, what distinguished girls and boys from adults was not lower probability of losing a job but greater probability of obtaining a new one, indicating the short term and insecure nature of much of their work.[102] The unemployment figures thus belie the fact that a large proportion of juveniles experienced short spells of unemployment prior to the 1940s, particularly in the depressed areas of north-west England's textile communities and the coalfields of north-east England, which contained over three-quarters of the juvenile unemployed in the interwar years.[103]

[99] Oldroyd, 'Sweetmaking', 7.

[100] W. R. Garside, 'Juvenile Unemployment and Public Policy between the Wars', *Economic History Review*, 30/2 (1977), 377; M. Thomas, 'Labour Market Structure and the Nature of Unemployment in Interwar Britain', in B. Eichengreen and T. J. Hatton (eds.), *Interwar Unemployment in International Perspective* (London: Kluwer Academic, 1988), 116.

[101] D. Fowler, *The First Teenagers: The Lifestyles of Young Wage-Earners in Interwar Britain* (London: Woburn Press, 1995), 21.

[102] W. H. Beveridge, *Unemployment: A Problem of Industry*, 2nd edn. (London: Longmans, 1930), 406.

[103] Garside, 'Juvenile Unemployment', 377.

Youth unemployment was largely involuntary. Some commentators claimed that it was frictional, caused by juveniles leaving jobs voluntarily, and that many girls registered as unemployed were in fact unpaid domestic helpers in the home.[104] Benjamin and Kochin have upheld this view, arguing that unemployment was confined to a small group of young people who found that state unemployment benefit, or parental support, compensated for their loss of wages.[105] Yet successive contemporary studies indicate that the great majority of the young unemployed had been dismissed for reasons beyond their control—this was true of 70 per cent of the 2,701 unemployed girls examined by a Ministry of Labour survey in 1925, with just 4 per cent of girls claiming to have left work for domestic reasons.[106] The unusually detailed records of Manchester's Juvenile Employment Bureaux also undermine the notion that youth unemployment was confined to a small, static, unemployable group. About 30 per cent of registrations by unemployed girls and boys at the Bureaux were re-registrations throughout the years 1932 to 1936, suggesting that many juveniles experienced one or two spells of short-duration unemployment, often occurring after the age of 16, and a smaller proportion experienced far more frequent unemployment.[107]

The most common reason young women became unemployed was their displacement by cheaper, younger workers. Fowler claims that there is no evidence that vulnerability to unemployment increased with age and wage rises.[108] Yet against this, successive contemporary studies demonstrate that young men and women's likelihood of losing their job rose substantially following their sixteenth or eighteenth birthdays, when they qualified for higher wage rates.[109] Benjamin and Kochin have argued that this was due to the increase in the indirect costs that employers incurred when a worker reached 16, due to the levying of insurance on them.[110] Contemporary studies, however, indicate that there was no significant difference in vulnerability to unemployment between those workers in

104 Ministry of Labour, *Report on an Enquiry into the Personal Circumstances and Industrial History of 3331 Boys and 2701 Girls Registered for Employment at Employment Exchanges and Juvenile Employment Bureaux in June and July 1925* (London: HMSO, 1926), 36.

105 D. K. Benjamin and L. A. Kochin, 'What Went Right with Juvenile Unemployment Policy between the Wars: A Comment', *Economic History Review*, 32/4 (1979), 523–8.

106 Ministry of Labour, *Personal Circumstances*, 53.

107 Manchester Juvenile Employment Bureaux, *Annual Reports, 1932–36* (Manchester: Manchester Education Committee, 1933–6).

108 Fowler, *First Teenagers*, 21.

109 Ministry of Labour, *Personal Circumstances*, 56; A. D. K. Owen et al., *A Survey of Juvenile Employment and Welfare in Sheffield* (Sheffield: Sheffield Social Survey Committee, 1933), 24–5; L. Beales and R. S. Lambert (eds.), *Memoirs of the Unemployed* (London: Gollancz, 1934), 82.

110 Benjamin and Kochin, 'What Went Right', 524–5.

insurable and those in uninsurable industries. The Ministry of Labour's 1925 investigation, for example, found that 4 per cent of those girls employed in insured occupations and the same proportion of those in uninsured jobs were discharged at 16.[111] This trend was reflected by an article that appeared in the *Woman Worker* in 1920, entitled 'Too Old at Eighteen', which documented the dismissal of female factory workers across the country 'to make room for juveniles'.[112] As such reports suggest, women's unemployment in the post-First World War years was not always due to the return of male troops; juveniles displaced adult and young adult women workers in unskilled and semiskilled work throughout the interwar years. Young women's domestic assistance in the home was thus frequently a consequence, rather than a cause, of their unemployment.

The young unemployed were significantly worse off than their wage-earning counterparts, further undermining the notion that they left work voluntarily. The Out of Work donation of 1918 and the operation of the subsequent 'piecemeal and adhoc'[113] benefits system for the unemployed categorized juveniles and to an extent young adults as dependants on their parents. This was reflected in the introduction of a household means test in 1922, which was explicitly aimed at 'young persons': boys under 18 and young women under 21.[114] Following its introduction, the proportion of disallowed claims leapt from 7.9 per cent to 15.4 per cent.[115] Its repeal in 1927 was accompanied by cuts to the benefit rate for younger claimants. Those under 16 were ineligible for benefit until the 1934 Unemployment Act, and unemployment benefit exhibited more significant gender and age differentials than wages. In the decade following the 1920 Unemployment Act, 16- and 17-year-old girls were paid 6s per week and then, following the 1927 Unemployment Act, 5s, whereas boys were paid 7s 6d and then 6s.[116] Although the real value of young people's benefits rose during the 1930s, Hatton and Bailey have shown that they did not reach a level comparable with average wages.[117] Moreover, the effect of this rise was partially offset by the institution of a household means test in 1931, which judged an individual's benefit entitlement according to entire household income, and cut the relief rate of one in

[111] Ministry of Labour, *Personal Circumstances*, 56.

[112] *Woman Worker*, October 1920, 7.

[113] A. Deacon, *In Search of the Scrounger: The Administration of Unemployment Insurance in Britain 1920–31* (London: Bell, 1976), 14.

[114] *Ministry of Labour Gazette*, 32/3 (1924), 79.

[115] Deacon, *Scrounger*, 28.

[116] T. J. Hatton and R. E. Bailey, 'Unemployment Incidence in Interwar London', *Economica*, 69/276 (2002), 646–8.

[117] Ibid.

three of the long-term unemployed.[118] This also increased the economic pressure on young wage-earners whose households also accommodated unemployed adults, as the following chapter will detail. The means test was finally revoked by the 1948 National Assistance Act, which assessed those aged over 16 on their own income; by that stage, however, young workers were far less vulnerable to unemployment. The fact that young wage-earners did not choose to leave work to rely on the improved benefit provision made for the unemployed following the Second World War is a further indication that unemployment was caused by the nature of labour demand rather than by the 'unemployability' of large numbers of young people.

'Blind Alley Labour'?: Gender, Age, and the Labour Market

Although young women were one source of low-cost labour, the preceding discussion has made clear that they were not the only one. Married women and young men were also cheap workers. Heim, and more emphatically Savage and Scott, have pointed out that young workers of both sexes were cheaper than adult women in most sectors.[119] In order to understand young women's occupational distribution, we must evaluate how employers chose between the different sources of low-paid labour available. It is first important to turn to contemporary explanations of the youth labour market, since it is here that we can find the foundations of historians' neglect of the relationship between gender, age, and class that shaped working patterns.

The use of young women as cheap labour was frequently ignored by contemporary concern over the 'boy labour problem'. The 'extent to which boys leaving the Elementary Schools are drafted into work which lasted only a few years and then flung out, unskilled and untrained, upon the casual labour market'[120]—so-called blind alley jobs, held by porters, delivery boys, and, by the 1930s, cinema ushers—had caused concern since the late nineteenth century as an alleged cause of adult

[118] N. Whiteside, 'Counting the Cost: Sickness and Disability among Working People in an Era of Industrial Recession, 1920–39', *Economic History Review*, 40/2 (1987), 238 and 242.

[119] C. Heim, 'Structural Transformation and the Demand for New Labor in Advanced Economies: Interwar Britain', *Journal of Economic History*, 34/2 (1984), 585–95; M. Savage, 'Trade Unionism, Sex Segregation, and the State: Women's Employment in "New Industries" in Interwar Britain', *Social History*, 13 (1988), 222–4 and 227; Scott, 'New Manufacturing Workforce', 460–6.

[120] *Majority Report of the Royal Commission on the Poor Law*, 4 (London: HMSO, 1909), 545.

'unemployability'.[121] No comparable 'girl labour' debate emerged. In the decades prior to 1914 anxiety was expressed by middle class social investigators over young women's industrial work, which by its nature, and because it brought young workers into close contact with adult workers, was viewed as morally problematic.[122] Such concerns were less commonplace by the 1920s, suggesting, contrary to Thom, that Woollacott is right to assert that the First World War normalized young women's industrial labour to a degree.[123] The economic responsibilities shouldered by young women in working class households, and the independence their wage-earning afforded them, were both of growing concern, as subsequent chapters will show. However, the nature of their work attracted relatively little concern. Indeed, as Bingham has shown, young women's expanding employment opportunities were regularly cited by the interwar press, particularly in the 1920s, as evidence of the emergence of a 'modern' post-war society.[124]

This neglect of young women's work was largely due to the view of many politicians, sections of the media, and some trade unionists that women's widespread 'retirement' from paid employment upon marriage justified their employment in low-paid work. The National Advisory Council for Juvenile Employment justified its exclusion of female shop and catering workers from a 1932 investigation of blind alley work because of 'marriage wastage', while London Trades Council reported in 1945 that 'the blind-alley problem is more serious for boys than for girls, because a high proportion of girls are prepared to accept the fact that their work is temporary' due to the prospect of retirement on marriage.[125] Yet as the earlier discussion on unemployment pointed out, young women, like young men, were likely to be made unemployed in their mid-teens, years before most of them expected to marry. Clearly, definitions of blind alley work were highly gendered and overlooked the poorly paid and insecure nature of young women's work, and the

121 A. Freeman, *Boy Life and Labour: The Manufacture of Inefficiency* (London: P. S. King and Son, 1914), 68–71; Juvenile Education (Employment after the War), Final Report, PP. 1917–18, xi, Cd. 8512, 3 and 5; National Advisory Council on Juvenile Employment for England and Wales, *Fourth Report: Hours of Employment of Boys and Girls in 'Unregulated Occupations'* (London: HMSO, 1932).

122 E. Cadbury, M. C. Matheson, and G. Shann, *Women's Work and Wages: A Phase of Life in an Industrial City* (London: T. F. Unwin, 1906), 194–5.

123 Woollacott, *On Her Their Lives Depend*, 215–16; D. Thom, *Nice Girls and Rude Girls: Women Workers in World War I* (London: I. B. Tauris, 1998), 44–5.

124 Bingham, *Gender and Modernity*, 96.

125 TNA, LAB 19/97, MS: Memorandum on Apprenticeship and Other Methods of Entry into Employment, November 1941.

significance of this for their own economic circumstances and for those of their families.

The other major reason for contemporary neglect of the insecure and poorly paid nature of young women's work was the existence of domestic service. The major political parties and most sections of middle class opinion viewed domestic service as a favourable alternative to less secure work and viewed it as training for marriage and motherhood. In 1922 women who refused to take up domestic service posts were made ineligible for unemployment benefit and in 1928 the Ministry of Labour introduced a labour transference scheme for young unemployed women in the depressed areas of northern England that sent thousands into domestic service.[126] The demise of domestic service, buoyant labour demand for young women in other sectors, and a growing degree of hostility towards the occupation within the labour movement prompted growing concern over the need to provide girls, as well as boys, with employment advice and guidance during the Second World War and following the election in 1945 of a Labour government.[127] The prevalence of domestic service prior to the Second World War thus accentuated differences between young men's and young women's employment; it was only after its decline that long-standing similarities in their working patterns became a matter for debate. Even then, emphasis was placed on advising young people on finding secure jobs, evading the fact that the nature of labour demand was far more important than personal choice in explaining young women's concentration in low-paid work.[128]

Why were young women such a popular source of cheap labour? Historians and sociologists have frequently ascribed trends in labour demand for women primarily to their gender. This overlooks the heterogeneity of the female workforce; as Fowler has pointed out, age was important in determining a worker's pay, conditions, and job.[129] An important reason for the low status of both female and male young workers was their lack of employment experience and representation, which made them a highly disposable section of the labour force. Juvenile workers were often excluded from trade unions, and thus from wage agreements.[130] Moreover, their lack of employment experience was

[126] See chapter 4.

[127] Ministry of Labour and National Service, *Report of the National Youth Employment Council on the Work of the Youth Employment Service 1947–1950* (London: HMSO, 1950), 14; B. H. Reed et al., *Eighty Thousand Adolescents* (London: Allen and Unwin, 1950), 34–5.

[128] Ministry of Labour and National Service, *Youth Employment Service.*

[129] Fowler, *First Teenagers*, 13.

[130] Scott, 'New Manufacturing Workforce', 466.

assumed by employers to make them a more docile and malleable section of the workforce.[131] The workplace disputes examined in chapter 6 of this study indicate that although this assumption was not always correct, the most militant young workers were frequently those with several years' employment experience and some knowledge of trade unionism.

Yet most important in constructing young people as a cheap and disposable workforce was their position as dependants within the nuclear family household. Married women's higher wages are largely explained by their domestic responsibilities, which meant that they required a greater financial incentive to work outside the home than was true of their sons and daughters. This, of course, made them highly suitable for casual and part-time work. Paying low wages to young workers was justified by and simultaneously strengthened their reliance upon parents, or, in the case of domestic servants, their employers, for board and lodging. In 1934, several local education authorities in the prosperous south-east informed the Ministry of Labour that it was inadvisable for the young unemployed to migrate to their districts in search of work, since the new industries providing local employment relied on paying juveniles and young women wages below subsistence level, assuming parental support.[132] During the Second World War, the Ministry of Labour observed that juvenile workers remained a ready source of labour for non-essential occupations paying low wages and offering temporary or casual work.[133] While the nuclear family could, as chapter 2 will show, provide a means of solace and support for its members, its survival also sustained capitalist interests, facilitating the growth of mass production.

Young workers' position in the family and their lack of employment experience explains their attraction vis-à-vis adult women, but these factors did not determine whether employers preferred young women over young men or vice versa. Fowler's argument that no significant sexual division of labour existed in the youth labour market[134] is undermined by the large concentration of young women in domestic service and, later in the period, in gender-segregated factory, shop, and office jobs. Historians have variously attributed the pattern of employers' demand for young female labour to three factors: their alleged possession of

131 Savage, 'Trade Unionism', 223; S. R. Dennison, *The Location of Industry and the Depressed Areas* (London: Oxford University Press, 1939), 78.

132 TNA, LAB 19/42, Memo 1484/1934, MS: 'Local Education Authorities Which Require Stimulation Either by Letter or Interview', 1934.

133 TNA, LAB 19/97, Memorandum on Apprenticeship and Other Methods of Entry into Employment, November 1941.

134 Fowler, *First Teenagers*, 13.

'feminine' attributes such as dexterity and docility, which made them a better source of unskilled and semiskilled labour than men;[135] their domestic and reproductive roles,[136] and their low cost.[137] Yet these explanations are largely self-fulfilling. The first is the least convincing. The suggestion that employers recruited women for jobs considered 'feminine' attributes coherence to conceptualizations of femininity, which is contradicted by the fact that 'housework consists of an almost infinite variety of tasks'.[138] Employers' rhetoric indicates the malleability of gender discourse. Many, across the whole range of sectors, represented those diverse tasks on which women and young people were employed as requiring 'care and dexterity'[139] rather than skill; the ambiguity of 'feminine work' was demonstrated by the use of this discourse to justify both the employment of women as munitions workers during two World Wars and their exclusion from many industrial jobs after 1918.[140] It would, however, be overly simplistic to claim that this was a strategy consistently and consciously operated by employers. Long-standing social and cultural factors shaped norms to which employers adhered. A government investigation of 1929 pointed out the importance of local custom in shaping women's work, noting that 'work which is considered to be too heavy for women in Birmingham is often done by women in the Black Country'.[141] The cultural construction of femininity and youth thus shaped the changing nature of labour demand, but was also fundamentally influenced by it.

Women's long-term domestic commitments clearly shaped their employment patterns.[142] The Ministry of Labour noted that few apprenticeships were open to young women because employers 'would not consider it worthwhile to spend their time teaching a woman, when the chance of her remaining in their service is so small.'[143] Consequently,

135 See, for example, Glucksmann, *Women Assemble*, 198–9.

136 See, for example, S. Alexander, 'Women's Work in Nineteenth-Century London: A Study of the Years 1820–60s', in ead. (ed.), *Becoming a Woman, and Other Essays in 19th and 20th Century Feminist History* (London: Virago, 1994), 21–2, although Alexander also cites tradition as a factor: see 27.

137 See, for example, Beddoe, *Back to Home and Duty*, 67.

138 Scott, 'New Manufacturing Workforce', 450.

139 London Advisory Council for Juvenile Employment, *Guide*, 130; Juvenile Education, PP. 1917–18, 4.

140 Thom, *Nice Girls and Rude Girls*, 53–77.

141 Ministry of Labour, A Study of the Factors Which have Operated in the Past and Those Which are Operating Now to Determine the Distribution of Women in Industry, xvii (1929–30), Cmd 3508, 13.

142 C. Hakim, 'Five Feminist Myths about Women's Employment', *British Journal of Sociology*, 46/3 (1995), 432–7.

143 A Study of the Factors, 30.

Savage and Scott found that employers in capital-intensive industries preferred young men, who were likely to work until retirement age. Among these industries were several that only expanded significantly in the later 1930s, including many branches of light manufacture.[144] This helps to explain why the labour transference scheme initiated by the Ministry of Labour in 1928 did not begin transferring young women into industry until the mid-1930s.[145] However, the nature of labour demand sustained this sexual division of labour. In areas like north-west Lancashire, many women worked after marriage throughout this period, as a consequence of low male wages and high labour demand in the textile industry.[146] Similarly, married women's labour increased dramatically during the Second World War across England. Employers' imposition of a marriage bar during the interwar years in sectors where labour supply outstripped demand indicates that a measure of compulsion was necessary to achieve a young, cheap, and ultimately disposable workforce.[147] That marriage bars were primarily economically motivated was evident when, in the late 1930s, the outstripping of labour supply by demand led firms such as Rowntree and Courtaulds—two of the main proponents of the argument that the marriage bar promoted family life—to lift it, rather than to employ men at higher wages.[148] Similar considerations meant that the marriage bar in clerical work, abolished during the Second World War, was not reinstated in the post-war years since employers could make profitable use of married women's part-time labour to supplement the full-time work of younger women. In teaching, where labour demand was still adequately met by the male workforce, and demand for part-time labour was low, the marriage bar remained. Employers promoted a correlation of femininity with domesticity only when it met their requirements.

The difference in the expected longevity of young women's and young men's working lives—shaped, as we have seen, by employers' preferences as well as by family commitments—primarily determined differences in the sorts of low-paid jobs they undertook. Boys were keener than girls to undertake casual, poorly paid, insecure jobs for a couple of years after

[144] Savage, 'Trade Unionism', 218–22; Scott, 'New Manufacturing Workforce', 460–1, 473–4.

[145] See chapter 4.

[146] See chapter 2 for more details of such regional variation.

[147] J. Castle, 'Factory Work for Women: Courtaulds and GEC between the Wars', in B. Lancaster and T. Mason (eds.), *Life and Labour in a Twentieth Century City: The Experience of Coventry* (Coventry: Cryfield Press, 1986), 144–7.

[148] Scott, 'New Manufacturing Workforce', 462; J. Childs, 'Quaker Employers and Industrial Relations', *Sociological Review*, 12/2 (1964), 298–300.

leaving school to mark time prior to competing for an apprenticeship at the age of 15 or 16. As chapter 2 details, this was often condoned by their parents since it was believed that a son's earnings and job security would markedly increase once he had learnt a skilled trade.[149] In the 1940s, military conscription and, after 1945, National Service, sustained this pattern of male entry to casual work in the mid-teens. Conversely, young women remained a valuable source of labour for more secure, unskilled and semiskilled labour-intensive industrial and retail work, and, increasingly, as typists and low-grade clerks.[150] They had less incentive than young men to move out of such work due to their more limited employment alternatives. As this suggests, no functionalist explanation can adequately explain young women's employment patterns, which were also influenced by their own expectations and aspirations. When their employment opportunities did expand due to rising labour demand in the 1940s, some employers clearly preferred to engage married women who were less likely to be occupationally mobile, as Cohn found was increasingly true of many clerical employers by the late 1940s.[151] However, married women's preference for part-time work, and young women's limited promotion prospects across all sectors, meant that young women continued to constitute a reliable but cheap labour force, distinguished from married women by their dependence on parents and ability to engage in full-time work, and from young men by their prospects of marriage and motherhood.

Conclusion

The period between 1918 and 1950 was one of great transition for young women. Their employment opportunities increased to include industrial and office jobs that offered higher earnings and a shorter, though still substantial, working week, than the domestic servants and textile workers of the 1900s had endured. The experience of paid work structured around the industrialized working day thus became central to young women's lifestyles. Moreover, these workers constituted a central, rather than a peripheral, section of the workforce in a range of occupational sectors and were affected by and in turn helped to shape the changing nature of work within these.

[149] TNA, LAB 19/97, Memorandum on Apprenticeship and Other Methods of Entry into employment, November 1941.

[150] Cohn, *Sex-Typing*, 219–20.

[151] Ibid., 221–3.

Despite these changes, significant continuities are evident. The turbulent transition to a largely clerical and industrial workforce has led too many historians to overlook the importance of domestic service in structuring a sexual division of labour among young workers and in shaping the working lives of a huge number of young women in the first half of the twentieth century. Moreover, young women continued to be valued as a cheap, ultimately disposable labour supply in all of the sectors that employed them. Although contemporaries recognized this, debate over blind alley employment, which has provided a structure for subsequent historiography, ignored the extent to which young women's employment was characterized by low security, poor pay, and limited promotion prospects, and overemphasized the importance of gender in shaping labour demand. Unlike married women, young women tended to seek full-time, permanent work, indicating that many women were not as disposable from the workforce as some historical and sociological accounts of women's labour have claimed. Young women constituted a distinct group of workers by virtue of their dependence within the household, which legitimated the payment of low wages to them, and their expectations of marriage and motherhood, which justified their sometimes forced departure from the labour force in their early twenties. As this suggests, young women's working lives affected and were in turn shaped by their familial roles and relationships, the subject of the following chapter.

2

Earning a Living: Daughters and the Family Economy

In 1919 the War Cabinet Committee on Women in Industry offered support to the existing gendered differential in earnings by recommending that women's pay should in future be of a level 'sufficient to provide a single woman over 18 years of age' with the means for her own subsistence and that juvenile girls should be paid lower wages than this.[1] This representation of girls as fully dependent on their parents and of young adult women as having economic responsibility only for themselves, both working only for 'pin money' to fund personal leisure expenditure, was widespread in political discourse and in the press.[2] It has remained largely unchallenged by the limited historiography on young people between 1918 and 1950, which has concentrated on the emergence of the youthful consumer, preceding the development of mass youth culture in the 1950s.[3] The assumption that a 'male breadwinner model' was established in most English communities by the beginning of the twentieth century, made by many historians of women's lives as well as by economic and labour historians, has also obscured the importance of young women as wage-earners.[4]

[1] Report of the War Cabinet Committee on Women in Industry, (1919), Cmd 135, xxi.241, 6–7.

[2] A. Bingham, *Gender, Modernity, and the Popular Press in Inter-war Britain* (Oxford: Oxford University Press, 2004), 61.

[3] J. Bourke, *Working Class Cultures in Britain 1890–1960* (London: Routledge, 1994), 45–6; A. Davies, *Leisure, Gender, Poverty: Working Class Cultures in Manchester and Salford, 1900–1939* (Buckingham: Open University Press, 1992), 83–9; D. Fowler, *The First Teenagers: The Lifestyle of Young Wage-Earners in Interwar Britain*, (London: Woburn Press, 1995), 99 and 110–11; C. Langhamer, *Women's Leisure in England 1920–1960* (Manchester: Manchester University Press, 2000), 101–3.

[4] S. O. Rose, 'Gender and Labor History: The Nineteenth-Century Legacy', *International Review of Social History*, 38/supplement (1993), 154; D. Beddoe, *Back to Home and Duty: Women between the Wars 1918–1939* (London: Pandora, 1989), 48–88; J. Giles, *Women, Identity and Private Life in Britain, 1900–50* (Basingstoke: Macmillan, 1995), 4–5 and 48–9; J. Humphries, 'Class Struggle and the Persistence of the Working Class Family', *Cambridge Journal of Economics*, 1/3 (1977), 241–58.

The focus of studies that have sought to contradict this view has not remedied this situation, since most have been primarily concerned with married women's often irregular earning patterns.[5] Young women's family relations were, as the report cited earlier suggests, central to their lives, with most women living in the parental home until marriage. However, closer scrutiny of their household roles and relationships with parents and siblings indicates that economic responsibility, as well as limited social and financial independence, distinguished young wage-earners from schoolchildren and adults.

Young women wage-earners' economic responsibilities caused great concern among socialist and liberal commentators, particularly when adult males' ability to support their families was threatened by war or unemployment. The Association of Women Clerks and Secretaries (AWCS) justified their campaign to protect young women's employment after the First World War by citing daughters' economic importance to families bereaved by the conflict.[6] High unemployment prompted the feminist writer Winifred Holtby to declare in 1934 that in the industrial areas

> a new element has entered into the relationship between parents and children. As it is often easier for women than for men to find employment, so it is easier for adolescents than for adults. It therefore often happens that young girls are working in factories, private domestic service, shops and laundries, and using their small wage to support their parents. . . . It is not always easy, even for generous and exploitable adolescence, to shoulder the adult burden of responsibility.[7]

Holtby highlights here the significance of the introduction in 1931 of a household means test, which assessed an individual's entitlement to benefit by assessing total household income. Young women, who were less likely to be unemployed than their fathers, consequently often found their economic responsibilities greatly increased. However, while unemployment rendered young workers' financial importance visible to middle class society, social surveys indicate that young workers remained important as breadwinners in a range of working class households across varied, regional labour markets between 1918 and 1950.[8]

Young women's role and status within the working class household underwent significant change. In the interwar years, many young women

[5] See, for example, T. J. Hatton and R. E. Bailey, 'Female Labour Force Participation in Interwar Britain', *Oxford Economic Papers*, 40/4 (1988), 711–12; E. Roberts, *A Woman's Place* (Oxford: Blackwell, 1984).

[6] *The Woman Clerk* (July 1921), 6.

[7] W. Holtby, *Women and a Changing Civilisation* (London: John Lane, 1934), 118.

[8] B. S. Rowntree, *Poverty and Progress: A Second Social Survey of York* (London: Longman, 1941), 27 and 158–9.

were expected to leave home at an early age to enter residential domestic service, while their wage-earning brothers enjoyed higher status within the family. Other young women remained unoccupied, in order to help their mothers with domestic responsibilities. The changes wrought in the working class standard of living by unemployment, particularly among adult males, in the late 1920s and early 1930s; increases in state welfare, particularly during the 1940s; rising wages; and a decline in average family size from 2.5 children in 1916–20 to 2.2 in 1946–50[9] altered the demands that the family economy made on young women, but the need for their earnings remained strong. Moreover, the expansion in their employment opportunities heightened young women's ability to be significant breadwinners, with consequences for their status and relations within the family.

The present chapter assesses young women's family relations, demonstrating that the family economy structured their educational and employment opportunities, and their domestic responsibilities. It begins by examining the effect of regional labour markets on household breadwinning patterns and on young women's role within the family. It then turns to the ways in which the family economy structured youth: educational opportunities depended on a family's financial circumstances, whereas wage-earning was central to this life stage for most women. The reasons their earnings were so important to the family economy, and the factors that determined young women's relative importance as household breadwinners, are then examined. In doing so the chapter offers a fresh perspective on the working class standard of living between 1918 and 1950, arguing that poverty remained central to the life experience of many, but that young wage-earners were also crucial in expanding working class leisure and luxury consumption. The needs of the family economy thus strongly shaped women's experience of youth, and this highlights how economic and social factors structured age and gender relations and roles within working class households.

Regional Labour Markets

Young women's employment patterns were shaped by two factors: employers' demands for certain types of labour, considered in chapter 1, and household breadwinning strategies. Consideration of such strategies

[9] D. Coleman, 'Population', in A. H. Halsey and J. Webb (eds.), *Twentieth-Century British Social Trends* (Basingstoke: Macmillan, 2000), 36, Table 3.

demonstrates that gender- and age-specific divisions of labour were shaped by historical circumstance, rather than simply by 'custom' or 'tradition'. Horrell, Humphries, and Oxley have demonstrated that in nineteenth-century England, sexual and age-specific divisions of labour were shaped by local opportunities for adult male employment.[10] Although the distinctiveness of regional labour markets diminished between the 1920s and the 1940s, they remained important, as is demonstrated by interwar concern over the economic division between the depressed, industrial communities of northern England and the more buoyant towns in the south-east where light manufacturing industries increasingly prospered.[11] The importance of region in shaping girls' labour force participation is demonstrated by the significant degree of variance in the proportion of those who were in the labour force, which ranged from 50 per cent in Northumberland to 89 per cent in Leicester in 1931, a degree of variation far greater than that which existed in boys' labour force participation rates.[12] While historians have paid limited attention to support and survival strategies at local level, studies have often focused on a single region[13] or solely on married women, whose unpaid domestic labour meant that their entry to paid employment was frequently a response to a particular economic need, caused, for example, by a husband's unemployment.[14] This, however, does not contradict the still widely held assumption that most working class households relied solely on a single, adult male breadwinner during our period. Scrutinizing young women's much more regular earning patterns challenges this, indicating that daughters' earnings were an integral, regular, and crucial component of the family economy in a wide range of working class households. However, young women's contributions to their households varied according to familial need and local labour demand, encompassing

[10] S. Horrell and D. Oxley, 'Crust or Crumb?: Intrahousehold resource allocation and male breadwinning in late Victorian Britain', *Economic History Review*, 52/3 (1999), 494–522; S. Horrell and J. Humphries, 'The Origin and Expansion of the Male Breadwinner Family: The case of Nineteenth Century Britain', *International Review of Social History*, 42/supplement. (1997), 64.

[11] S. R. Dennison, *The Location of Industry and the Depressed Areas* (London: Oxford University Press, 1939).

[12] Cambridge and Oxford had far lower participation rates among boys: 44 and 56 per cent, respectively, but this was due to the large proportion of university students among 18 to 20 year olds; the rates for younger juveniles (14 to 17 year olds) were much nearer the mean for England: 67 per cent in Cambridge and 74 per cent in Oxford.

[13] Davies, *Leisure*.

[14] Hatton and Bailey, 'Female labour force participation', 711–12; C. M. Moehling, 'Women's Work and Men's Unemployment', *Journal of Economic History*, 61/4 (2001), 928–9; Roberts, *Woman's Place*, 159–61.

domestic labour as well as wage-earning. In many cases, the support they offered, in both financial and domestic terms, surpassed that given by their brothers or fathers.

Here, four areas—London, Northumberland, Blackburn, and Coventry—are briefly examined to highlight regional and household factors that influenced girls' labour force participation and employment patterns. Juvenile girls are the focus, since the census offers detailed records of their employment at local level. London has been selected due to its significance as the largest urban labour market in England, representing 15 per cent of the interwar labour force and still 9 per cent in 1951.[15] Northumberland's strong sexual division of labour was typical of many rural localities, and indicates how the interaction of domestic responsibilities with the needs of the family budget shaped girls' labour force participation. Blackburn, conversely, recorded the highest rate of adult female labour force participation of any English county and highlights how mothers' labour force participation, high adult unemployment, and the decline of the textile industry affected girls' employment patterns. By the 1930s, a more buoyant type of labour market was emerging, typified here by Coventry, which was characterized by a sexual division of labour stronger than that of Blackburn, but was increasingly dominated by light manufacturing industries and by the retail and clerical sectors.

In rural communities, limited employment for women increased reliance on male breadwinners. Northumbrian communities remained heavily reliant upon agriculture and mining for adult employment throughout this period; in 1931, 34 per cent of men were employed as miners and 10 per cent in agriculture. Traditionally, miners enjoyed relatively high wages, and this, together with a lack of alternative local industrial employment, increased reliance upon male breadwinning; just 7 per cent of women were engaged in paid employment in 1931, and 43 per cent of girls compared with 78 per cent of boys.[16]

[15] D. Baines and P. Johnson, 'In Search of the "Traditional" Working class: Social Mobility and Occupational Continuity in Interwar London', *Economic History Review*, 52/4 (1999); B. Eichengreen, 'Juvenile Unemployment in Twentieth-Century Britain: The Emergence of a Problem', *Social Research*, 54/2 (1987).

[16] Figures derived from *Census of England and Wales, 1921: County Tables* (London: HMSO, 1924), Table 16; *Census of England and Wales, 1931: Occupation Tables* (London: HMSO, 1934), Tables 2, 3, and 18. It is impossible to provide a meaningful comparison with juveniles' participation rates in 1921, since the definition of juvenile in the 1921 Census included a large number of children of compulsory school age, although the proportion of those unoccupied is included in the graphs presented here for both years.

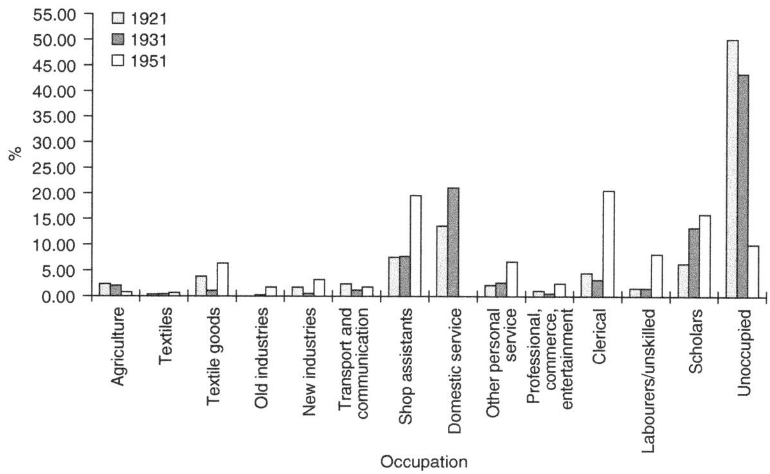

FIGURE 2. Occupational distribution of girls, Northumberland, 1921, 1931, and 1951

Source: *Census of England and Wales, 1921: County Table for Northumberland* (London: HMSO, 1923), Table 18; *Census of England and Wales, 1931: Occupation Tables* (London: HMSO, 1934), Table 18; *Census of England and Wales, 1951: Occupation Tables* (London: HMSO, 1954), Table 18.

In such communities, maintaining a daughter at home denoted respectability, a variable concept which in this localized context signified males' ability to support their families, but also a maternal need for domestic assistance. Figure 2 shows that in 1931 44 per cent of Northumberland girls were unoccupied, as Linda Thew, who grew up in a Northumbrian mining family in the interwar years, recalled:

I remember one father saying of his daughter who left the secondary school at 14 because he wasn't going to have her worry herself into an early grave with all that 'book stuff'. 'With three men working, it's a pity if we can't keep one lass at home without her having to work.'[17]

This practice of keeping a daughter at home, due to 'the demand for [daughters'] services'[18] and their father's ability to support them, was

[17] L. M. Thew, *The Pit Village and the Store* (London: Pluto Press, 1985), 124.

[18] A. D. K. Owen et al., *A Survey of Juvenile Employment and Welfare in Sheffield* (Sheffield: Sheffield Social Survey Committee, 1933), 16; D. Caradog Jones, *The Social Survey of Merseyside*, 2 (Liverpool: Liverpool University Press, 1934), 320; D. Gittins, *Fair Sex: Family Size and Structure, 1900–39* (London: Hutchinson, 1982), 70; Roberts, *Woman's Place*, 39–40.

evident in households headed by skilled manual workers elsewhere in interwar England. A daughter maintained at home was important in sustaining wage-earners and relieving her mother's domestic burden, as the *Social Survey of Merseyside* noted.[19] Some certainly became 'the family drudge', their domestic obligations limiting opportunities for courtship, marriage, and thus independence from the parental home.[20] Although the practice declined in the 1940s, investigations of rural areas noted strong parental opposition to daughters' war work because of the loss of their domestic labour.[21] The proportion of girls who were neither wage-earners nor at school dropped significantly in the 1930s and 1940s, but 10 per cent of Northumberland girls remained unoccupied in 1951, whereas the national average was just 5 per cent.

Yet the 'male breadwinner model' that historians have often used to categorize such households[22] requires great qualification. Even those agricultural and mining households that appeared to conform to this relatively recent 'tradition' could not in fact afford to support a large number of non-earners. This had greater consequences for older children's labour force participation than for married women's. Boys could find local employment as miners (34 per cent in 1931), agricultural workers (12 per cent), or messengers and delivery boys (11 per cent), but their wages were not high enough to support their sisters, whose migration to domestic service employment was often essential to the social economy of the rural poor.[23] This movement is partially captured by Figure 2, although not fully; many residential servants would have been recorded at the household of their employer, which might well be outside their home region, and were thus not enumerated on the local census. By providing board and lodging, residential domestic service reduced spatial and financial demands upon

[19] Caradog Jones, *Merseyside*, 2, 320.

[20] Thew, *Pit Village*, 124; see also R. Roberts, *The Classic Slum* (Harmondsworth: Penguin, 1973), 53; and L. Davidoff et al., *The Family Story: Blood, Contract and Intimacy, 1830–1960* (London: Longman, 1999), ch. 8.

[21] Mass-Observation, *War Factory* (London: Gollancz, 1943), 41; TNA, LAB 19/99, Note on Youth Advisory Council Paper No. 1; LAB 19/99, YAC Minutes no. 1/42, Mon 29th June 1942.

[22] Horrell and Humphries, 'Male Breadwinner Family'; C. Creighton, 'The Rise of the Male Breadwinner Family: A Reappraisal', *Comparative Studies in Society and History*, 38/2 (1996); Beddoe, *Home and Duty*, 89; Giles, *Women, Identity and Private Life*, 5 and 50.

[23] On the long-term importance of young women's wages to the rural family economy see Horrell and Humphries, 'Male Breadwinner Family', 89–117; N. Verdon, 'The Rural Labour Market in the Early Nineteenth Century: Women's and Children's Employment, Family Income, and the 1834 Poor Law Report', *Economic History Review*, 55/2 (2002), 299–323.

overcrowded households. The importance of this during periods of high unemployment is demonstrated by the decline in the proportions of Northumbrian girls who were unoccupied or employed as clerks between 1921 and 1931, and the corresponding increase in domestic servants.

The need for supplementary earners continued through the 1930s and 1940s, and helped to shape the dramatic changes that occurred in girls' and women's employment patterns between 1931 and 1951. The proportion of adult women in employment rose from 7 to 31 per cent, with most finding employment in offices (10 per cent) or as cleaners (7 per cent). Yet the increase in the proportion of occupied girls was even more dramatic, rising by 30 to 73 per cent, emphasizing the importance of the war and its aftermath for rural young women. The rapid decline of domestic service and personal service (included as a single category in the 1951 data here) was accompanied by an expansion in clerical and retail employment, due to rising labour demand and young men's transference into the lucrative and relatively secure engineering sector. Girls' willingness to take advantage of these opportunities points to the fact that many households valued daughters' economic contribution more than their full-time domestic help in the home, when local jobs were available.[24] The Second World War thus had a dramatic effect on young women's earning patterns, economic status, and lifestyles in rural communities.

In communities where households required more than the adult male wage, women's and particularly young workers' labour force participation was often long established. This pattern prevailed in many Lancashire textile towns, like Blackburn. In the interwar years the largest employers of men were the textile industry (22 per cent in 1931) and labouring and unskilled work (17 per cent)—low-waged occupations. Consequently, 62 per cent of women and 79 per cent of both girls and boys were in the labour force in 1931. Although textile employment for girls declined following the First World War, it continued to be their largest employer throughout the period, as Figure 3 shows. Low male wages and high labour demand meant that many young women expected to remain in full-time employment after marriage.[25] One lace worker from Nottingham, where a similar pattern of employment among textile workers prevailed,

[24] On the insecurity of agricultural work and wages in this period see A. J. Howkins, *The Death of Rural England: A Social History of the Countryside since 1900* (London: Routledge, 2003), 127–8.

[25] J. and S. Jewkes, *The Juvenile Labour Market* (London: Gollancz, 1938), 16–17; Roberts, *Woman's Place*, 36.

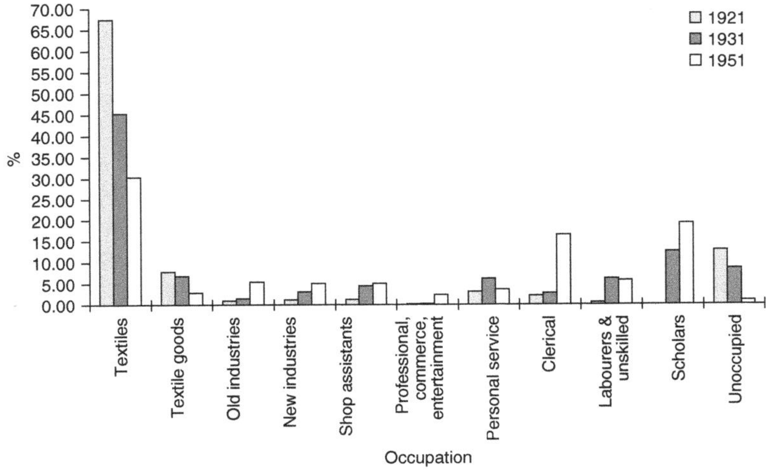

FIGURE 3. Occupational distribution of girls, Blackburn, 1921, 1931, and 1951
Source: *Census, 1921: County Table for Lancashire* (London: HMSO, 1923), Table 18; *Census, 1931: Occupation Tables*, Table 18; *Census, 1951: Occupation Tables*, Table 18.

explained that she continued working after her marriage in the 1930s—with the support of her husband—because, 'if you're a lace worker, you're a lace worker, it's in you, and that's it'.[26]

In Blackburn, as in Northumberland, the value of girls' earnings to their households changed over time. Young textile workers were vulnerable to unemployment in the late 1920s and early 1930s, but the fact that they *had* to work for economic reasons is highlighted by the concurrent increase in the proportion employed in personal service (most as domestic servants), from 2 per cent in 1921 to 6 per cent in 1931. Nora Holroyd, who began her working life in a textile mill, was made unemployed in the early 1930s: 'So my mother had two girls out of work. So I went down to—what did they call it—Junior [Employment] Exchange. And they found me a job with—a woman, looking after her family—service.'[27] The decline in the proportion of unoccupied girls over the same period strongly suggests that the unemployment of other household members prompted girls to enter the labour force in areas where jobs were available to them.

26 Nottingham Local Studies Library (NLSL), Making Ends Meet collection, A85/c/1, interview with Edna.

27 Lancashire Records Office (LRO), North West Sound Archive (NWSA), 2000.0651A, interview with Nora Holroyd.

Girls' high level of labour force participation in the early 1930s was, then, largely explained by economic need and their likelihood of obtaining work being greater than that of their fathers or brothers. This is demonstrated by the decline in the proportion of occupied girls from 79 to 73 per cent between 1931 and 1951. This was not true of boys, whose labour force participation remained static at 79 per cent, or of adult women, whose labour force participation rose from 62 to 68 per cent. This pattern points to the increasing availability of part-time work for married women as cleaners or office workers during the 1940s, and to the potential advantages that secondary education could provide to girls in a labour market where clerical opportunities expanded dramatically during and after the war. Boys, on the other hand, could get secure and skilled employment by entering an engineering apprenticeship, which increased in availability. Their earnings and those of adult women could thus help families to afford girls' schooling, and consequently aid their attempts to obtain lucrative office jobs.

In areas where a significant proportion of men were skilled workers, young women often ceased full-time employment upon marriage, but their earnings still had great short-term value for the household. In Coventry the largest employer of males was the metal industry, which employed 38 per cent of the city's men in 1931 and 37 per cent twenty years later. Metal work paid relatively high wages—an adult male's mean weekly earnings stood at 75s in 1938[28]—and only 22 per cent of adult women were in the workforce in 1931. However, entry to the metal industry was largely restricted to apprenticeships, generally limited to boys aged 15 or 16. The very low wages of metal apprentices, and the limited availability of paid work for married women, enhanced the value of a daughter's employment in the interwar years. Consequently, in 1931 75 per cent of girls and 90 per cent of boys were in the labour force, reflecting the buoyancy of the local labour market.

Girls' employment and earning patterns were influenced by those of their brothers. Many male school leavers in Coventry entered 'blind alley' work—14 per cent of 14-year-old boys were messengers or porters in 1931, the second-largest employer after metal work—to mark time before competing for an apprenticeship. The Ministry of Labour noted the continuation of this trend during the Second World War, when 'in the Distributive trades and the Textile industry boys of 14–15 taking "blind alley" jobs, regard these merely as a stop-gap, until they can enter

[28] Ministry of Labour, 'Average Earnings and Hours Enquiry, October 1938', *Ministry of Labour Gazette* (February–July 1944).

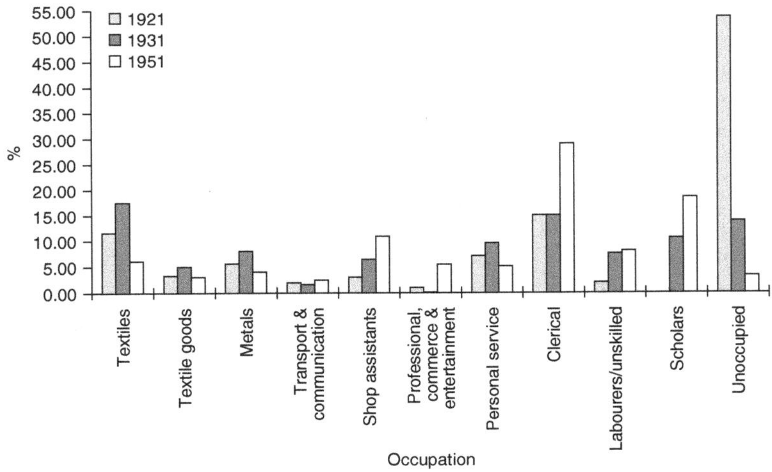

FIGURE 4. Occupational distribution of girls, Coventry, 1921, 1931, and 1951
Source: *Census, 1921: County Table for Warwickshire* (London: HMSO, 1923), Table 18; *Census, 1931: Occupation Tables*, Table 18; *Census, 1951: Occupation Tables*, Table 18.

apprenticeships, which the majority succeed in doing before becoming redundant.'[29] Consequently, girls were in demand for relatively secure industrial or clerical work. Figure 4 demonstrates that between 1921 and 1951 the labour force participation of Coventry girls rose dramatically, from 46 to 78 per cent, largely because of expanding earning opportunities in industry and retail work from the mid 1930s. Doris Addicott, who began work at Coventry's Courtaulds firm in 1924, remembered that 'You had no choice except GEC or Courtaulds in those days',[30] but by 1936 many of Mrs Johnson's workmates at GEC were leaving for work at Armstrong's, one of the expanding arms manufacturers.[31] Of greater significance by the late 1940s was the expansion of clerical work, reflecting the city's continued economic growth. The proportion of adult women employed rose to 37 per cent in 1951, enabling more girls to benefit from post-compulsory education, but the proportion at school was lower than the national average (13 per cent compared with 19 per cent) largely

[29] TNA, LAB 19/97, Memorandum on Apprenticeship and Other Methods of Entry into Employment, November 1941, 2.

[30] Modern Records Centre, University of Warwick (MRC), Coventry Women's Work Collection, MSS 266/6/1, interview with Doris Addicott.

[31] MRC, Coventry Women's Work Collection, MSS 292/6/3, interview with Mrs E. Johnson.

because lucrative and secure employment was available for those who left school at 15.

This pattern also points to the growing importance of young women's earnings relative to those of other family members when their employment opportunities increased from the mid-1930s and especially in the 1940s. Mary Collins, the daughter of a skilled factory worker, recalled of her youth in Manchester during the Second World War:

> I worked in Hawker Siddeley, my father was a bus-driver, I was only 18. He had to do compulsory overtime, I had to do a 12 hour shift, we used to compare wages. Before that I'd never known what my dad earned. We were having races and I used to feel sorry for my dad because I was earning perhaps a shilling or two more than he was, it was a great boon. I was earning over £5 a week, which was good money.[32]

Post-war studies suggest that maintaining a wife outside the workforce remained a sign of affluence in many working class communities in the early 1950s, particularly after she had had her first child.[33] However, this pattern actually relied upon the continued contributions of wage-earning daughters who were actively contributing to a rising level of income in many households.

The data provided on London differ from those presented on the provincial areas discussed previously. The computerized dataset of the *New Survey of London* is used to provide a snapshot of working class occupational distribution across 26,915 (over 2 per cent of) working class households in thiry-eight London boroughs between 1929 and 1931. These data enable an analysis to be made of wage-earners according to their family position, as daughters or as heads of the household for example, rather than simply on the basis of their age and gender. However, its wide coverage means that comparisons can also be made with the 1951 census returns for the same districts, and these data are presented in Figure 5.

While 10 per cent of male heads of household enumerated by the *New Survey of London* were employed in the metal industry, and 48 per cent altogether were employed on skilled work, 29 per cent were unskilled workers, most commonly as labourers employed on casual, insecure work in the transport and communications sector. The 1951 Census enumerated 65 per cent of the adult male workforce as employed in unspecified unskilled occupations. Consequently, relatively large proportions of other

32 Tameside Local Studies Library (TLSL), Manchester Studies collection, tape 1075, interview with Mary Collins.

33 M. Young and P. Wilmott, *Family and Kinship in East London* (Harmondsworth: Penguin, 1963), 18–20.

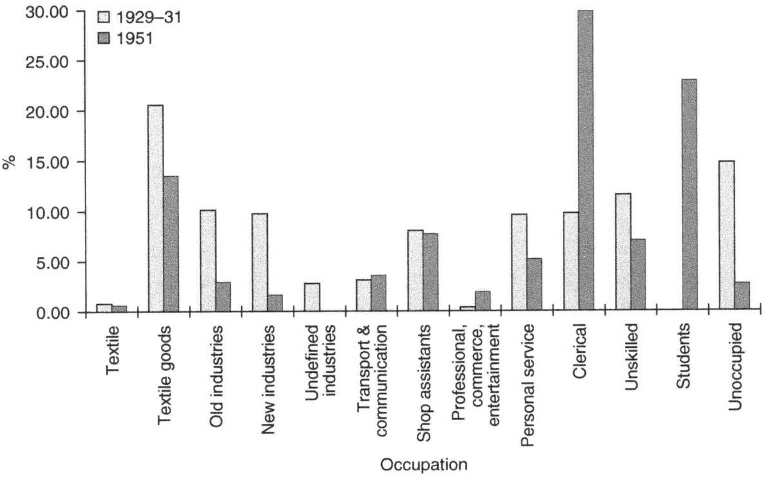

FIGURE 5. Occupational distribution of girls, London, 1929–1931 and 1951
Source: UK Data Archive, University of Essex, SN3758, *New Survey of London* datafiles; *Census, 1951: Occupation Tables*, Table 18.

groups—36 per cent of adult women, 85 per cent of girls, and 89 per cent of boys—were in the labour force in 1929–31.

London girls benefited from the expansion of retail, clerical, and light industrial work earlier than those in most provincial areas. Between 1929 and 1931, boys could earn relatively high wages as either metal workers (8 per cent), clerical workers (8 per cent), or in blind alley, but relatively well-paid, jobs in transport and communications (30 per cent). This led employers in the growth industries to employ girls on lucrative and relatively secure semiskilled work. Thirty-four per cent of girls were thus employed, mainly in the expanding metal and food-processing trades. However, the expansion of 'new' industries was slower than sometimes assumed. Textile goods manufacture, a large employer of London girls since the nineteenth century, continued to dominate the labour market until the Second World War, and remained girls' largest industrial employer in 1951. Of greater significance than industrial expansion was the proliferation of clerical jobs, which enabled a far higher proportion of girls in London than in many provincial areas to obtain relatively well paid non-manual work by the early 1950s, raising their financial value to families relative to that of their brothers, 30 per cent of whom were employed in unskilled industrial work and another 13 per cent in poorly paid metal apprenticeships in 1951. Just as was the case nationally, so in London girls' employment patterns underwent a far more dramatic change between the end of the First World War and the beginning of the 1950s than did those of boys, with implications for their economic status in the household.

Schooling

The importance of children as wage-earners is demonstrated by the difficult decisions taken by parents about education. Most secondary schools charged fees before 1944. Under 7 per cent of 15 to 18 year olds attended school in the interwar years.[34] Even if a scholarship was obtained, families faced the cost of uniform, travel expenses, and, indirectly, loss of juvenile earnings. Price lists and personal testimonies indicate that a uniform for a selective grammar school cost between £2 10s and £5 in the mid-1930s, when the average adult male wage was £3 4s per week.[35] Following the introduction of compulsory, free secondary education by the 1944 Education Act, the family economy continued to shape decisions about whether young people experienced post-compulsory education; 27 per cent did so in 1950.[36] Selective grammar schools remained expensive, despite abolition of fees. In the late 1940s a uniform cost up to £10;[37] average weekly male earnings stood at £7 1s in 1949. Since grammar schools were generally in middle class suburbs, transport costs were another important consideration.

Existing historical studies of the subject have suggested that widespread bias towards boys shaped the allocation of education,[38] and a notable number of women in my sample concurred with this, particularly those whose education took place before the 1944 Education Act. Dolly's father, a plumber, 'believed the lads should go to High School. I passed a scholarship to go, but wasn't allowed to. We were short of money, and he considered that lads would need the education more than a girl. I felt badly

[34] A. H. Halsey, *British Social Trends since 1900*, 2nd edn. (Basingstoke: Macmillan, 1988), 230.

[35] See 'Farnworth Grammar School: Girls' Uniform Prices *Ca.* 1936', http://www.fgs.utvinternet.com/36_Uniforms.html (retrieved 20 August 2004).

[36] Annual Report of the Ministry of Education, 1950 (PP 1950–51), Cd.8244, 142–3.

[37] Janet Cook, cited on http://clutch.open.ac.uk/schools/bushfield00/uniform.html (retrieved 28 August 2004).

[38] S. Alexander, 'Becoming a woman in London in the 1920s and 1930s', in ead., *Becoming a Woman and Other Essays in 19th and 20th Century Feminist History* (London: Virago, 1994), 213; Beddoe, *Home and Duty*, 41; J. Kamm, *Hope Deferred: Girls' Education in English History* (London: Methuen, 1965), 233.

about that at the time.'[39] Joyce Shaw, the daughter of a stevedore, left school aged 14 in the 1940s. She judged that 'We must have been more comfortable than most people because we always had very good meals and good clothes', but even so, 'with the boys, I think it's an old feeling that, well, lads need an education, girls don't, girls can always, er, get work.'[40]

Such views were particularly widespread in those communities where a girl's earning potential was limited. In Northumberland, ' "Educate a boy and dress a girl" was a maxim still prevalent' in the 1930s and Linda Thew's paternal grandparents opposed her parents' decision to send her, as well as her brother, to secondary school.[41] In the mid-1940s, social investigator Pearl Jephcott quoted a parent who represented the views of a significant proportion of her sample taken from a northern, semi-rural district: 'If Nesta had gone to the secondary it would only have meant an office instead of that good shop job that she's got now. Schooling is different for her brother, of course, because he has his living to make for always.'[42]

Interesting and insightful though such testimonies are, no existing study has produced quantitative proof of gender bias in the allocation of education, or examined the influence of household breadwinning patterns upon this. The Censuses of 1931 and 1951 enable such an analysis. They strongly suggest that although gender did influence the allocation of education, particularly prior to the 1950s, family income was the most important determinant. Consequently, a girl's chances of receiving extended education varied according to local employment opportunities. As Figure 6 shows, across England as a whole, 24 and 26 per cent of 14-year-old girls and boys, respectively, were in full-time education in 1931, suggesting that boys were slightly more likely to have their schooling extended, probably as a result of their longer working lives. However, regional variation was marked. In Northumberland, just 10 per cent of 14-year-old girls were at school compared with over 25 per cent of boys, demonstrating that girls' limited employment opportunities and short working lives discouraged poorer households from extending their education. In Blackburn, the converse was true. A greater proportion of households were able and willing to invest in secondary education, with 44 per cent of girls and 33 per cent of boys being recorded as scholars,

[39] Lifetimes History Group, *Something in Common* (Manchester: Manchester Polytechnic, 1975), 13.

[40] LRO, NWSA, 1993.0020, interview with J. Shaw.

[41] L. M. Thew, *A Tune for Bears to Dance to: A Childhood* (Berwick-upon-Tweed: Bridge Studios, 1992), 145.

[42] P. Jephcott, *Rising Twenty: Notes on Some Ordinary Girls* (London: Faber and Faber, 1948), 99.

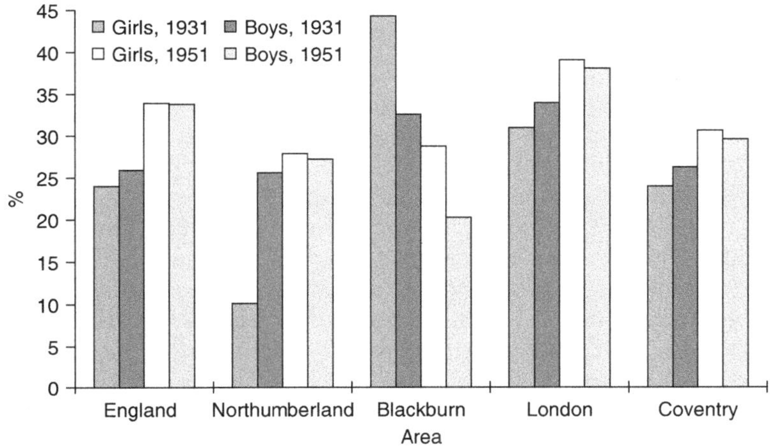

FIGURE 6. Percentage of 14 year olds in full-time education, England and selected localities, 1931, and percentage of 15 year olds in full-time education, England and selected localities, 1951

Source: *Census, 1931: Occupation Tables*, Table 18; *Census, 1951: Occupation Tables*, Table 18.

demonstrating the long-term importance of women as household breadwinners in this textile community, and the value of some secondary education for girls as better-paid, secure, clerical, and retail employment expanded.

Girls' high educational participation in Blackburn also hints at a less patriarchal form of household decision-making than some historians have suggested existed. Whereas Davies has argued that the division of labour had little impact upon patterns of household decision-making,[43] Roberts and Gittins have suggested that women's paid work contributed to (but did not determine) a more equal marital relationship in which decisions over the family economy might be shared.[44] Griffiths has shown that maternal concern to keep daughters out of dangerous, dirty, and insecure mill jobs when possible had become a powerful sentiment in textile communities by the 1930s[45] and education increasingly offered a passport to better employment.

By 1951 a greater proportion of juveniles were likely to stay on at school and gender bias was not significant nationally; in fact, as Figure 6 shows,

43 Davies, *Leisure*, 55–8. 44 Gittins, *Fair Sex*, 134–6; Roberts, *Woman's Place*, 116–18.

45 T. Griffiths, *The Lancashire Working Classes c.1880–1930* (Oxford: Clarendon Press, 2001), 126–7.

20 and 19 per cent of 15-year-old girls and boys, respectively, were recorded at school that year. This testifies to a rise in both the standard of living, which meant that many households did not have to limit education to certain children, and the value of educational qualifications for girls as clerical employment expanded across a range of regional labour markets. Boys, on the other hand, could continue to benefit from entering apprenticeships in the skilled trades at the age of 15 or 16, reducing the value of further schooling for them. These developments, together with the prominence of young women as war workers, and the 1944 Education Act, shaped an attitudinal shift towards an acceptance of the equal value of education for boys and girls. Hilda Fielding believed that this cultural change meant that her younger sister had far less of a struggle to obtain further education in the late 1940s than she herself had faced ten years earlier.[46] The effect of gender on the life course, particularly in the short to medium term, was thus largely determined by family composition, household income, and local labour demand, rather than by static, unchanging, prescriptive gendered roles.

The extent of consensus between husbands and wives over the allocation of education should not be overemphasized. Young and Wilmott noted that in 1950s Bethnal Green, mothers provided far greater encouragement than most fathers to daughters who passed their eleven-plus exam for grammar school. Many juggled the household budget or went out to work to fund educational expenses that their husbands could not or would not meet.[47] This trend partially explains why the proportion of adult women in the London workforce rose to 47 per cent between 1931 and 1951 while the proportion of girls and boys dropped to 75 and 77 per cent, respectively. Carolyn Steedman recalls that maternal pleasure at her entry to grammar school contrasted with her father's greater indifference or ambivalence:

> the uniform I needed for grammar school was the subject of angry debate. [My father had] been approached for money for the gabardine mac, the tunic, the shoes, and he had handed some over, but not a lot. . . . The issue, this Saturday afternoon, is the blouses that I will have to wear. . . . I approach him at my mother's persuasion and drag his attention away from the form on telly. He asks why I can't wear the one I've got on.[48]

Memoirs like Steedman's indicate that differences in attitudes towards education were not simply shaped by notions of a child's economic 'value'. For aspirant women like Steedman's mother, who had themselves been

46 TLSL, Tameside tapes collection, tape 244, interview with Miss Fielding.
47 Young and Wilmott, *Family and Kinship*, 177–9.
48 C. Steedman, *Landscape for a Good Woman* (London: Virago, 1986), 57.

denied a secondary education in the pre-1944 years, their daughters often became a repository for their thwarted ambitions. This adds support to Jerry White's conclusion, based on his North London case study, that women found less consolation for material deprivation in working class culture than men did, largely because of the gender discrimination they faced in the allocation of financial and social independence, and in employment opportunities. As a consequence, they more frequently looked for avenues of escape.[49] It is a theme returned to throughout this study, particularly in chapter 4.

Even in 1951, most young people did not remain at school after finishing their compulsory education. Older children, who were often expected to begin earning as early as possible to help to maintain younger siblings, were particularly disadvantaged.[50] Mrs Savage, who entered industrial employment in Manchester during the early 1920s, as the oldest of five, recalled that her wage was necessary 'bread for the kids. Because I was the oldest girl.'[51] Conversely, Rose Gamble was able to take up a scholarship to secondary school in 1930s London due to the earnings of her two older sisters.[52] In the post-war years, Young and Wilmott noted that the younger daughters of large families in Bethnal Green were more likely to be permitted to take up a grammar school place than their elder sisters were, whereas boys' family position had little effect on their greater chances of entering grammar school.[53]

Many more parents simply could not afford secondary education for any of their children, particularly prior to the late 1940s. For many girls and boys, the restrictions placed on their schooling served as a powerful realization of the limitations imposed by poverty. Lavinia Swainbank, who became a domestic servant in the early 1920s, responded with realism and resentment: 'Passing the eleven-plus exam was just a matter of pride of achievement. . . . the English teacher . . . who tried so hard . . . to open the way to a career in journalism for a promising pupil must have realised from the start that he was fighting a losing battle'.[54] Ten years later,

[49] J. White, *The Worst Street in North London: Campbell Bunk, Islington, between the Wars* (London: Routledge, 1986), 188.

[50] Rowntree, *Poverty and Progress*, 23–6, 158; Davies, *Leisure*, 98; J. Smyth, ' "Ye never got a spell to think aboot it." Young Women and Employment in the Inter-War Period: A Case Study of a Textile Village', in E. Gordon and E. Breitenbach (eds.), *The World is Ill Divided* (Edinburgh: Edinburgh University Press, 1990), 107.

[51] TLSL, Manchester Studies, 61, interview with Mrs Savage.

[52] R. Gamble, *Chelsea Child* (London: BBC, 1979), 120.

[53] Young and Wilmott, *Family and Kinship*, 179–80.

[54] Lavinia Swainbank, 'Housemaid', in J. Burnett (ed.), *Useful Toil* (Harmondsworth: Penguin, 1974), 221.

Margaret Sharp entered mill work in Clitheroe, Lancashire but 'I hated it, I'll tell you that. I were clerically minded. I wasn't a bad student, I won a scholarship—I never went'.[55] A study of Bristol's young people undertaken in 1942 found that many blamed poverty for their limited education, and that girls were less likely to have received secondary education; similar results were obtained in the subsequent ten years by other studies, although those carried out in the early 1950s suggest that gender differentiation may have declined, with similar proportions of boys and girls expressing dissatisfaction that they had had to leave school at fifteen.[56] The London Advisory Council for Youth Employment warned in 1949 that 'Many parents, especially now that their children have remained an extra year at school, expect them to receive wages to keep and clothe themselves.'[57] Of course many families simply did not have to make such calculations, the notion that a meritocratic education system had been established by the 1944 Education Act being undermined by the low eleven-plus pass-rate among working class children.[58] Most attended non-selective, vocational secondary moderns.

Earning a Living: From Schoolgirl to Breadwinner

By the time they left school, young women were clearly aware of the importance of their earnings to the household. Fowler has suggested that by the 1920s the main appeal of work for young people was the opportunity to earn some spending money,[59] and this certainly was an attraction for many. Nellie Hilton recalled that she voluntarily became a half-time mill worker at the age of 12 in the early 1920s, although her mother told her she did not need to, because 'I saw these girls, being, "oh, I'm getting so much money" and I said to my mother "why can't I go half-time?" '[60] By the late 1940s, an increasing number of schoolchildren

[55] NWSA, 1994.0128, interview with M. Sharp.

[56] B. A. Fletcher et al., *The Welfare of Youth: A City Survey* (Bristol: University of Bristol, 1945), 19; F. Zweig, *Labour, Life and Poverty* (London: Gollancz, 1948), 16–17; B. H. Reed et al., *Eighty Thousand Adolescents* (London: Allen and Unwin, 1950), 26, 34; L. Wilkins, *The Adolescent in Britain*, Social Survey, Reports, New Series, no. 148 (1955), 17.

[57] London Advisory Council for Youth Employment, *Annual Report for the Year 1948* (London: HMSO, 1949), 6.

[58] R. McKibbin, *Classes and Cultures in England 1918–1951* (Oxford: Oxford University Press, 1998), 231, 268–9.

[59] Fowler, *First Teenagers*, 29; McKibbin, *Classes and Cultures*, 135.

[60] NWSA, 1999.03040, interview with Nellie Hilton. See also East Sussex Records Office (ESRO), Lewes in Living Memory collection, 6416/1/7/51, tape-recorded interview with Joan Perry.

were benefiting from pocket money, but the London Advisory Council for Youth Employment was still able to note that 'on going out to work they expect still more.'[61] However, as the previous discussion highlights, most young women also recognized the need to earn their keep and many welcomed the opportunity to 'repay' their parents for childhood dependency, expressing the reciprocity of familial relationships. As Dolly, who began work in Manchester in 1938, explained:

> I know what I felt when I started work, I'd been kept until I was 14, and it was my turn to put something back into the house. I'd got younger brothers and sisters, and my wage—it was 10 shillings a week—I'd got to put back into the house. You'd got the feeling you wanted to help.[62]

Others were less keen to begin work, particularly those entering domestic service, but recognized their family's need for their earnings. Explaining why she had entered service at the age of 14 in 1929, Edith Edwards simply stated, 'we were very, very poor'.[63]

As this indicates, children were acutely aware of their family's economic needs from an early age. This realization was heightened for many children not only by the limitations that poverty placed on their educational opportunities, but also by their need to begin earning while still at school. Increasingly conscientious state regulation of children's employment dramatically reduced their importance as breadwinners, accentuating the distinction between dependent childhood and wage-earning youth over the first three decades of the twentieth century.[64] Fowler's claim that many children continued to undertake full-time work illegally in interwar England is based on the erroneous assumption that the 12 and 13 year olds recorded in employment by the 1921 Census were below the school-leaving age.[65] In fact, the 1918 Education Act, which raised the school-leaving age to 14, was not enforced until 1921, when it also abolished the half-time system that had previously allowed schoolchildren to undertake substantial amounts of part-time employment, particularly in textile and agricultural districts. Nevertheless, throughout our period, and particularly prior to the Second World War, it was not uncommon for schoolchildren to undertake some paid work, particularly if they came from poorer households. Margaret Sharp, born in 1919, could weave 'before I ever left

61 London Advisory Council on Youth Employment, *Annual Report for the Year 1948*, 6.
62 Lifetimes, *Something in Common*, 35.
63 TLSL, Manchester Studies, 36, interview with Edith Edwards.
64 A. Davin, *Growing Up Poor* (London: Rivers Oram, 1996), 10–11, 214–16.
65 Fowler, *First Teenagers*, 18.

school because mother and granny worked in the mill . . . and when I came out of school I used to go up to granny's [mill] or mum's . . . and I used to run looms for them while they went and did the jobs at home'.[66] White noted that the daughters of poorer London families came under pressure to leave school a year or two early, as factory job opportunities expanded in the interwar years.[67] As this suggests, schoolchildren's labour remained integral to some families' budgeting strategies, particularly prior to the Second World War.

The decline of schoolchildren's paid work did not diminish girls' understanding of their obligation to the family economy. Steedman suggests that young women were even more aware of their financial importance to the family than their brothers, since their early participation in domestic tasks meant they had a greater understanding of their mother's struggle to make ends meet.[68] The evidence presented here supports this; whether eager to enter employment or not, most young women felt that as dependants in their parents' home, their contribution was an obligation. Added to this was, for most young women, the awareness that, unlike their brothers, they would probably leave paid work in early adulthood. Their employment was an initiation into a role that would structure their adult lives only inasmuch as it implicated them in the planning of the family economy; their paid labour was prompted solely by their own and their families' immediate need for their earnings.

The nature of young women's financial contribution to the household changed as they grew older, and over time. Most young school leavers 'tipped up' their wage packet to their mother when they received it. Eileen's experience was typical of the 1920s:

> you had to hand over the pay packet unopened to mothers in those days, and this applied to most children. I can't remember—I think in the beginning I was allowed about a shilling . . . a week. Later I got half a crown a week when I earned a bit more money, spending money.[69]

Social surveys and subsequent studies have noted that this was a widespread custom across labour markets as diverse as York, Manchester, and London,[70] and it is a process recalled by all of my own sample.

66 LRO, NWSA, 1994.0128/Margaret Sharp.

67 White, *Worst Street*, 200.

68 Steedman, *Landscape for a Good Woman*, 89.

69 NLSL, Making Ends Meet collection, A14/a/2, interview with Eileen.

70 Rowntree, *Poverty and Progress*, 27; Mass-Observation Archive (M-OA): FR 1353, 'The Service of Youth', July 1942, xiii; London Trades Council, *Juvenile Employment* (London: Trades Council, 1945), 4–5; Davies, *Leisure*, 92.

Contributing to the family economy continued until young people left home, although workers in their late teens and early twenties were often allowed to retain their earnings, paying board and lodging from these. This practice was particularly common in more affluent households and increased in the later 1940s due to rising adult wages and an improved standard of living; Jephcott found it to be generally practised among her London sample.[71] Being a breadwinner, as well as becoming a consumer, thus distinguished young workers from children. Dependence on parents was not the corollary of youth in many working class households, although it had been established as such in middle class society for at least fifty years.[72]

Becoming a wage-earner was thus a significant step towards adulthood in most communities. Many young women were convinced that, in the words of Linda Thew, who became a shop assistant in Northumberland in the early 1930s, 'Adolescents had no clout until they started work'[73] and welcomed the change to their status that employment brought. This transition was not only marked by an increase in their financial independence. Marie Paneth was concerned to discover that it was still the case in the working class district of London where she worked in the early 1940s that wage-earners had first rights to food in poorer households, while schoolchildren 'have to snatch the food from the stove or from the table which is laid for the older brother or sister, or for father, on whom mother waits.' As she noted, schoolchildren had 'no claims to make'.[74] Rituals around the collection and treatment of the first wage signify appreciation of the contribution that a young worker's earnings made to the family budget. Rose Lowe was one of many women who vividly recalled the pride she felt upon collecting her first pay packet; her older brother stuck the envelope on the kitchen wall in her honour.[75] In more affluent households, particularly by the late 1940s, young workers were sometimes allowed to keep their first wage packet for themselves.[76] A degree of financial independence was, then, widely accepted as the right of wage-earners, and was not simply the prerogative of males in the household.

71 Jephcott, *Rising Twenty*, 126–7.

72 J. Gillis, *Youth and History: Tradition and Change in European Age Relations, 1770–Present* (New York: Academic Press, 1974), 87–93, 123–5.

73 Thew, *Tune for Bears*, 209.

74 M. Paneth, *Branch Street* (London Allen and Unwin, 1944), 37.

75 R. Lowe, *Daddy Burtt's for Dinner: Growing up in Hoxton between the Wars* (London: Centreprise, 1976), 19.

76 See, for example, Langhamer, *Women's Leisure*, 101; Smyth, 'Young Women and Employment', 107.

Whereas the increasing number of factory, shop, and office workers found that the transition from schoolgirl to worker raised their status in the parental home, servants frequently experienced their entry to employment as a brutal wrench from family and friendship ties. Mrs Hevness, for example, 'cried herself silly' on her first Christmas day in service, but when homesickness led her to return to her parents, she quickly realized that her presence in the home was a financial burden and felt 'they were glad to be rid of me'.[77] Entering service could sharpen a young woman's sense of gender difference—and disadvantage—as was true of Winifred Foley who hated leaving her family home to enter service, and was acutely aware that, had she been a boy, her presence would not 'add to the burden of the little ones'.[78] The demise of domestic service thus changed young rural women's lives in some important ways. Linda Thew, who left school in the early 1930s, was aware that just ten years earlier domestic service would have been the only employment open to her, and welcomed the additional freedom but also ability to make a substantial contribution to the family home that her job as a shop assistant allowed her.[79] Mass-Observation found that the wartime expansion of industry in rural and semi-rural areas greatly increased young women's earning potential and contributions to the family budget.[80] As more young women entered industrial, retail, and clerical jobs, so a more homogeneous experience of youth began to emerge, but it remained fractured by social class, and was characterized for working class girls by economic and social responsibility as well as by a degree of independence.

Wage-Earning and the Family Economy

The contribution that daughters were expected to make to the family economy was shaped by several factors. Young wage-earners' importance to the family economy is largely explained by the high proportion of working class households that continued to live in poverty between the end of the First World War and the beginning of the 1950s. Assessing the extent of this is problematized by the lack of a uniform poverty line, but most contemporary surveys drew on Bowley and Hogg's stringent 1925

[77] NLSL, Making Ends Meet collection, A78/a/1, interview with Mrs Hevness.
[78] W. Foley, *Child in the Forest* (London: BBC, 1974), 141, 190.
[79] Thew, *Pit Village*, 123–4.
[80] Mass-Observation, *War Factory*, 23.

definition of 37s 6d per week.[81] Theirs and subsequent interwar surveys found that between 4 and 20 per cent of the working class population lived in primary poverty, with adult men's low wages and unemployment being the major causes of this.[82] Even in Bristol, in the economic recovery of the late 1930s, 7.2 per cent of working class families lacked the basic means of subsistence.[83] Rowntree, who used a revised 'human needs' minimum, of 53s per week for an average working class family,[84] found that 31 per cent of his sample in relatively affluent York were still living in poverty in 1936.[85]

The situation improved in the 1940s. Full employment eradicated a major cause of interwar poverty and food rationing[86] and a growth in average earnings of almost 25 per cent between 1938 and 1948 also helped to reduce want. However, large families in particular remained vulnerable to poverty.[87] In 1942, interviews with 16 and 17 year olds in connection with the Youth Registration Order of December 1941 led the Ministry of Labour's Youth Advisory Committee to conclude that 10 per cent of young workers' families lived in poverty and another 30 per cent experienced great economic insecurity.[88] The introduction of family allowances in 1945 eased the financial situation of many, but Ferdynand Zweig's investigation of 400 working men and their families in 1946 found that a significant proportion of households remained reliant on more than one wage for the basic means of subsistence.[89]

As this suggests, the presence of supplementary earners could mitigate the effects of poverty, or even provide an escape from it. Horrell and Humphries have pointed out that family breadwinning patterns continued to be 'pluralistic and multifaceted' in late nineteenth-century

[81] A. L. Bowley and M. H. Hogg, *Has Poverty Diminished?* (London: P. S. King and Son, 1925), 12–17.

[82] Ibid.; H. Llewellyn Smith, *The New Survey of London Life and Labour*, 3 (London: P. S. King and Son, 1932), 78–96; Caradog Jones, *Merseyside*, 1, 156–60; P. Ford, *Work and Wealth in a Modern Port: Southampton* (London: Allen and Unwin, 1934), 114–16; Rowntree, *Poverty and Progress*, 30–1; H. Tout, *The Standard of Living in Bristol* (Bristol: Arrowsmith, 1938), 21.

[83] Tout, *Bristol*, 25–6.

[84] Rowntree, *Poverty and Progress*, 28–9.

[85] Rowntree, *Poverty and Progress*, 32 and 108–9. See Davies, *Leisure*, 14–29 for a discussion of measurements of poverty, 1900–39.

[86] I. Zweiniger-Bargielowska, *Austerity in Britain: Rationing, Controls, and Consumption, 1939–1955* (Oxford: Oxford University Press, 2000), 31–45.

[87] I. Gazeley, *Poverty in Britain, 1900–1965* (London: Palgrave, 2003), 129–58, offers a comprehensive summary of these changes. See also Paneth, *Branch Street*, 36–7.

[88] The National Archives (TNA), LAB 19/99, Youth Advisory Committee Paper No. 10, 'A Youth Movement. Memorandum by Lt Col the Hon A Lytton Milbanke', 1942.

[89] Zweig, *Labour*, 15–16.

England.[90] The high proportion of young women in the labour force between 1918 and 1950 indicates that breadwinning strategies remained flexible and transient. The major causes of interwar poverty—adult male unemployment and low pay—raised the importance of other household wage-earners. Even among Rowntree's relatively affluent sample, the life cycle remained crucial in determining a household's economic state: whereas those families with young children, or headed by pensioners, were most likely to experience poverty, those with children at work were least likely to fall below the poverty line.[91] Clearly, poverty was not confined to a small minority of households, but affected a large number of individuals at different points in their lives; the majority of young wage-earners had already experienced it by the time they began work.

Despite the eradication of unemployment and a rise in earnings during the 1940s, young wage-earners remained important to working class households. Family size shaped the relative importance of young workers; Zweig found that young wage-earners' contributions were often crucial for households with more than two children under 14, or which lacked an adult male wage-earner.[92] The poverty cycle continued to exist, meaning that the 'best earning age of a worker is . . . the time when his children live with him, while already working'.[93] Of the 12,911 households studied by the Ministry of Labour's Household Expenditure survey of 1953–4, 40 per cent of those relying on a single earner lived on less than £10 per week, but only 14 per cent of those with three or more earners.[94] In rural areas, the continuing insecurity and low wages of agricultural employment, and limited job opportunities for adult women meant that, as Howkins has noted, 'children's earnings [continued to be] central to country [family] budgets' across 1940s England.[95] Young workers thus continued to shoulder partial responsibility for maintaining a large proportion of working class families at subsistence level into the 1950s.

The earlier discussion on schooling indicates that family size and a young woman's position within her family were also important. Elsie Lee, who entered factory work in Coventry in 1924, explained that 'I had to because I came from a big family. There was eight of us.'[96] Parental earnings and expenditure were also crucial. The *New London Survey* indicates

[90] Horrell and Humphries, 'Male Breadwinner Family', 64.

[91] Rowntree, *Poverty and Progress*, 155–71. See also Ford, *Southampton*, 136.

[92] Zweig, *Labour*, 15–16.

[93] Ibid., 15.

[94] Derived from Ministry of Labour and National Service, *Report of an Enquiry into Household Expenditure in 1953–54* (London: HMSO, 1954), 18, Table 5.

[95] Howkins, *Rural England*, 126.

[96] MRC, Coventry Women's Work Collection, MSS 266/6/5, interview with Elsie Lee.

that maternal absence from households headed by low-waged male workers increased daughters' likelihood of entering the labour force,[97] highlighting the importance of married women as casual workers as well as household managers, in families headed by poorly paid men in areas offering work to adult women. However, in households where male earnings did not require substantial supplement, the converse was often true, with daughters being expected to take over the role of domestic manager when a mother was ill or absent. As the oldest daughter in her family of six, Grace Foakes was expected to leave work to keep house at the age of 15, when her mother became an invalid in the early 1920s.[98] Doris Addicott's younger sister was expected to do likewise, because she earned less than anyone else in the family,[99] demonstrating that careful evaluation of the respective value of earnings and unpaid domestic labour governed such decisions.

When married women worked outside the home, their daughters frequently shared their 'double burden' of paid employment and domestic work. Rose Gamble's sister Luli followed their mother into part-time cleaning when she left school in London's East End in the mid-1930s, in order to supplement her parents' wages and help to care for younger siblings while her mother was at work. A lack of well-paid jobs in the district made this a more rational choice than entering full-time work.[100] In the 1940s, conscription and the increased employment of married women exacerbated such pressures. Pearl Jephcott cited a case of a 'girl (who had abandoned a succession of jobs between 14 and 15) [who] at this latter age took over the housekeeping for a family of four, so that her mother could go out to a full-time job in munitions.'[101]

By the early 1950s, the expansion of full-time, relatively lucrative employment for young women, and the introduction of the National Health Service, meant that few daughters were likely to be completely withdrawn from the labour force to take on domestic or nursing responsibilities. The conscription of young women in wartime, beginning with those aged over 20 from March 1941, but eventually extending to all those over 16, also meant that entering employment became a more common experience in those areas, like many rural communities, where relatively few girls had entered the labour force before the War, encouraging households to value

97 Eichengreen, 'Juvenile Unemployment', 289.

98 G. Foakes, *Between High Walls: A London Childhood* (London: Shepeard-Walwyn, 1972), 70–2. See also MRC, Coventry Women's Work Collection, MSS 266/6/1, interview with Doris Addicott.

99 MRC, Coventry Women's Work Collection, MSS 266/6/1, interview with Doris Addicott.

100 Gamble, *Chelsea Child*, 124.

101 Jephcott, *Rising Twenty*, 43.

daughters' economic contributions. Nevertheless, daughters' double burden continued to be heavy when illness afflicted their family or when their mothers went out to work. A study of Nottingham young people in 1950, for example, quoted the example of 'Sally', a 17-year-old machinist who spent her evenings caring for her invalid father and younger siblings while her mother went out to work.[102] At the end of our period, such heavy domestic responsibilities were shouldered by only a small minority of young women, but such cases are a reminder that young women's responsibilities towards parents and siblings never disappeared.

Paternal absence or unemployment also affected a young woman's responsibilities, although, once again, this varied according to the local labour market. The sexual division of labour meant that a father's lack of earnings were more likely to prompt sons' labour force participation than daughters', as Eichengreen found in interwar London.[103] However, this chapter has made clear that the majority of working class juveniles entered the labour force regardless of their father's occupation, because of their household's need for supplementary earnings. Consequently, analysis of young people's labour participation rates is of limited value in tracing the effect of paternal unemployment; more significant were the less obvious emotional and economic pressures that a father's lack of earnings placed on their wage-earning children. Young men often bore the brunt of this. Eleven per cent of households in the *New Survey of London* were headed by males other than a husband and father, including sons.[104] In 1950 Wilkins was struck by the fact that paternal unemployment continued to place pressure on sons to obtain better-paid jobs, although the decline in unemployment meant that this affected fewer young men than twenty years earlier.[105]

Although the lack of paternal earnings often affected young women less directly, it nonetheless placed significant pressure upon them. In the aftermath of the First World War, Rowntree and Stuart carried out an extensive study of 13,637 wage-earning women across 67,333 households in eleven towns. They found that the most common cause of women's

[102] P. Jephcott, *Some Young People* (London: Faber, 1954), 51.

[103] Eichengreen, 'Juvenile Unemployment', 288.

[104] Derived from UK Data Archive, University of Essex, SN3758, *New Survey of London* datafiles.

[105] C. Cameron, A. Lush, and G. Meara, *Disinherited Youth: A Report on the 18+ Age Group Enquiry Prepared for the Trustees of the Carnegie United Kingdom Trust* (Edinburgh: T. and A. Constable, 1943), 60–2; Rowntree, *Poverty and Progress*, 188–9; L. Beales and R. S. Lambert (eds.), *Memoirs of the Unemployed* (London: Gollancz, 1934), 40–1; Wilkins, *Adolescent*, 47.

responsibility for dependants was the death of their father, accounting for 53 per cent of cases.[106] In the 1930s, Percy Ford found that the operation of the household means test introduced in 1931 greatly increased men's dependence on sons, daughters, and wives, in that order.[107] Peggy, who grew up in Nottingham, recalled that when, as a teenage factory worker in the mid-1930s, she received a wage rise, her father's dole money was stopped:

> he cried like a baby and so did I, he fetched me out of work to tell me . . . and I said 'It don't matter daddy, it don't matter, we'll get through somehow, we'll get through somehow.'[108]

Investigations undertaken by Beales and Lambert, the National Unemployed Workers' Movement (NUWM), and the Pilgrim and Carnegie Trusts indicate that Peggy's example was typical, and highlight that by forcing paternal dependency on children, the means test could severely strain familial relations.[109]

Unemployment was greatly reduced during the 1940s, but paternal absence and death placed pressure on their children. Opportunities for married women's paid employment increased, as did their earnings, which in industry rose from a weekly average of 31s 1d in 1935 to 74s 6d by 1948.[110] However, even in the latter year this amount represented just 54 per cent of average adult male earnings, and domestic commitments continued to restrict married women's job opportunities. Consequently, young earners continued to be important to families lacking an employed male head. In 1944 the Ministry of Labour recognized that 'It is useless for [the Juvenile Employment Service] to advise a boy or girl to take up this or that calling if for instance . . . a widowed mother needs the highest wage that the child can earn immediately to keep the home together'.[111]

A man's leisure expenditure could, as Davies points out, affect the family economy as much as the size of his wage packet.[112] Winifred Cotterill

[106] B. S. Rowntree and F. D. Stuart, *The Responsibility of Women Workers for Dependants* (Oxford: Clarendon Press, 1921), 33.

[107] P. Ford, 'Means Tests and Responsibilities for Needy Relations', *Sociological Review*, 28 (1937), 186.

[108] NLSL, Making Ends Meet collection, A66/a, interview with Peggy.

[109] Beales and Lambert, *Memoirs*, 20, 40–1, 82–7; W. Hannington, *The Problem of the Distressed Areas* (London: Gollancz, 1937), 46–8; Pilgrim Trust, *Men Without Work* (Cambridge: Cambridge University Press, 1938), 147–8; Cameron et al., *Disinherited Youth*, 75; see also J. Beauchamp, *Working Women in Great Britain* (New York: International Publishers, 1937), 51.

[110] Ministry of Labour, 'Average Earnings and Hours Enquiry, October 1948', *Ministry of Labour Gazette*, 1949.

[111] Ministry of Labour, *The Young Worker* (London: HMSO, 1944), 9.

[112] Davies, *Leisure*, 98.

recalled that her father, a skilled factory worker, 'earned good money but he didn't know how to look after it because he drank.'[113] Rose Gamble's father stole or pawned his children's possessions in the years preceding the Second World War to increase his beer money after spending his wage. Only loyalty to their mother kept them from confronting him, and Rose's eldest sister continued to contribute to the household income even after she had moved out, for this reason.[114] By the late 1940s, Zweig noted paternal expenditure on drinking, smoking, and gambling as important causes of secondary poverty;[115] similar conclusions were reached by Rowntree in the early 1950s.[116] For young workers in households affected by this, contributing to the family economy could be a means of expressing emotional as well as financial support for their mother and distancing themselves from their father's irresponsibility, but it could also be experienced as a heavy, exploitative obligation.

The rise in the working class standard of living from the mid-1930s is frequently viewed as diminishing the importance of young wage-earners to the family economy, but their earnings were in fact largely responsible for the increase in working class leisure and luxury consumption. Eileen, who began work in the early 1920s, was aware that any little luxuries in her family's life were connected to the wage packets that she and her eldest brother brought home. She recalled that at the age of 15:

> Mother still had my wage packet, and that was half a crown a week, I know, because the family then would probably be feeling a little bit better off because my eldest brother would then be at work . . . [our standard of living] did improve slightly then because I think we began to get—I can recall having more for Sunday tea than we had [had]. Probably there would be a jelly or something like that. . . . but yes, things were improving slightly so far as food was concerned, and things in general.[117]

Similarly, Molly Weir recalled a friend whose 9s per week 'meant potatoes and cabbage and ham for . . . her mother, unemployed dad, and three brothers and sisters. . . . Besides many a wee "extra" for their teas during the week.'[118]

By the late 1930s, a diminishing proportion of working class households considered the provision of Sunday tea to be a luxury, but young

[113] MRC, Coventry Women's Work Collection, MSS 266/6/2, interview with Winifred Cotterill.

[114] Gamble, *Chelsea Child*, 135.

[115] Zweig, *Labour*, 21.

[116] B. S. Rowntree, *English Life and Leisure: A Social Study* (London: Longman, 1951), 160.

[117] NLSL, Making Ends Meet, A14/b/2, Eileen.

[118] M. Weir, *Best Foot Forward* (London: Pan, 1974), 35.

women's earnings were essential in expanding working class consumption of consumer durables and commercial leisure. The economic recovery meant that by 1936, Bowley recorded the average weekly income of working class families as 76s. This included a margin of 20s for non-essential expenditure, a 'very important and modern gain'[119] that increased leisure and luxury consumption. Yet this margin was too large to be entirely accounted for by a single adult male's wage in many households, since mean adult male earnings were recorded by the Ministry of Labour as 64s 6d per week in 1935. Young wage-earners were thus crucial in increasing working class consumption of such luxuries as the wireless, which achieved mass ownership by the outbreak of the Second World War, or even renting or buying a new home. Housing developments—local authorities built 1,136,457 houses between 1919 and 1939, with 31 per cent being built after 1934[120]—meant that by the late 1930s home ownership, or tenancy of a nicer house, had become a realistic aspiration of more affluent working class households, which young women shared and contributed to. For Dolly, as for many young women who began work from the late 1930s onwards, 'My ambition was to have a nice home, more than ever when I started work', an aspiration she shared with her mother.[121] It was achieved while Dolly was still a teenager in her parents' home; they could afford the rent on the new house because 'several of us were out at work by then'.[122] During the Second World War, Mass-Observation noted that young workers' substantial wage increases did not greatly increase their personal affluence; rather, they continued to be contributed to the family economy, being used to buy better quality clothing and commodities like wirelesses or medicines.[123] In 1947 Zweig noted that six out of twenty-seven families he studied were in 'a comfortable position'—able to afford regular leisure consumption—as a result of the financial contributions made by children in their early twenties.[124] Young women's expanding earning opportunities increased their value to such strategies relative to that of other household members. Security, and to an even greater degree affluence, thus remained transient states for many, facilitated by childlessness or the presence of supplementary earners, of whom young women constituted a significant proportion.

[119] A. L. Bowley, *Wages and Income in the United Kingdom since 1860* (Cambridge: Cambridge University Press, 1937), 39.

[120] J. Burnett, *A Social History of Housing 1815–1970* (Newton Abbot: David and Charles, 1978), 246.

[121] Lifetimes, *Something in Common*, 15.

[122] Ibid., 16. See also White, *Worst Street*, 216–17.

[123] M-OA: FR 1053, 'A Savings Survey (Working Class)', January 1942, 49–53; FR 1353, 'The Service of Youth', xiii.

[124] Zweig, *Labour*, 16.

Conclusion

While young women's increasing social independence was highlighted by contemporary commentators and has been focused on in subsequent historiography, their youth was shaped by household responsibilities and the family economy. Most working class households depended on two or more earners, and young women were increasingly prominent among these. Daughters' economic responsibilities were increased by paternal unemployment and death following the First World War, male unemployment in the 1930s, and paternal absence during and after the Second World War. The heavy domestic burden that their mothers struggled with added to young women's responsibilities. However, the expansion of their employment and earning opportunities, together with a decline in family size, significantly raised the value of their paid employment over their assistance in the family home. This had repercussions for the value placed on their education and training by many families.

This indicates that explanations of young women's labour force participation that focus solely on gender, drawing on an abstract 'domestic ideology', or 'male breadwinner model' are inadequate. Regional variance in employment and earning patterns, together with family composition, strongly influenced young women's educational opportunities and the amount of economic or domestic assistance they were expected to offer. Nevertheless, the working class experience of youth was increasingly homogeneous, largely due to the increasing likelihood that young women would enter the workforce, and would not become domestic servants.

Despite the differences in income levels between working class households, young women's importance as wage-earners highlights certain common elements of the working class family economy. Breadwinning strategies were transient and flexible; few households relied on a single wage if other members of the household could enter the labour force without jeopardizing domestic management. Young women's wages were often essential to make ends meet in poorer households, but they were also crucial to a wider range of working class families. Increased working class leisure and luxury consumption cannot be attributed to an abstract 'rising standard of living', but was in fact often dependent upon the continuing contributions of young wage-earners to the family economy. The expansion of young women's employment and earning opportunities consequently profoundly affected relationships between young women, their families, communities, and the state, which are highlighted by the search for work, the subject of the following chapter.

3

Entering Employment

Entering paid employment was an abrupt, often bewildering change for young school leavers. Joan Perry's experience—'I left school on the Friday and started work on the Monday'[1]—was typical, and unsurprisingly many young women experienced this as 'a sudden, sudden break-off from one kind of life.'[2] For Rose Lowe among others, leaving school was 'the thing she had always dreaded'; she 'did not even know what jobs there were in that great big world outside her world'.[3] This chapter is concerned with how these young women, who often felt so unprepared for the world of work, conducted their job search. In doing so, it explores their relations with family, community, and the state; engages with ongoing debates about the nature of intergenerational occupational and social mobility; and examines the changing role of work in social class formation between 1918 and 1950.

Social class composition and identity are highly contested entities. Recent historical and sociological investigations have suggested that class identities were relatively fluid in the period under study, citing the limited degree of direct occupational continuity between parents and children as evidence that a homogeneous working class did not exist.[4] Yet the assumption that intergenerational occupational continuity was a feature of a 'traditional' working class has been undermined by Reid, Thompson,

[1] East Sussex Record Office (ESRO), Lewes in Living Memory collection, AMS 6416/1/7/51, interview with Joan Perry. See also Modern Records Centre, University of Warwick (MRC), Coventry Women's Work Collection, MSS 266/6/5, interview with Mrs Mullis.

[2] Nottingham Local Studies Library (NLSL), Making Ends Meet collection, A14/a/2, interview with Eileen.

[3] R. Lowe, *Daddy Burtt's for Dinner: Growing up in Hoxton between the Wars* (London: Centreprise, 1976), 15.

[4] D. Baines and P. Johnson, 'In Search of the "Traditional" Working Class: Social Mobility and Occupational Continuity in Interwar London', *Economic History Review* 52/4 (1999), 692–713; D. Fowler, *The First Teenagers: The Lifestyles of Young Wage-earners in Interwar Britain* (London: Woburn Press, 1995), 7–42; T. Griffiths, *The Lancashire Working Classes c.1880–1930* (Oxford: Clarendon Press, 2001), 101–46.

and Savage and Miles, who have shown that such continuity was very limited before the First World War. They have convincingly argued that the study of the social distance travelled as a result of intergenerational occupational mobility can shed more light on class homogeneity or heterogeneity than simply the existence of mobility per se.[5] Care is taken throughout this chapter to distinguish between occupational and social mobility. The study of young women's work can in fact offer a re-evaluation of both. Although studies of male mobility often assume a clear social division between manual occupations, considered working class, and non-manual occupations, categorized as middle class, the occupational hierarchy was in reality more complex. Women's clerical employment has fuelled unease about how they fit in social relations and class formation, but as chapter 1 showed, vertical segregation characterized most occupational sectors, including clerical work, and women's opportunities for promotion from low-grade non-manual work were extremely limited.[6] Women's occupational continuity and mobility thus necessitates a revision of existing mobility models and offers fresh insights into the interaction of class and gender in shaping employment choice.[7]

This approach also challenges the purely quantitative methodology employed by many studies of mobility. The substantial interruptions that women's employment faced over their life course, the low labour force participation rate among married women—10.4 per cent in 1931[8]—and differences in the jobs held by young women and older, married women mean that even where data on mothers' and daughters' employment pathways exist, it is difficult to identify links between their occupations. The sexual division of labour that characterized most regional labour markets prevented much direct occupational continuity between fathers and daughters. Consequently, numerous sociologists and historians, led by Goldthorpe, have justified omitting women from studies of occupational mobility.[9] However, an investigation of the wider importance of kinship

[5] A. Reid, *Social Classes and Social Relations in Britain, 1850–1914* (Basingstoke: Macmillan, 1992); M. Savage and A. Miles, *The Remaking of the British Working Class 1840–1940* (London: Routledge, 1994), 33–5; P. Thompson, *The Edwardians: The Remaking of British Society* (London: Paladin, 1975), 194–5.

[6] See, for example, F. D. Klingender, *The Condition of Clerical Labour in Britain* (London: M. Lawrence, 1935), 64–7.

[7] G. Payne and P. Abbott, 'Origins and Destinations', in eid. (eds.), *The Social Mobility of Women: Beyond Male Mobility Models* (London: Falmer, 1990), 11.

[8] *Census of England and Wales 1931: Occupation Tables* (London: HMSO, 1934), Table 5.

[9] J. H. Goldthorpe with C. Payne, 'The Class Mobility of Women', in Goldthorpe et al., *Social Mobility and Class Structure in Modern Britain* (Oxford: Oxford University Press, 1987), 277–8, 294–6.

and social background on young women's occupational choices is possible and worthwhile. Ross, Roberts, and White have shown that maternal household management, parental support, and kinship and neighbourhood networks influenced families' and individuals' social status and choices.[10] This chapter draws on contemporary data-sets to trace links between parents' and daughters' occupational status, but also uses personal testimonies to examine indirect connections between social background and occupational choice. In doing so, it argues that the existence of intergenerational occupational mobility does not necessarily signify a weakening of family and community ties. Contrary to Griffiths's assertions, a lack of direct occupational continuity between parents and daughters did not denote an absence of familial influence; a family's contacts and social status had a strong influence on job choices.[11] Moreover, a lack of occupational continuity does not signify significant social fluidity; the social distance travelled through intergenerational mobility was frequently limited.

This study draws on the huge amount of contemporary interest shown in juveniles' job search. Social investigations were provoked by concern over the lack of security and progression available in many juveniles' first jobs; although such anxiety was primarily focused on boys, girls' employment patterns were increasingly subject to scrutiny as unemployment increased in the late 1920s, and domestic service declined during the subsequent two decades. Investigations included a national study of 2,701 unemployed girls and 3,331 unemployed boys undertaken in 1925;[12] the Sheffield Social Survey Committee's *Survey of Juvenile Employment*, which examined 500 boys' and 500 girls' entry to employment in 1927 and 1928;[13] the *Social Survey of Merseyside*'s assessment of intergenerational occupational continuity between 2,239 sons and their fathers, and between a further 164 boys and 102 girls and their fathers, in 1930 and 1931;[14] a study of how 1,040 boys and 998 girls in Lancashire found work

[10] E. Ross, 'Survival Networks: Women's Neighbourhood Sharing in London before World War I', *History Workshop Journal*, 15 (1983), 4–27; E. Roberts, *A Woman's Place: An Oral History of Working Class Women 1890–1940* (Oxford: Blackwell, 1984), 48–50; J. White, *The Worst Street in North London: Campbell Bunk, Islington, between the Wars* (London: Routledge, 1986), 62–90.

[11] Griffiths, *Lancashire*, 101–46.

[12] Ministry of Labour, *Report on an Enquiry into the Personal Circumstances and Industrial History of 3331 Boys and 2701 Girls Registered for Employment at Employment Exchanges and Juvenile Employment Bureaux in June and July 1925* (London: HMSO, 1926).

[13] A. D. K. Owen et al., *A Survey of Juvenile Employment and Welfare in Sheffield* (Sheffield: Sheffield Social Survey Committee, 1933), 18.

[14] D. Caradog Jones, *The Social Survey of Merseyside*, 3 (Liverpool: University of Liverpool, 1934), 203; Caradog Jones, *Merseyside*, 2, 33.

between 1934 and 1936;[15] and L. Wilkins's national study in 1950 of the employment patterns of 1,400 young men and 450 young women aged between 15 and 19.[16] Smaller-scale investigations were also undertaken by Mass-Observation[17] and Pearl Jephcott[18] in the 1940s. These studies are used extensively in the first section of the chapter, which examines family involvement in the job search.

Increasing state intervention in the juvenile labour market offers a wealth of material, which is drawn on in the discussions of the changing roles of education and of employment exchanges that structure the second and third sections of this chapter. Juvenile Employment Advisory Committees were established under the auspices of the Ministry of Labour from 1909, and had responsibility for Juvenile Employment Bureaux (JEBs). Regional Juvenile Choice of Employment Committees, directed by Local Education Authorities (LEAs), were also formed, and co-ordinated Juvenile Employment Exchanges (JEEs). The overlapping functions of the Ministry and Local Authorities was a cause of administrative confusion and some tension, leading to the establishment of the National Advisory Council for Juvenile Employment in 1928 to co-ordinate local Committees. One hundred and eighty Committees were recorded in England and Wales in 1944.[19] These bodies were replaced by the Youth Employment Service (YES) in 1948. All of them produced regular reports drawn on here.

Following in Their Parents' Footsteps? Intergenerational Occupational Continuity

Direct occupational continuity was, even in the 1920s, limited to certain skilled trades and to areas dominated by just one or two industries. This reflected a longer term trend of kinship recruitment in skilled occupations, operated by fathers and sons in trades like building, but also by mothers and daughters in trades such as millinery and weaving.[20] The importance of mothers in this respect was recalled by almost every

15 J. and S. Jewkes, *The Juvenile Labour Market* (London: Gollancz, 1938), 12–13.

16 L. Wilkins, *The Adolescent in Britain*, Social Survey, Reports, New Series, no. 148 (1955).

17 Mass-Observation Archive (M-OA): TC 'Youth', 51/1/C, in particular CF, unpublished ms: 'Attitudes towards Work—Girls and Young Women', 18 November 1940.

18 P. Jephcott, *Rising Twenty: Notes on some Ordinary Girls* (London: Faber and Faber, 1948).

19 Ministry of Labour, *The Young Worker* (London: HMSO, 1944), 3.

20 Jewkes, *Juvenile*, 32–3. See also Roberts, *Woman's Place*, 59–62.

woman in my sample who entered the clothing and textile trades. For Eileen, beginning work in the 1920s, 'my mother was the one who determined where I was going'; she secured Eileen's first job in the reputable clothing factory where she herself had been a skilled worker before marriage.[21] Edna, whose mother was a middle-woman in the Nottingham lace trade, helped with clothing homework deadlines from the age of 9—'I was born on a lace work-cot'—and entered the industry as an errand girl at 14. Although she found her first job herself, her mother's experience was influential: 'I went and knocked at the door, said me mum did lace work and you know, talked meself into a job.'[22] Limiting entry to such work helped to preserve the skilled status and bargaining rights of those thus employed.

However, declining demand for skilled workers in industries such as textiles meant that occupational continuity was often an expression of limited employment choice, rather than skill preservation. This was demonstrated by the very restricted intergenerational occupational mobility of workers featured in Ginsberg's 1927 study of small labour markets.[23] Many schoolgirls took it for granted that they would enter the same mill where parents or older siblings worked,[24] like Nora Holroyd, who had only one day between leaving school and entering employment: 'I was pushed into the mill, straightaway.'[25] Although employment opportunities expanded in wartime, this pattern did not entirely disappear. In 1941, for example, Amy Cowie entered the mill where her mother worked, due to a lack of other options.[26] Sarsby has shown that a similar pattern was sustained in the Potteries until the late 1950s.[27] In the north-east coalfield, occupational continuity was very strong until at least the late 1930s among both men and women. In Northumberland, girls continued to enter the same occupation their mothers had followed in their youth—domestic service. It was a trend characteristic of many rural communities.[28]

21 NLSL, Making Ends Meet collection, A14/a/2, Eileen. See also Lancashire Records Office (LRO), North West Sound Archive (NWSA), 2000.0529, interview with Dorothy Raby; NLSL, Making Ends Meet collection, A85/a/1, interview with Edna.

22 NLSL, Making Ends Meet, A85/a/1, Edna.

23 M. Ginsberg, 'Interchange between Social Classes', *Economic Journal*, 39 (1929), 554–65.

24 LRO, NWSA, 1999.0343, interview with Olive Jones.

25 LRO, NWSA, 2000.0651A, interview with Nora Holroyd. See also LRO, NWSA, 1998.0201, interview with Martha Ellen Pennington.

26 LRO, NWSA, interview with A. Cowie, 2002.0224.

27 J. Sarsby, *Missuses and Mouldrunners: An Oral History of Women Pottery-Workers at Work and Home* (Milton Keynes: Open University Press, 1988), 59.

28 *Census of England and Wales, 1921: County Table of Northumberland* (London: HMSO, 1924); *Census of England and Wales, 1931: Occupation Tables* (London: HMSO, 1934), Table 18.

One woman from Oxfordshire who entered employment in the early 1920s recalled that 'on the last day at Goring school the local gentry came round and offered jobs. My first job was as a between maid.'[29]

Outside these areas, opportunities for intergenerational occupational mobility grew between 1918 and 1950. This does not, however, prove that social mobility was also rising. Studies of males suggest that intergenerational occupational mobility was a long-term characteristic of the youth labour market, but that movement was constrained by class background. Just 18 per cent of the *Social Survey of Merseyside*'s male sample were following the same occupation as their father[30] and only 8 per cent of Baines and Johnson's sample, derived from the *New Survey of London Life and Labour*, did so, testifying to the interwar growth of employment opportunities in the capital. Surveys in the 1940s provide less information, but just 4 per cent of Wilkins's male sample were working for their fathers and he judged that only a minority were following the same occupation as their parent.[31] However, 50 per cent of Baines' and Johnson's sample were in the same occupational group as their fathers (classified as unskilled-manual, semiskilled-manual, skilled-manual, and non-manual), and although the rest had an almost equal chance of ascending or descending, movement was usually over no more than two grades.[32] This trend was also evident among the *Social Survey of Merseyside*'s male sample, 37 per cent of whom shared their father's occupational grade, while 28 per cent were in higher grades and 35 per cent in lower grades.[33] Wilkins noted a similar pattern in 1950.[34] This testified to continuity in boys' established employment pathways. In the industrial areas, as chapter 2 pointed out, many continued to enter casual, unskilled work after leaving school, prior to competing for an apprenticeship in a skilled trade at the age of 15 or 16. Twenty-three per cent of 14 year olds were employed as delivery boys in 1931,[35] and although this was true of just 6 per cent of 15-year-old boys by 1951, another 11 per cent were included in the new census classification of 'unskilled occupations'. Opportunities for social mobility were thus clearly very limited.

Young women's opportunities for occupational mobility were increasingly greater than those of young men, but their chances of experiencing

[29] Oxfordshire Federation of Women's Institutes, *Oxfordshire within Living Memory* (Newbury: Countryside Books, 1994), 145. Thanks to Alun Howkins for this reference.

[30] Caradog Jones, *Merseyside*, 2, 44.

[31] Wilkins, *Adolescent*, 31.

[32] Baines and Johnson, 'Occupational Continuity', 704.

[33] Caradog Jones, *Merseyside*, 2, 34–5.

[34] Wilkins, *Adolescent*, 47.

[35] *Census of England and Wales 1931: Occupation Tables.*

social mobility were also restricted. Girls' employment patterns changed more markedly than those of boys, particularly among the children of unskilled and semiskilled industrial workers in urban communities. The *Social Survey of Merseyside* found that girls from such backgrounds were slightly more likely to find work in an occupational grade higher than that of their brothers, and much more likely to move two or more grades upwards from their father's occupation.[36] This trend testifies to the long-term effects of the First World War upon young women's work. The contrast is marked between those who experienced the expansion of light industrial and non-manual work between the 1920s and the 1950s and David Vincent's pre-1918 sample of women, who were more likely to experience downward progression from their father's last occupational grade.[37]

From the mid-1930s the expansion of employment opportunities in retail and light industry was significant enough to weaken young workers' reliance upon familial recruitment networks in the more buoyant labour markets. Dolly Scannell obtained a clerical post in interwar London 'with a large good firm and considered to be a plum job. Such jobs were never advertised, going to families who "spoke" for each other, but I happened to write in at a time when no relation of the office staff was available.'[38] Rising wages and job security meant that the daughters of relatively affluent working class families could spend some time searching for work, or benefit from an extended education, rather than taking the first available job. Those who moved into housing developments on the outskirts of cities like London and Manchester frequently benefited from the local expansion of light manufacturing, which tended to be concentrated in such areas, and the cultural shift involved in moving to a new area. Alice Bates, who moved onto a housing estate in Greater Manchester at the age of 4 in 1924—earlier than most—recalled that this 'took away from families the idea of having to go into the local industry and the local workshop so that the horizon was opened up a bit for children like myself who moved up.'[39] She, the youngest of five, benefited from further education. Fathers

[36] Caradog Jones, *Merseyside*, 2, 335; 3, 216.

[37] D. Vincent, 'Mobility, Bureaucracy and Careers in Early-Twentieth-Century Britain', in A. Miles and D. Vincent (eds.), *Building European Society: Occupational Change and Social Mobility in Europe 1840–1940* (Manchester: Manchester University Press, 1993), 234–5.

[38] D. Scannell, *Mother Knew Best: An East End Childhood* (London: Macmillan, 1974), 180.

[39] LRO, NWSA, 2000.0900, interview with Alice Bates. On this point see B. Jones, 'Social Life and the Built Environment: Council Housing in Brighton 1918–1940', MA dissertation (Sussex, 2003).

and brothers, on the other hand, frequently continued to travel long distances to skilled manual employment in the inner cities.[40]

Such changes in the labour market gradually affected rural young women, too, although to a much more limited extent prior to the 1940s. Roberts noted that rural women were increasingly able to place their daughters in occupations other than domestic service during the interwar years.[41] Edith Edwards, who grew up near Macclesfield, had no choice of occupation except domestic service in 1929, but her sister 'was ten years younger than me, and times had changed by the time she left school—and—she went into a shop in Knutsford'.[42] Joan Perry, who grew up in the rural town of Lewes, Sussex, also became a shop assistant when she left school in 1939, and felt more fortunate than her older sisters, who had entered domestic service 'because that was the only thing then, you had to go'.[43]

Intergenerational occupational mobility was accelerated by increased demand for young women's labour in the Second World War. Those women who entered employment during the early 1940s often expressed an awareness of expanding job opportunities, similar to that articulated by the women who had begun work in the aftermath of the First World War. Mary Gregory, who grew up in a Lancashire textile town, and became a munitions worker during the Second World War, recalled that 'it was a case of something different. Up to the war, everyone left school at 14 and in this district went in the cotton mill. . . . But then the war started, we were 16 and we fancied it, kind of thing.'[44] It is notable how many of Jephcott's London sample, whose older sisters had entered industrial work, were able to find clerical employment by the mid-1940s, while in smaller, less prosperous northern towns and villages, an increasing proportion of the daughters of former servants were becoming shop workers.[45] The trend is similar to that traced by the Scottish Mobility Study, which noted a sharp increase in non-manual employment, particularly among young women, from the mid-1930s to the early 1940s.[46] Structural

[40] Ministry of Labour, *Report on Juvenile Employment for the Year 1934* (London: HMSO, 1935), 4; K. Hunt and A. Hughes, 'A Culture Transformed?: Women's Lives in Wythenshawe in the 1930s', in A. Davies and S. Fielding (eds.), *Workers' Worlds: Cultures and Communities in Manchester and Salford, 1880–1939* (Manchester: Manchester University Press, 1992), 42.

[41] Roberts, *Woman's Place*, 56.

[42] Tameside Local Studies Library (TLSL), Manchester Studies, tape 36, interview with Edith Edwards.

[43] ESRO, Lewes in Living Memory, AMS 6416/1/7/51, interview with Joan Perry.

[44] LRO, NWSA, 2000.0292, interview with Mary Gregory.

[45] Jephcott, *Rising Twenty*, 128–9.

[46] G. Payne, J. Payne, and T. Chapman, 'The Changing Pattern of Early Career Mobility', in Payne and Abott (eds.), *Women*, 51.

changes in British industry, and the attraction of young women as a cheap labour supply for semiskilled or lower-grade non-manual work, meant that by the 1940s they were increasingly likely to enter employment different to that of mothers who had begun work in the 1920s. Young women's increasing degree of occupational mobility distinguished them both from their parents and from their brothers.

However, geographic and social background continued to shape girls' ability to obtain different kinds of work, and thus the degree of social mobility they experienced. In rural areas, young women's employment opportunities continued to be far more limited than in large urban conurbations, a pattern highlighted by domestic service recruitment. In London, the expansion of light manufacture provided jobs for girls from the poorest backgrounds by the late 1920s,[47] while migrants from the provinces filled the less lucrative domestic service jobs.[48] While demand for female migrant labour had increased in other large towns by the early 1940s, it was concentrated in the industrial sector, as local young women moved into more prestigious retail and clerical occupations.[49] Moreover, while the Second World War led to an expansion of industrial and clerical employment outside the largest towns, Jephcott found that locality and parental background continued to shape employment prospects for girls in the mid-1940s, with those in London enjoying greater choice of employment than young women living in small northern towns.[50]

Family background was also crucial. Even in the more buoyant areas, a noticeable distinction in employment opportunities existed between the girls from non-manual and those from manual backgrounds, and between the daughters of skilled-manual and unskilled-manual workers. In 1930s Manchester, growth industries were concentrated in the south of the city, offering light industrial employment to daughters of more affluent working class families living in the southern suburbs and Cheshire. Girls from poorer families, and those commuting into the city from poorer northern towns, were employed in the clothing trade or as domestic servants.[51] A similar social division was evident on Merseyside, but a lack of industrial employment meant that daughters of the 'better artisan class' worked as servants in private households, while 'A rougher type of

47 White, *Worst Street*, 191.

48 H. Llewellyn Smith, *New Survey of London*, 3 (London: P. S. King and Son, 1932), 266.

49 C. V. Butler, *Domestic Service*, reprint of 1916 edn. (London: Garland, 1980), 73; P. Scott, 'Women, Other "Fresh" Workers, and the New Manufacturing Workforce of Interwar Britain', *International Review of Social History*, 45/3 (2000), 466–8.

50 Jephcott, *Rising Twenty*, 128–9.

51 Hunt and Hughes, 'Culture Transformed?', 87.

girl, but still not from the slum districts associated with casual labour, is employed in Institutions.'[52] The 'very large number of clerks living in working class families'[53] were in most labour markets largely drawn from the upper echelon of the working class.[54] Rising labour demand in the 1940s eroded this to some extent, but while *Woman's Own* declared in 1942 that 'there is no such thing as a typical factory girl these days', listing ballet dancers and society girls among the workforce of one Royal Ordnance Factory,[55] social background in reality continued to shape young women's employment prospects. Juveniles' exemption from conscription meant that disruption to established employment recruitment practices was very limited. Mass-Observation investigations recorded that throughout the war the majority of female factory operatives were from unskilled or semiskilled manual backgrounds whereas clerks tended to be recruited from households headed by a skilled-manual or non-manual worker.[56]

The importance of social background in structuring young women's employment opportunities indicates that occupation remained strongly correlated with social status in working class life. Although Davies and Roberts have shown how non-work factors such as women's household management and men's leisure activities shaped a family's status and wider social networks,[57] a father's occupation and income were clearly still extremely influential. White has noted that coming from a street or family known to be very poor or to accommodate criminals could greatly disadvantage young people in the interwar labour market, and that these were generally the children of unskilled, casual workers.[58] Young women themselves recognized the importance of social selection. Dolly, who entered factory work in Manchester in 1938, was typical in feeling that 'a lot is where you're brought up—the little narrow place you see, what your parents have done. You're expected to go into a certain little niche.'[59] Any assessment of the connections between family and workplace needs to take account of the indirect influences of gender and social background

[52] Caradog Jones, *Merseyside*, 2, 320.

[53] Llewellyn Smith, *London*, 8/3 (1933), 273. See also Klingender, *Clerical Labour*, 58–66.

[54] Caradog Jones, *Merseyside*, 3, 216; G. Anderson, *The White-Blouse Revolution: Female Office Workers since 1870* (Manchester: Manchester University Press, 1988), 10–13.

[55] *Woman's Own*, 3 April 1942.

[56] Mass-Observation, *War Factory* (London: Gollancz, 1943), 31–2, 50, and 56; M-OA: FR 2117, 'Women at Work: The Attitudes of Working Women towards Postwar Employment and Some Related Problems', June 1944, 8–11.

[57] Davies, *Leisure*, 48–54; Roberts, *Woman's Place*, 148–68.

[58] White, *Worst Street*, 164.

[59] Lifetimes, *Something in Common* (Manchester: Manchester Polytechnic, 1976), 35.

upon occupational recruitment that accounts like Dolly's point up, and to which this chapter now turns.

The Family and the Job Search

The limitations on young women's employment choices imposed by social background are partially explained by the importance of the family in advising on and finding work, a factor missed by purely quantitative analyses that concentrate on direct occupational continuity between parents and children. Table 5 shows that parents and relatives were extremely influential in obtaining a young worker's first job. At least one-third of John and Sylvia Jewkes's sample obtained their first job as a result of parents or friends, and relatives played a large part in the recruitment of another third who claimed to have found work by themselves.[60] This high degree of familial involvement was partially explained by the study's concentration on Lancashire towns dominated by one or two industries, but even in larger labour markets, and in periods of full employment, parental influence remained important in finding a first job, with 21 per cent of girls in the Sheffield sample and 26 per cent of those in Wilkins's sample finding their first job through family members, chiefly parents.

TABLE 5. Percentage of Girls and Boys Using Various Methods of Obtaining First Jobs Nationally (1925 and 1950), in Sheffield (1927), Merseyside (1930), and Lancashire (1934)

Method	National (1925)		Sheffield		Merseyside		Lancashire		National (1950)	
	Girls	Boys	Girls	Boys	Girls	Boys	Girls	Boys	Girls	Boys
Own efforts	54	62	36	40	31	37	33	38	28	28
Family	27	24	21	25	9	16	28	34	26	32
Friends	N/A	N/A	26	20	9	5	N/A	N/A	N/A	N/A
JEB	16	10	14	13	41	32	34	24	25	27
School	2	2	N/A	N/A	3	4	2	2	15	9

Source: Caradog Jones, *Merseyside*, 3, 212; Jewkes, *Juvenile Labour Market*, 35; Ministry of Labour, *Personal Circumstances*, 36; A. D. K. Owen et al., *Sheffield*, 17; Wilkins, *Adolescent*, 32.

[60] Jewkes, *Juvenile*, 34.

The relative influence of fathers and mothers varied in this respect. The earlier discussion of women's entry to the textile and clothing trades indicates that mothers could be very important in obtaining jobs for daughters in sectors that employed women on skilled work. Conversely, where a strong sexual division of labour existed, male industrial workers frequently secured unskilled or semiskilled jobs for daughters, a practice particularly common in textile and light manufacturing firms such as Courtaulds in Coventry, Players in Nottingham, and Huntley and Palmer's in Reading.[61] Fathers' wider workplace networks could also be important, as Jean Garstang's experience highlights. When she left school in 1940

> My father, he was training special constables . . . and one of the chaps who was being taught he was the manager of Barratt's shoe shop. And I had always wanted to work in a shoe shop so my father talked to him and he said bring her along for an interview.[62]

Yet personal testimonies suggest that across the full range of labour markets mothers more frequently played an influential, if indirect, role in recruitment.[63] A long neglected role of the support networks developed among working class women[64] was the provision of advice on and the location of employment for children, particularly daughters. Mary Welch's mother found her daughter her first job in a London café in the early 1920s, just as Grace Wardle's first job in a bakery in her home town of Ashton, Lancashire, was obtained for her by her mother when Grace left school in 1948.[65] However, the situation of these two girls differed in some significant ways. Mary, who had grown up with her sister, was taken in by her mother when she left school because 'she wanted my dibs from work. I can understand that'. Her mother was primarily concerned with the contribution her daughter would be able to make to the family economy and with finding her a job in an area where few posts were available for poor girls.[66] Although Grace's earnings were also important to the family economy, she was able to express an opinion on the type of

[61] See, for example, MRC, Coventry Women's Work Collection, MSS 266/6/1, interview with Doris Addicott; NLSL, Making Ends Meet collection, A66/a/1, interview with Peggy; Reading Museum Archive (RMA), 1997.127.26, interview with Mrs Cottrell.

[62] LRO, NWSA, 1999.0445, interview with Jean Garstang.

[63] S. Alexander, 'Becoming a Woman in London in the 1920s and 1930s', in ead. (ed.), *Becoming a Woman and Other Essays in 19th and 20th Century Feminist History* (London: Virago, 1994), 212.

[64] Ross, 'Survival Networks', 4–27.

[65] TLSL, Tameside tapes, tape 101, interview with Grace Wardle.

[66] M. Welch, 'Leather Worker', in Hackney People's Autobiography (ed.), *Working Lives* (London: Centreprise, 1976), 50.

employment she wanted, and her mother was able to fulfil her daughter's wishes.[67] This difference is partly explained by distinctions between the two women's relationships with their mothers, but it also points to a generational change, shaped by expanding employment opportunities and a rising standard of living between the 1920s and late 1940s, which reduced the necessity for girls to take the most lucrative job available, expanded their employment options, and, as chapter 2 suggested, raised maternal aspirations for their daughters—and the ability to realize them.[68]

Reliance on the family could ease a girl's job search, but could also limit her occupational choices. Mothers frequently accompanied daughters as they looked for their first job, often by approaching local employers directly. Doris Bailey, who was keen to obtain clerical work in the 1920s, was advised by her father, a French polisher, to seek work in Shoreditch:

> So we set out, Mum and I, past big box making factories, 'machinists wanted' signs and 'girls to learn upholstery' notices. Everyone wanted girls to use their hands, not brains, and it never occurred to my poor Mum that we were in the wrong area.[69]

Irene Moore, who was evacuated from London to Reading in 1940, and was eventually adopted by the family she was billeted with, recalled that her mother's limited employment experience shaped her own entry to employment: 'My [adoptive] mother thought I should go into service. I suppose in their day they did, so I had to do a year in service'.[70] By contrast, Miss Cotterill, whose background was lower middle class, obtained a clerical job in 1941 because 'my mother, who played a tremendous amount of bridge, met someone who knew the regional co-ordinator of the Ministry of Labour, Mr Blakeman, and he said "we're short of shorthand typists, tell her to come and see me." '[71]

As employment opportunities expanded, many women invested time and energy in endeavouring to improve daughters' chances of entering secure, respectable, and possibly satisfying employment. An increasing number attended the conferences and meetings organized by local Juvenile Employment Advisory Committees.[72] Others asked for advice from a wide

[67] TLSL, Tameside tapes, tape 101, interview with Grace Wardle.

[68] Roberts, *Woman's Place*, 64–5.

[69] D. Bailey, *Children of the Green* (London: Stepney Books, 1981), 106.

[70] RMA, 1997.127.1b, interview with Irene Moore.

[71] RMA, 1997.127.26, Miss Cotterill.

[72] Ministry of Labour, *Annual Report on the Work of the Advisory Committees for Juvenile Employment for the year 1933* (London: HMSO, 1934), 5.

range of sources. Doris Bailey's mother, unable to advise her daughter on the non-manual work that Doris desired, asked the insurance man what she should do.[73] Nellie Oldroyd's mother persuaded a local clerk to give her daughter shorthand lessons to improve her employment prospects.[74] So important was adult influence considered that when Rose Lowe's mother was unable to accompany her daughter on her job search, she arranged for a female friend to take her place.[75] Leaving school did not mark a simple transition from child to adult; daughters were, as Roberts found, still subject to parental, particularly maternal, authority.[76]

Familial recruitment practices were encouraged by many employers, particularly prior to the Second World War, for they facilitated social selection and forged ties of obligation between new recruits and the workplace. Marion Kent was clear that domestic servants had to bring their mothers to interviews so that prospective employers could assess their social background, trustworthiness, and cleanliness, a conclusion supported by other servants.[77] Many clerical employers[78] and reputable industrial firms used similar methods: to obtain a job at a prestigious clothing firm in Nottingham, Eileen had to be spoken for by her mother and 'I was generally inspected and I had to be of a good type and all the rest of it to get into a job of this kind'.[79] Ida Hackett, who became a Co-op shop assistant in 1928, was sure that 'my mother being an active Co-operator had a big influence on the Co-op board'.[80] Such experiences were typical, although other relatives and friends were also influential. At Nottingham's Players factory, where Mrs Mead began her first job in 1926:

> Someone spoke for me, a friend of my father's 'cos you couldn't get in Players in those days, you know, you had to have someone speak for you. It was a family affair sort of thing, and er, Jack Edwards spoke and said, saw someone and I went and I got the job in the Leaf Room.[81]

The Factory Inspectorate noted that this strategy was widely operated among industrial employers when labour supply outstripped demand

[73] Bailey, *Children*, 106.

[74] N. Oldroyd, 'Sweetmaking', in R. Van Riel (ed.), *All in a Day's Work* (Pontefract: Yorkshire Art Circus, 1982), 9.

[75] Lowe, *Daddy*, 15.

[76] Roberts, *Woman's Place*, 42–3.

[77] LRO, NWSA, 1988.0060, interview with Marion Kent. See also TLSL, Manchester Studies, tape 28, interview with Mrs Cleary; TLSL, Manchester Studies, tape 26, interview with Mrs Hughson.

[78] Llewellyn Smith, *London*, 8/3, 288.

[79] NLSL, Making Ends Meet, A14/a/2, Eileen.

[80] LRO, NWSA, 2000.1010, interview with Ida Hackett.

[81] NLSL, Making Ends Meet collection, A23/a-b/1, interview with Mrs Mead.

in the 1930s.[82] Even in the 1940s non-manual employers, particularly in smaller labour markets, were able to remain quite selective over who they employed. Amy Cowie, who entered employment in 1941, recalled:

> I always wanted to work at Woolworths . . . but when I went, they said you've got all the qualities, you know, of a shop girl, but when they found out me mother and dad were parted they said no. You'd to have a good family relation to work in a shop.[83]

Consequently, Amy followed her mother into the local mill, remaining there until she obtained a shop job at the age of 50. Her testimony is a reminder that although, as Davin and Davies have pointed out, definitions of roughness and respectability could be fluid,[84] they were nonetheless shaped by a range of social, economic, and cultural factors, such as a father's occupation, or parents' marital status, outside an individual's control.

High unemployment in the early 1920s and early 1930s adversely affected occupational mobility, with employers frequently giving preference to the children of existing workers or favoured employees or customers when the supply of young workers exceeded demand.[85] Nellie Hilton obtained work at Glen Mill in Lancashire in the early 1920s only because her older sister worked there and her mother persuaded the foreman to put Nellie's name down for a job while she was still at school.[86] The increase in domestic service employment during the 1920s is a sign that employment contraction forced many young women into downward occupational mobility.[87] Young people were forced to search for jobs outside local family networks: the National Advisory Council for Juvenile Employment noted in 1934 that unemployment was responsible for juveniles' increasing willingness to undertake long daily journeys to work.[88] Swindon LEA was one of several that felt unable to accommodate any of the juvenile workers transferred by the Ministry of Labour from depressed areas in the early 1930s, since local employers preferred the children of current employees.[89] Parental unemployment could thus disadvantage job-seeking children, by eroding those social networks drawn upon in the job search.

82 Report of the Chief Inspector of Factories and Workshops for the Year 1937 (PP 1937–8), x, Cmd 5802, 21.

83 LRO, NWSA, 2002.0224, interview with Amy Cowie.

84 A. Davin, *Growing Up Poor* (London: Rivers Oram, 1996), 69–74; Davies, *Leisure*, 61–73.

85 Ministry of Labour, *Report on Juvenile Employment . . . 1933*, 6; Owen et al., *Sheffield*, 17.

86 LRO, NWSA, 1999.0340, interview with Nellie Hilton.

87 Roberts, *Woman's Place*, 55.

88 Ministry of Labour, *Report on Juvenile Employment . . . 1933*, 4.

89 The National Archives, LAB 19/24, MS: 'Juvenile Transference 1934–1937', *c.* 1937.

Although an increase in labour demand from the mid-1930s eroded the value of having a family member available to 'speak for' a girl starting work, the family economy continued to constrain the effects of employment expansion. Several Juvenile Employment Advisory Committees reported that applicants' inability to afford travel significantly hindered their placement of juveniles in jobs throughout the 1930s.[90] In 1948, the London Advisory Council for Youth Employment noted that on 'the outskirts of London, where choice of employment is necessarily more limited, many parents prefer their children to take unskilled employment near home rather than undertake the daily journey involved in the acceptance of progressive employment'.[91] Zweig found that money continued to shape parental decisions about the type of job a child should take in the late 1940s. Although he identified a significant proportion of families who were able and willing to allow sons to enter apprenticeships or other poorly paid forms of work, he also noted that a small proportion encouraged sons to take the highest paid job available, 'and we must bear in mind that in many cases real misery, and not greed, is the cause of such an attitude.'[92] The London Trades Council concurred with this.[93] Poverty, then, remained an important determinant of young women's job opportunities.

The expectation that a woman's working life would be shorter than a man's could also restrict young women's employment choices. In those areas of England where men were the main breadwinners, like Greater London, parents' investment in their children's job search frequently demonstrated the same bias towards males that chapter 2 showed was evident in the allocation of education. A survey of Becontree and Dagenham in the 1930s found that parents were reluctant to let girls incur travel costs to and from work, particularly as relatively lucrative shop work was available locally.[94] Mass-Observation found that girls' employment choices continued to be constrained by a lack of suitable clothes in the early 1940s, which reduced their likelihood of obtaining employment as clerks or shop assistants in the smartest stores. Families appeared more

[90] London Advisory Council for Juvenile Employment, *Annual Reports 1929–1935* (London: HMSO, 1930–6); Ministry of Labour, *Report on the Work of Advisory Committees* (London: HMSO, 1930–8); T. Young, *Becontree and Dagenham* (London: S. Sidders and Son, 1936), 122.

[91] London Advisory Council on Youth Employment, *Annual Report for the Year 1948* (London: HMSO, 1949), 6.

[92] F. Zweig, *Labour, Life and Poverty* (London: Gollancz, 1948), 17.

[93] London Trades Council, *Blind Alley Labour* (London: London Trades Council, 1944), 10.

[94] Young, *Becontree*, 121–2.

willing to spend money on a son's work clothes.[95] However, the social and geographic limitations of familial recruitment networks faced a potential challenge as working class participation in secondary education increased, and state involvement in juvenile employment recruitment grew, particularly during the 1930s and 1940s.

Education

By the end of the First World War, elementary education had been compulsory for almost 50 years. This, together with the expansion of the labour market and formalization of recruitment strategies in the non-manual sector, extended schoolteachers' influence over job recruitment, primarily through the provision of written testimonials.[96] Their importance varied according to an applicant's locality, social background, and occupational aspirations. For young women in labour markets dominated by a single industry, testimonials—also called characters—'didn't make a lot of difference to your job. As long as they said you were on the level, that was all that mattered.'[97] Less than 4 per cent of girls and boys in the Jewkeses' sample found employment through a schoolteacher.[98] Testimonials proved more important for girls aspiring to enter clerical or upmarket retail work.[99] Dolly Scannell attributed her office job to her teacher's reference: 'Characters were . . . passports to livelihood to be cherished'.[100] Testimonials were also used by JEBs to direct juveniles to jobs.[101] Mabel Morrison's analysis of her limited choice of job relates to the interwar years, but, as she suggests, had relevance for the 1940s and 1950s as well:

> you wouldn't get into an office unless somebody spoke for yer, or you were the top of the class! And, er, you would probably get—they would pick the cream of the class—like they do now! And they forget that other people—you had to go where you could get a job![102]

However, less than 56 per cent of the Jewkeses' sample,[103] and a similar proportion of Manchester JEBs' applicants between 1932 and 1936,[104]

95 M-OA, FR 1353, 'The Service of Youth', July 1942, xi.

96 Vincent, 'Mobility', 223.

97 Welch, 'Leather worker', 52.

98 Jewkes, *Juvenile*, 34–5.

99 Vincent, 'Mobility', 222–3.

100 Scannell, *Mother*, 146–7.

101 See, for example, Manchester Juvenile Employment Bureaux, *Annual Report, 1932–3* (Manchester: Manchester Juvenile Employment Bureaux, 1933), 5; Manchester Juvenile Employment Bureaux, *Annual Report, 1936* (Manchester: Manchester Juvenile Employment Bureaux, 1937), 3; Vincent, 'Mobility', 223.

102 LRO, NWSA, 1992.0103, C. Curlett. Mabel Morrison is a pseudonym.

103 Jewkes, *Juvenile*, 35.

104 Manchester JEBs, *Reports, 1932–6*.

actually obtained the work recommended by their teachers. In the 1940s, the expansion of employment opportunities for young women outside established family networks and in clerical and shop work increased the importance of teachers' testimonials, but in 1948 the London Regional Council for Youth Employment noted that their influence was still limited compared with that of parents and friends.[105] While connections between education and employment grew, limited labour demand prior to the Second World War; the wartime direction of labour by the state; and full employment all limited, in different ways, the formalization of occupational recruitment.

It is impossible to use existing quantitative data to test the hypothesis that secondary education improved occupational choice. The cross-sectional nature of the large data-sets available prevents cohort analysis of juveniles' progression from school to work. Baines and Johnson have concluded from their *New Survey of London* data-set that an additional year of schooling did improve working class London boys' chances of entering higher status employment, but stress that their conclusion is based on the hypothesis that most unoccupied juveniles were in full-time education.[106] Their results are nonetheless convincing, but since a smaller proportion of unoccupied girls were in education than boys in the interwar years, and less is known about girls' labour force distribution, attempting such an analysis for them would be problematic. Moreover, conclusions based on London, where educational participation was relatively high, cannot be applied to other areas.

The 1931 Census can, however, offer some insight into the effects of extended education on occupation, by providing a national snapshot of occupational distribution and educational participation. This indicates that a combination of advancing age, extended education, and social background affected job prospects. In 1951, girls' probability of being in clerical employment increased by 14 per cent between the ages of 15 and 17, while the likelihood that they would be in full-time schooling fell by 24 per cent. These figures, together with personal testimonies, indicate that whereas secondary schooling alone could not guarantee white-collar employment, it enhanced a girl's chances of obtaining such work. This was recognized by young women themselves; after secondary schoolgirl Linda McCullough Thew's success in the Co-operative Society's competitive examination for job applicants, one unsuccessful girl 'put out

[105] London Regional Advisory Council for Youth Employment, *Annual Report for the Year 1948* (London: HMSO, 1949), 6.

[106] Baines and Johnson, 'Occupational Continuity', 707.

her tongue and said, "Secondary school snobs. You shouldn't be allowed to try" '.[107] For the great majority, schooling and its connection to job selection reinforced, rather than challenged, the limitations imposed by social background.

Formal qualifications were less important than schooling prior to the introduction of compulsory secondary education in 1944. Many shops and offices that recruited secondary schoolgirls nonetheless imposed an upper age limit of 16 on applicants—thus keeping wage costs low—which prevented entrants from taking public examinations.[108] This caused difficult choices for working class secondary schoolgirls and their parents. Linda Thew had to evaluate the benefits and risks of remaining in secondary education when she turned 14, against those of taking a job at the Co-op, which operated an age limit of 16. She was acutely aware of the cost of her education and 'had no vocation whatever for nursing and I most definitely did not want to teach. Neither did I want to leave school. . . . thus, I was in a dilemma.'[109] Ultimately, she took the job. The fact that extended education could limit young women's job choices to a greater extent than qualifications could expand them was one reason only approximately 40 per cent of secondary school entrants sat the School Certificate during the interwar years.[110]

In the post-1944 era, academic qualifications—the signifier of a selective grammar school education—became increasingly important as secondary education was made universal and compulsory. A large number of the non-manual occupations open to girls, including laboratory assistants and technicians, nursing and school teaching, and many branches of clerical work, required at least a School Certificate.[111] However, job opportunities, and thus the value of qualifications, continued to be differentiated by gender. Higher grade clerical posts continued to be a largely male preserve, and although demand for school teachers rose after the Second World War, opportunities continued to be greater for men, since educational expansion was concentrated in the male-dominated secondary sector.[112] Few other jobs available to working class girls demanded extended schooling, a factor that

[107] L. M. Thew, *The Pit Village and the Store* (London: Pluto Press, 1985), 133.

[108] London Advisory Council for Juvenile Employment, *Report for the Year 1928* (London: HMSO, 1929), 93.

[109] Thew, *Pit Village*, 128.

[110] E. W. Bakke, *The Unemployed Man: A Social Study* (London: Nisbet and Co, 1932), 172–3; Ministry of Labour, *Report of the Committee on Education and Industry (England and Wales)*, 2 (London: HMSO, 1928), 34; Vincent, 'Mobility', 221.

[111] *Ministry of Labour Gazette* (July 1943), 97.

[112] G. Routh, *Occupation and Pay 1906–1979* (London: Macmillan, 1980), 34; R. McKibbin, *Classes and Cultures in England 1918–1951* (Oxford: Oxford University Press, 1998), 48.

Jephcott found provided a disincentive for many girls to pursue post-compulsory education, as well as reducing its value in the eyes of their families.[113] The sexual division of labour thus limited the effect of extended educational opportunities on young women.

The influence of social background was not overcome by the extension of secondary schooling. The Ministry of Labour revealed that of their 1925 sample of 2,701 girls and 3,331 boys, 30 per cent of 'Class A' girls (those expected to obtain skilled or white-collar work, usually having had some secondary education), and 50 per cent of 'Class A' boys failed to obtain 'appropriate' situations,[114] indicating that secondary schooling did not guarantee to improve job prospects. Baines and Johnson convincingly argue that the prospects of juveniles from skilled manual backgrounds were enhanced by additional schooling more than those of the lower classes.[115] Likewise, the Carnegie Trust's survey of young men in 1937 noted that the selective nature of secondary schooling made it difficult to separate the significance of extended education upon employment prospects from that of social class.[116] This continued in the post-1944 era. Wilkins noted that clerical employers preferred former grammar school pupils.[117] These students were chosen for their high level of education, which the 1944 Education Act had made accessible to a larger number of working class children. However, the disproportionately large number of middle- and upper-working class pupils in such schools[118] facilitated social selection. Whereas secondary schooling could improve girls' prospects of obtaining office or retail jobs, then, it did not guarantee to do so and could not overcome the effects of social background.

Girls' own attitudes to school were shaped by their awareness of the influence of social background on their job prospects and future lives. Many viewed school subjects as an irrelevance. Jephcott noted disapprovingly that her sample 'see formal education as something which should have an immediate market price'; those who expressed a positive view of school referred to the general advantages offered by secondary education in helping ' "you to get a better job" '.[119] This is, however, unsurprising, given the

[113] Jephcott, *Rising Twenty*, 98–100.
[114] Ministry of Labour, *Personal Circumstances*, 73.
[115] Baines and Johnson, 'Occupational Continuity', 707–8.
[116] C. Cameron, A. Lush, and G. Meara, *Disinherited Youth: A Report on the 18+ Age Group Enquiry Prepared for the Trustees of the Carnegie United Kingdom Trust* (Edinburgh: Edinburgh University Press, 1943), 20–1.
[117] Wilkins, *Adolescent*, 31.
[118] McKibbin, *Classes and Cultures*, 267–70.
[119] Quoted in Jephcott, *Rising Twenty*, 99.

economic pressures that the family economy exerted upon most working class girls and the ethos of formal education, which was clearly designed to prepare working class pupils for the job market. Moreover, the quality of such preparation did not inspire young women with confidence. The 'vocational' curriculum implemented in elementary and central schools and, after the 1944 Act, secondary modern schools centred on homecraft for girls. Wilkins found that young men were more likely than young women to view their education as vocationally valuable, since the subjects taught correlated with the skills required by some of the skilled manual occupations they hoped to enter.[120] Joyce Shaw, however, although proud to have won a scholarship to a central school in the 1930s, commented that 'I didn't seem to learn much at all. What they wanted you to learn was domestic work. . . . you were supposed to clean out the flat for the two teachers who lived in!'[121] Other women did value such lessons, viewing them as preparation for marriage and motherhood, as many of Jephcott's sample did in the mid-1940s.[122] However, most of her sample also recognized that they would acquire domestic skills from mothers or older sisters, and had no desire to use such training in their paid employment, due to the disadvantages associated with domestic service, which was anyway in rapid decline by the late 1940s.[123]

The ability of selective secondary education to facilitate upward social mobility was limited due to the small proportion of working class children allowed through the doors, but the experiences of women in secondary education indicate that even those who experienced it were disadvantaged by gender and class. Over the past 40 years the narrative of upward social mobility through selective secondary education has characterized a large proportion of working class male autobiographies. Far fewer women's autobiographies adopt such an unproblematic narrative; most of those that do are the work of authors from lower middle or middle class backgrounds.[124] Working class girls who attended selective secondary schools often articulated a sense of ambivalence and loss. Rose Gamble, who attended secondary school in the 1930s, recalled, 'I wanted to be like the girls in my class when I was with them, but I honestly had to admit that I enjoyed myself much more

120 Wilkins, *Adolescent*, 45.

121 LRO, NWSA, 1993.0020, interview with Joyce Shaw. Central Schools were vocational secondaries.

122 Jephcott, *Rising Twenty*, 99.

123 Ibid., 42–4.

124 For example, A. Hennegan, '. . . And Battles Long Ago', in L. Heron (ed.), *Truth, Dare or Promise: Girls Growing Up in the Fifties* (London: Virago, 1985), 149–50.

back in the yard.'[125] Doris Bailey was proud of having passed the entrance exam to a London girls' high school, but, like Rose Gamble, she suffered bullying from other pupils when they discovered she came from a working class area. She also disliked the difference this created between herself and her siblings and neighbours, particularly when her sister began work while Doris remained at school:

> Gwen started work at the Holborn factory and I felt, for the very first time, that she and I were drifting apart. We had always done things together; and when she offered me a threepence pocket money, I felt dreadful. I was afraid she would gang up on me with Eva [their older sister], who kept making comments about me being kept as a lady by her.[126]

Many working class girls who had some form of selective secondary education valued the opportunity, but the social consequences could seem a high price to pay for the limited opportunities that such an education offered.

Directed to Work: The State and Employment

Many more young women came into contact with state employment exchanges and bureaux than attended selective secondary schools. Baines and Johnson have argued that the increasing concern expressed by the government, educationalists, and social investigators over the need to provide vocational guidance for young people—by 1935 there existed 192 Local Advisory Committees for Juvenile Employment and 107 Local Choice of Employment Committees in Britain,[127] and by 1949 129 of 181 local authorities were providing a Youth Employment Service[128]—is proof that familial recruitment strategies were weakening.[129] Yet the rhetoric used in the debate over vocational guidance in fact expresses anxiety that traditional recruitment methods persisted in the face of industrial and technological change. In the aftermath of the First World War, concern to bring about national physical and economic renewal by developing the 'industrial efficiency' and 'character' of juvenile 'citizens in training', together with post-war unemployment, increased support among policy makers for state direction of the juvenile labour market

125 R. Gamble, *Chelsea Child* (London: BBC, 1979), 172.

126 Bailey, *Children*, 104.

127 Political and Economic Planning, *The Entrance to Industry* (London: PEP, 1935), 25.

128 Ministry of Labour, *Report of the National Youth Employment Council on the Work of the Youth Employment Service 1947–1950* (London: HMSO, 1950), 9.

129 Baines and Johnson, 'Occupational Continuity', 709.

through the extension of JEBs.[130] By the late 1920s, rising unemployment, coupled with fears that a falling birth rate would provoke a shortage of juvenile labour in those areas where growth industries were expanding, heightened interest in regulating and directing juvenile labour.[131] In 1929, the National Advisory Council for Juvenile Employment expressed anxiety that 'there are considerable numbers of boys and girls who are unemployed or unsuitably employed and are not brought into contact with any official machinery or voluntary agency which could help them.'[132]

Whereas unemployment provided the initial impetus for the establishment of state employment exchanges, it was the increased demand for young workers' labour from the mid-1930s and young people's expanding job choices that heightened interest in employment guidance between the mid-1930s and the early 1950s. In 1935 the influential think tank Political and Economic Planning declared that employment guidance was the 'work of the expert',[133] requiring professional intervention to ensure that young people were matched with jobs that would train them for adult responsibility, while also promoting national economic efficiency. This was increasingly accepted during the 1940s, as wartime production necessitated the training and direction of labour. However, it was also accepted that major job expansion would be in unskilled and semiskilled labour; as a consequence, plans for the post-Second World War reorganization of education and the establishment of a youth employment service placed great emphasis on equipping school leavers with 'adaptability . . . to meet the demand of any sudden turnover to new materials or fundamental revision of technique'.[134] Such perspectives were influential in designing the vocational curriculum of the secondary modern schools in which the vast majority of working class people were educated following the 1944 Education Act.[135] A Ministry of Labour report on post-war reconstruction, published in 1943, emphasized the

130 Juvenile Education (Employment after the War), Interim Report, PP 1916, viii, Cd 8374, 3–4; Juvenile Education (Employment after the War), Final Report, PP 1917–18, xi, Cd 8512, 26–7.

131 Ministry of Labour, *Memorandum on the Shortage, Surplus and Redistribution of Juvenile Labour in England and Wales during the Years 1930–1938* (London: HMSO, 1931).

132 Second Report of the National Advisory Council for Juvenile Employment (Age of Entry into Unemployment Insurance), PP 1929–30, xv, Cmd 3427, 4.

133 Political and Economic Planning, *The Entrance to Industry* (London: PEP, 1935), 25.

134 London Advisory Council on Youth Employment, *Annual Report for the Year 1942* (London: HMSO, 1943), 9.

135 TNA, LAB 19/236, Committee on the Recruitment and Training of Juveniles for Industry, MS: 'Report on Consultations with Representatives of Industries', *c.*1945, 2.

importance of vocational guidance within a labour market characterized by full employment: 'employers wanting juveniles may compete more keenly and it may not always be the best or the most progressive jobs which will carry the highest wages. . . . [consequently] experienced guidance will be very necessary'.[136] Young people were construed as a potential problem, who required training for the labour market. The nature of labour demand, which sustained the use of young workers in poorly paid, insecure posts, was left largely untouched.

The effects of state employment guidance and direction were extremely limited prior to the depression of the early 1930s, but subsequently expanded. The numbers placed in employment by JEBs rose from less than 20 per cent of young workers in 1926[137] to 33 per cent by 1933.[138] This reflected a degree of compulsion: following the 1920 Unemployment Act, juveniles' benefit eligibility was dependent on their registration at a JEB, a regulation tightened by the 1934 Unemployment Act. Girls, who were less likely to experience direct occupational continuity than boys, were consequently more receptive to using the state as a means of obtaining work. Among the *Merseyside* sample, particularly hard hit by unemployment, 41 per cent of girls found their first job through the JEBs.[139] Economic depression thus eroded one of the functions of the working class household and of wider neighbourhood networks.

Economic expansion extended the JEBs' influence in buoyant labour markets from the mid-1930s. The Ministry of Labour noted that this was particularly the case among young women, who used the Bureaux to locate jobs that were opening up in sectors with which their families were unfamiliar.[140] Consequently, connections between family background and occupational choice did begin to weaken among girls rather more than among boys prior to the Second World War. In the 1940s, the expansion of employment for young men in office and technical work, as well as semiskilled factory work, raised the proportion of both girls and boys using the Bureaux. The London Regional Advisory Council for Juvenile Employment attributed its increased placement of juveniles in 1943 and 1944 to the fact that 'boys and girls have a much greater choice of employment than ever before, which, of course, makes vocational guidance much more realistic than in the days when juveniles

136 Ministry of Labour, *Young Worker*, 11.
137 Ministry of Labour, *Committee on Education and Industry*, 1 (London: HMSO, 1926), 16.
138 Ministry of Labour, *Report on the Work of the Advisory Committees, 1933*, 4.
139 Caradog Jones, *Merseyside*, 3, 202–4.
140 Ministry of Labour, *Report on Juvenile Employment . . . 1933*, 5.

had to grasp at almost any job, blind alley or otherwise, rather than be unemployed.'[141] The establishment of the national Youth Employment Service in 1948, which forged close links with secondary schools, extended the state's influence further, with 25 per cent of girls in Wilkins's sample and 27 per cent of boys finding their first job through a JEB, and a further 15 per cent of girls and 9 per cent of boys using their school.[142]

Despite the growth of state intervention, its effects clearly remained limited. Parents—and employers—preferred to rely on traditional recruitment strategies, particularly outside the largest urban conurbations. In their search for new employment opportunities, young women were more likely to turn to relatives and friends than to the Bureaux or careers adviser. Friends, who chapter 4 will show were particularly significant in shaping young adult women's mobility between jobs, were increasingly important in a girl's entry to employment. Within the Sheffield sample, 26 per cent of girls found their first post through friends.[143] In 1937, the Factory Inspector for the south-east division noted that prospering manufacturing firms in need of young workers were offering 'substantial inducements' to workers who recruited friends. One firm in Suffolk 'offered a bonus to anyone who introduced a friend who remained for six months.'[144] Such recruitment methods were familiar to employers, and reflected the nature of labour demand for young women: cheapness and reliability, rather than specific skills, were prioritized. This continued during wartime, when Jephcott noted the importance of mothers, older sisters, and friends in young women's job search.[145] In 1948, the London Advisory Council for Youth Employment noted that the 'influence of parents and friends [on recruitment] is still very marked', and was disappointed at parents' poor attendance at vocational guidance interviews.[146] Jobs were also increasingly advertised in the local press. None of the young women in my sample who entered employment in the 1920s found their first job in this way, but a small number of those who began work twenty years later did, like Joyce Shelley, the daughter of a manual worker, who secured a job at a Liverpool department store in 1942 in this way: 'I saw an advertisement when I was leaving school . . . and I replied to it.'[147] However, these remained a minority.

[141] TNA, LAB 12/215, London Regional Advisory Council for Juvenile Employment, MS: 'Survey for 1943 and 1944', 1944, 6.

[142] Wilkins, *Adolescent*, 31.

[143] Owen et al., *Sheffield*, 17.

[144] Report of the Chief Inspector of Factories and Workshops for the Year 1937, x (1937–8), Cd. 5802, 16.

[145] Jephcott, *Rising Twenty*, 120.

[146] London Advisory Council on Youth Employment, *Annual Report, 1948*, 6.

[147] LRO, NWSA, 2000.1174, interview with Joyce Shelley.

Even in 1950, 24 per cent of those girls included in Wilkins's study attributed their choice of employment to the influence of relatives or friends,[148] a pattern also noted by Young and Wilmott in the mid-1950s.[149]

Girls' unwillingness to use Employment Bureaux or, later, the YES was compounded by the association of employment exchanges with the implementation of interwar unemployment policy, and, from 1941 until 1945, with conscription. Parents and juveniles were suspicious of unemployment registration at the Bureaux since this was combined with assessment of eligibility for benefit. Hostility increased when a labour transference scheme was established by the government in 1928. This placed pressure on unemployed juveniles to migrate to work—particularly girls, who could be used to meet demand for servants. It was further exacerbated by the introduction of the household means test in 1931, which meant a juvenile's benefit eligibility or refusal to take work could reduce the benefit entitlement of other household members, and by the 1934 Unemployment Act, which made registration at a JEB compulsory for all unemployed juveniles, regardless of benefit entitlement. In the early 1940s young women questioned by Mass-Observation expressed suspicion of interfering and incompetent Bureaux personnel. One unemployed 18-year-old former shop assistant commented disparagingly on the employment exchange: 'It's not much good here . . . they're nosy but they don't get you nothing. I'd rather get a job for myself really.'[150] In addition, parents and their daughters were aware that employers were often reluctant to use JEB applicants, to the frustration of the Ministry of Labour and its subsidiaries.[151] Jephcott found that many girls 'regard [the employment office] as the last resort of the lazy. They are apt to think of it in connection with unemployment rather than employment.'[152]

Reluctance to use the Bureaux was also due to the recognition that they upheld the effect of social class upon employment choice, rather than eroding it. State employment agencies discriminated on the basis of

148 Wilkins, *Adolescent*, 37.

149 M. Young and P. Willmott, *Family and Kinship in East London* (Harmondsworth: Penguin, 1957), 95–7.

150 M-OA: TC 51/2, CF, unpublished MS: 'Attitudes to Jobs—Girls and Young Women', 18 November 1940.

151 National Advisory Council for Juvenile Employment for England and Wales, *Fifth Report: Provision of Courses of Instruction for Unemployed Boys and Girls* (London: HMSO, 1934), 10–12.

152 Jephcott, *Rising Twenty*, 120. See also M-OA, TC 51/2, V.T., MS: 'Juvenile Wages', 6 February 1942.

an applicant's appearance, health, and family background; 'indifferent character' was blamed throughout the late 1920s and the 1930s for a failure to place up to 25 per cent of applicants.[153] While unemployment declined from 1941, similar criteria continued to be used to discriminate between applicants for sought-after non-manual work. The type of professional psychological vocational guidance adopted after the Second World War advised employment officers to consider juveniles' 'bearing, their cleanliness and the goodness of their speech' when selecting a suitable job for them. Shop assistants, for example, needed 'Good personality and address', whereas clerical workers required 'above average' intelligence,[154] despite the fact that much junior office work was menial. Moreover, although more girls than boys sought, and used, employment guidance, particularly after unemployment began to fall from the mid-1930s, the choices with which they were presented were constrained by gender. May Hobbs felt keenly that her interview with the youth employment officer when she left school aged 15 in 1953 was shaped by his assumptions about the proper role of working class girls:

> A right old git, he was. His advice was, don't think of making a career out of anything because you'll only give it up to get married and have kids. Either be a secretary, he said, or, better still, go into a factory. That way, he implied, it wouldn't rock the foundations too much when you left.[155]

State rhetoric increasingly emphasized the importance of vocational guidance as a means of creating a meritocratic society, but official agencies were ultimately concerned with fitting young people for the changing demands of employers. This was, as many young women recognized, an approach that continued to discriminate by gender and class.

Conclusion

Young women's entry into employment demonstrates that direct occupational continuity is not and never has been the only employment pattern that defines a working class community, and its absence does not necessarily signify a socially fluid society. Family and neighbourhood networks remained strong between 1918 and 1950. Parents, particularly

[153] London Advisory Council, *Report*, 1928–35; Ministry of Labour, *Personal Circumstances*, 9–15, 65–9; Ministry of Labour, *Report on the Work of the Advisory Committees* 1933–6; Owen et al., *Sheffield*, 20, 38.

[154] TNA, LAB 12/215, 'Survey for 1943 and 1944', 31–2.

[155] M. Hobbs, *Born to Struggle* (London: Quartet Books, 1973), 28.

mothers, were extremely influential in determining where a daughter began her working life, and frequently drew on friends and neighbours for advice. This testified to limited employment choices in the 1920s and early 1930s, but the persistence of this trend into the 1940s highlights the strength of parental authority in young women's first years of employment. While young women's employment choices grew, they remained concentrated in poorly paid occupations offering few prospects of promotion. State provision of employment guidance upheld, rather than challenged, existing class and gender divisions in the labour market and in particular the use of young, working class women as cheap and disposable workers. Entering employment thus emphasized a girl's position as a subordinate member of her household and society.

Nevertheless, young women's employment pathways underwent some significant changes over this period, which altered their relationship to their household and defined them as agents of social, economic, and cultural change in many working class communities by the 1940s. They witnessed greater expansion in their employment opportunities and experienced a greater degree of occupational and social mobility than young men. Social investigators, and women themselves, were conscious that a generational shift had occurred between the 1900s and the 1930s, and that another occurred between the 1930s and the 1950s. This centred on the expansion of young women's employment opportunities, which were therefore integral to young women's, social investigators', and politicians' understanding of what made these generations distinctively different from their mothers or grandmothers. The consequences of these changes for young women's lifestyles and social identity provide a focus for the remainder of this book.

4

Mobility, Migration, and Aspiration

The previous two chapters have provided an overview of the family's strong influence on young women's social and economic roles. The focus of the book now turns directly to young women themselves: their choices, aspirations, and identity. Young, working class women were distinguished from their fathers, mothers, and brothers, as well as from their more affluent counterparts, through their workplace culture, their leisure, and, the focus of this chapter, their mobility: occupational, geographic, and social. Young women's mobility challenges some established myths about working class communities and class status. Firstly, young women's occupational mobility undermines the notion that until very recently, a job for life was the expectation of, and reality for, most workers. The importance of intragenerational occupational mobility continues to be neglected by historians, who assume that strong, static, occupational affiliation was central to class identity within our period. Consequently, those who lack lifelong occupational affiliation, such as many women, have often been presented as an aberration or a problem within histories of employment and social class. In fact, this chapter shows that most workers held at least two jobs in their first decade of employment and that this was one of the features that distinguished young from older workers. Their mobility does not signify weak class affiliation, but rather demonstrates how social identity was forged in more complex and nuanced ways than is sometimes considered. Friends were particularly significant in prompting mobility between jobs, which did not usually constitute social mobility.

Secondly, the frequency of young women's geographic mobility contradicts the image of working class communities as cohesive parochial units, unified by neighbourhood and family lives in which women were extremely important. In fact, many working class girls left home at an early age to enter domestic service or, by the 1940s, industrial work elsewhere. They constituted a significant proportion of migrants from rural to urban areas, thus influencing migration and employment trends, as well as the composition of working class communities.

Finally, young women's mobility offers insights into their own occupational and wider aspirations. The lack of social mobility that resulted from their occupational choices has led historians and social scientists like Vincent and Summerfield to suggest that young women simply 'drifted' between jobs.[1] Yet as well as ignoring reasons for involuntary occupational mobility, this representation also reflects a subjective 'philosophy of femininity'[2] and an adherence to a paradigm of career development shaped by wider opportunity and a longer working life than most young working class women could expect. It therefore profoundly misreads and simplifies young women's own responses to structural change in the labour market between 1918 and 1951, and the location of work within their own occupational and social aspirations and desires, the subject of the final section of this chapter.

Occupational Mobility

Young women's increasing ability, and propensity, to move between jobs was one of the distinguishing features of their lifestyle, responsible for bringing them to the attention of contemporary politicians, educationalists, and social investigators. This concern arose partly because of the trend's novelty. Whereas young men's labour mobility had been discovered in the late nineteenth century,[3] it remained very limited among young women until the end of the First World War, and was still a new phenomenon in many smaller towns and rural areas in the late 1940s. In addition, young women's occupational mobility did not fit a clear-cut route of self-improvement and endeavour. The established male career trajectory began with casual work in the teens, during which time mobility between jobs could be quite frequent, followed by an apprenticeship and skilled manual work or non-manual work in

[1] D. Vincent, 'Mobility, Bureaucracy and Careers in Early-Twentieth-Century Britain', in A. Miles and D. Vincent (eds.), *Building European Society: Occupational Change and Social Mobility in Europe 1840–1940* (Manchester: Manchester University Press, 1993), 221; P. Summerfield, *Reconstructing Women's Wartime Lives* (Manchester: Manchester University Press, 1998), 93.

[2] S. Alexander, 'Men's Fears and Women's Work: Responses to Unemployment in London between the Wars', *Gender and History*, 12/2 (2000), 416.

[3] A. Freeman, *Boy Life and Labour: The Manufacture of Inefficiency* (London: P. S. King and Son, 1914).

adulthood, when mobility declined. This did not threaten perceived notions of class formation, or change dramatically prior to the 1950s. No such work ethic appeared to underpin young women's job changes. Many contemporaries concurred with the Pilgrim Trust that '[t]he prospect of marriage . . . conditions a girl's outlook on industry. . . .the girl of 14 tends to drift into the most remunerative employment immediately available'.[4]

This concept of 'drifting' remained central to discussions of girls' employment choices during and after the Second World War.[5] Rose has shown that young people's leisure activities became a site of moral anxiety in wartime,[6] but this was also true of their employment, with juvenile boys but particularly girls and young adult women being problematized as lacking the qualities of the selfless and responsible citizen. Social investigators Jephcott and Wilkins lamented girls' inability to recognize their work as 'a service to other people as well as a way of earning a living', even in the midst of war.[7] Although full employment in the post-war years increased tolerance for young workers' occupational mobility, this was conditional on their job changes being aimed at establishing a secure and stable career. The Ince Committee, established to reform the juvenile employment service in 1944, approved of the fact that 'the main hopes and ambitions that youth has are related to the job' and designed post-war youth employment provision to fit juveniles to 'suitable' jobs.[8] Young women's 'drifting' and their apparent lack of ambition thus became a matter for disapproval and concern. [9]

Young women's mobility also suggested an assertiveness and inability to know their place that caused great unease. Just as their leisure activities and appearance made it increasingly difficult to define a young woman's class in the decades following the First World War,[10] so their

[4] Pilgrim Trust, *Men without Work: A Report Made to the Pilgrim Trust* (Cambridge: Cambridge University Press, 1938), 231.

[5] P. Jephcott, *Rising Twenty: Notes on Some Ordinary Girls* (London: Faber, 1948), 134; Mass-Observation Archive (M-OA): TC 51: Youth, 51/2/C, CF, unpublished MS: 'Attitudes to Work—Young Women and Girls', 18 November 1940.

[6] S. O. Rose, 'Sex, Citizenship and the Nation in World War II Britain', *American Historical Review*, 103/4 (1998), 1147–76.

[7] Jephcott, *Rising Twenty*, 134; L. Wilkins, *The Adolescent in Britain*, Social Survey, Reports, New Series, no. 148 (1955), 68.

[8] Board of Education, *Report on the Youth Service after the War* (London: HMSO, 1944), 42; see also Ministry of Labour, *The Young Worker* (London: HMSO, 1944), 10.

[9] Jephcott, *Rising Twenty*, 134; Wilkins, *Adolescent*, 69.

[10] S. Alexander, 'Becoming a Woman in London in the 1920s and 1930s', in ead. (ed.), *Becoming a Woman and Other Essays in 19th and 20th Century Feminist History* (London: Virago, 1994), 213.

employment mobility meant that their jobs were no longer a stable signifier of their social status. Domestic servants were increasingly able to become factory girls who looked like actresses; and by the 1940s factory workers could increasingly aspire to donning the white blouse of the office worker. A series on 'Girls We All Know' in the *Manchester Evening News* in 1930 expressed optimism about this but also a sense of anxiety, noting that 'the average mill girl is as well dressed as the average typist. If you were to meet her in a Rawtenstall street, Mr Southerner, you would think that she was the millowner's daughter'.[11] Young women's occupational mobility thus provided a focus for unease over the decline of deferential domestic service, and the shift in office work from a predominantly middle class, male occupation to one increasingly dominated by lower-middle and working class women whose independence and affluence was funded by their wages. The concern provoked by these changes emphasizes their rapidity and highlights the importance of the economic context in shaping the interwar anxiety over gendered and social identities that cultural historians have highlighted.[12]

Occupational mobility could be involuntary, where labour supply outstripped demand, or voluntary, as a means of improving pay or conditions. Prior to the mid-1930s, the former dominated. As chapter 1 pointed out, the rate of youth unemployment between the wars, together with its comparatively short duration, demonstrates that many young women experienced this form of involuntary mobility.[13] Many were consequently forced to enter domestic service, experiencing a cut in wages and a decline in working conditions when they did so. Mrs Halliday, who began her working life as a laundry assistant, was one of many women to be forced to take a domestic service post in the early 1930s when she was made unemployed.[14] Mrs Cleary was sent into domestic service by her mother after ill-health cost her her industrial job. She was typical of most servants surveyed here in attributing this to her family's poverty and limited choice in the local labour market: 'there was nothing then—actually I wasn't given any time to consider [alternative jobs] and—as

[11] *Manchester Evening News* (May 14, 1930), 3. Thanks to Claire Langhamer for bringing this series to my attention.

[12] Alexander, 'Becoming'; M. Houlbrook, ' "Lady Austin's Camp Boys": Constituting the Queer Subject in 1930s London', *Gender and History*, 14/1 (2002).

[13] W. H. Beveridge, *Unemployment: A Problem of Industry*, 2nd ed. (London: Longman, 1930), 406. See also N. F. R. Crafts, 'Long-Term Unemployment in Britain in the 1930s', *Economic History Review*, 40/3 (1987), 431.

[14] Lancashire Records Office (LRO), North West Sound Archive (NWSA), 1999.0088, interview with Mrs Halliday.

I say my mother was desperately poor—and I just—in those days, it was usual to do as you were told sort of thing—I wasn't actually consulted about it.'[15] This sense of thwarted aspiration is a subject returned to at the end of the chapter.

An increasing number of young women experienced voluntary occupational mobility, however. Prior to the mid-1930s, this was most evident among domestic servants. Labour demand for servants had outstripped supply since the nineteenth century, meaning that leaving a job, or threatening to, was the greatest power a servant possessed. Press and government reports suggest that servants in general became more assertive during the interwar years, their awareness that demand for their labour outstripped supply encouraging them to initiate negotiation with employers.[16] Many servants respectfully and regretfully handed in their notice in order to force a wage rise or improvement in their working conditions. In 1936, after three years in service at a large country house, 18-year-old Marion Kent informed her employer that she would leave to take a better paid job as housemaid to her brother's employer. Her good work, and the servant shortage, meant that she secured a substantial wage rise and remained where she was.[17] As opportunities for progression in a single household were reduced by the decline of employment in large, wealthy households that maintained a hierarchy of staff, so incentives for moving between jobs to improve pay and conditions increased. Winifred Foley, for example, moved between five domestic jobs in as many years.

By the mid-1930s, voluntary occupational mobility was also evident among young workers in other sectors, although this was confined to the largest and most buoyant urban labour markets prior to the Second World War. In London, demand for young industrial and office workers was sufficiently high to mean that many moved voluntarily between jobs throughout the 1920s and 1930s. Dolly Scannel, for example, had eight different clerical jobs between leaving school in 1924 and

[15] Tameside Local Studies Library (TLSL), Manchester Studies Collection, tape 28, interview with Mrs Cleary. See also East Sussex Records Office (ESRO), Lewes in Living Memory collection, AMS 6416/1/6/13, interview with Joan Whitfield.

[16] Ministry of Labour, *Second Interim Report of the Central Committee on Women's Training and Employment for the Period Ending Dec. 31st 1922* (London: HMSO, 1923); Ministry of Labour, *Report of the Committee Appointed to Enquire into the Present Conditions as to the Supply of Female Domestic Servants* (London: HMSO, 1923), 8.

[17] LRO, NWSA, 1988.0060, interview with Marion Kent. See also W. Foley, *A Child in the Forest* (London: BBC, 1974), 126.

marrying about nine years later.[18] As employment opportunities expanded from the mid-1930s, young women also increasingly moved between occupational sectors. Many had unusual and varied employment pathways: Eileen, for example, moved from a factory job to office work, and then to another factory, before becoming a hairdresser in interwar Nottingham.[19] All of the young women questioned by Mass-Observation at a London employment exchange in 1940 had held jobs in at least two occupational sectors: one had moved between shop, factory, and clerical work in the space of two years.[20] In 1950, 78 per cent of the 1,400 young men in Wilkins's sample and 72 per cent of the 500 young women he surveyed had worked in at least two occupational sectors.[21] A narrowing of wage differentials between semiskilled industrial jobs and low-grade clerical work, and the limited promotion prospects of the latter, increased the incentive for workers to change jobs. At the same time, rising labour demand made it easier for young women with little previous experience to enter shop or office work in their later teens if they wished to.

Young women changed jobs voluntarily for better pay or conditions, more congenial company, or more interesting work. The importance they attributed to wages was a matter of concern for many social investigators and for the Ministry of Labour, who felt that this encouraged young people to enter highly paid but insecure jobs. Manchester's Juvenile Employment Bureaux were typical in warning school leavers in the 1930s that 'It does not follow that a job is a good one because you are going to start at a high wage. . . .IT WILL PAY TO LOOK AHEAD AND BE CONTENT WITH A SMALL WAGE AT FIRST IF THE PROSPECTS ARE GOOD.'[22] In the 1940s, the Ministry of Labour under Bevin's leadership became more receptive to trade unionists' argument that juveniles' job choices were greatly restricted by the needs of the working class family economy and employers' demand for cheap labour. However, continued concern that juveniles lacked discernment fuelled support for their inclusion in Essential Work Orders within reserved industries, because 'they give a measure of stability at a time when high wages lured

[18] Manchester Juvenile Employment Bureaux, *Annual Report for the Year 1934–35* (Manchester: Manchester Juvenile Employment Bureaux, 1935), 6.

[19] Nottingham Local Studies Library (NLSL), Making Ends Meet collection, A14/a/2, interview with Eileen.

[20] M-OA, TC 51/2/C, 'Attitudes to Jobs—Young Women and Girls'.

[21] Wilkins, *Adolescent*, 55.

[22] Manchester Juvenile Employment Bureaux, *Advice to Boys and Girls about to Leave School* (Manchester: Manchester Juvenile Employment Bureaux, *c.*1933), 1.

youngsters into unsteady or unsuitable employment'.[23] Yet it remained extremely important for many young wage-earners to obtain the highest possible wages. As Jephcott noted in the mid-1940s, 'poverty, hardship and insecurity' made wage-earning 'a deadly serious matter' for young working class women.[24]

Young women's bargaining potential grew as labour demand increased from the mid-1930s. Mass-Observation noted disapprovingly that 'casualness, sometimes combined with some defiance or truculence' characterized the attitudes of young women seeking work in London in 1940. One 18-year-old London office worker who wanted to enter munitions or government work told a Mass-Observer, 'I want to better my money. It's not much, what I get. They think they can pay you what they like when you're young. I can do the work as well as an older girl, why shouldn't I get the money?'[25] Similarly Mrs Howard, who grew up in Exeter and became a shop assistant at Woolworths after leaving school, entered war work at the age of 16 'because I wanted to earn more money, so I went to [a factory] that was making er, er parachutes at the time, er, as a machinist.'[26]

Considerations other than wages increased in importance as labour demand, and young women's earnings, rose. This was summed up by one 20-year-old former domestic servant questioned in London in 1940: 'I'm trying the factory, if I don't like it I'll walk out. I don't put up with no nonsense!'[27] Similarly, Joan Geary, who grew up in Manchester, began work in 1941 in a warehouse, quickly followed by factory work, but at 15 'I got fed up and decided I'd see if I could get a job in a hat shop, so I went round all the hat shops in the area and I picked the one that was the best.'[28] In 1950, only 2 per cent of Wilkins's female sample gave wages as a reason for taking their first job; many were concerned with finding interesting work.[29] By their late teens and early twenties, though, young women's priorities had changed. Many had exhausted the avenues of employment open to them, and faced limited subsequent wage increases and few promotion prospects. Consequently, as Jephcott found, many chose to remain in the same job if it offered wages that enabled them to save for marriage, which

23 TNA, LAB 12/215, London Regional Advisory Council for Juvenile Employment, ms: 'Survey for 1943 and 1944', 1944, 30.

24 Jephcott, *Rising Twenty*, 125.

25 M-OA, TC 51/2/C, 'Attitudes to Jobs—Young Women and Girls'. See also Reading Museum Archive (RMA), tape 1997. 127.36, interview with E. V. Ellingham.

26 Imperial War Museum Sound Archive (IWM), tape 14993, interview with Mrs Howard.

27 M-OA: TC 51/2/C, 'Attitudes to Jobs—Young Women and Girls'.

28 LRO, NWSA, 2002.0722, interview with Joan Geary.

29 Wilkins, *Adolescent*, 37.

many knew, or hoped, would take them out of the workforce within a few years.[30]

The 'alarmingly influential'[31] role of young women's friendship networks in shaping their employment choices was of great concern to social investigators, politicians, and educationalists.[32] The declining importance of the family in young women's job choices as they got older reflected the transition from schoolchild to adult. A survey of 1,031 women in 1941, for example, found that 30 per cent of those aged between 17 and 20 were reluctant to enter the Forces because of parental objections.[33] Women who became industrial war workers often attributed this to parental insistence that they stay at home; Kitty Burn recalled that when she reached 18 in 1942, 'I was given the choice in the Women's Army, the Air Force, Land Army or munitions works, but I really had no choice because my father told me I had to go to the munitions factory so that I would be home every night and not away from home.'[34] However, only 13 per cent of those questioned who were aged between 20 and 25 gave any weight to parental opinion in their decision about whether to enter the Forces.[35] The social independence that Davies and Langhamer have noted was granted to young adult wage-earners reflected the value of these relatively affluent wage-earners to the household,[36] which manifested itself in a weakening of parental authority—although this certainly did not disappear completely.

The importance of friends was twofold. Their role testified to the value young women gave to sociability in monotonous jobs. Betty Ferry was one of many young women to leave one job, in her case in the 1920s, in order to work with friends employed at a different factory.[37] Similarly,

[30] Jephcott, *Rising Twenty*, 136; R. McKibbin, *Classes and Cultures in England, 1918–1951* (Oxford: Oxford University Press, 1998), 134–5.

[31] Jephcott, *Rising Twenty*, 120.

[32] A. D. K. Owen et al., *A Survey of Juvenile Employment and Welfare in Sheffield* (Sheffield: Sheffield Social Survey Committee, 1933) 23; J. and S. Jewkes, *The Juvenile Labour Market* (London: Gollancz, 1938), 34–5; B. A. Fletcher et al., *The Welfare of Youth: A City Survey* (Bristol: University of Bristol, 1945), 15.

[33] Mass-Observation, *ATS: An Investigation of the Attitudes of Women, the General Public, and ATS Personnel to the Auxiliary Territorial Service*, Social Survey, New Series, Reports, 5, 1941, 6.

[34] IWM, 19686, interview with Anon. See also IWM, 19696, interview with Anon.

[35] Mass-Observation, *ATS*, 6.

[36] A. Davies, *Leisure, Gender and Poverty: Working-Class Culture in Salford and Manchester, 1990–1939* (Buckingham: Open University Press, 1992), 85–6; C. Langhamer, *Women's Leisure in England, 1920–60* (Manchester: Manchester University Press, 2000), 102–3.

[37] B. Ferry, 'Boot and Shoe Maker', in R. Gray (ed.), *Working Lives*, 1 (London: Centreprise, 1976), 109.

in London during the early 1950s, May Hobbs and her friend Jean always sought new factory jobs together, changing about every fifteen or eighteen months.[38] The lack of opportunity for promotion meant that, as Jephcott noted, even when a young woman was proud of technical skills acquired at work, as a minority of her sample were, 'a girl will change her type of work for such an apparently ephemeral reason as to keep a friend company.'[39]

Friends were also an increasingly important source of information about job opportunities, since employment expansion meant that young women were often better informed about potential jobs than their parents. Eileen, who originally followed her mother into the clothing trade, changed jobs after being informed of a clerical vacancy by friends.[40] The need to be 'spoken for' by a relative in order to obtain jobs with popular firms declined with full employment in the 1940s, making friends even more important. Twenty-two per cent of Wilkins's sample of young women found their first job through friends, and many more found second or subsequent posts this way.[41] Midge Harris, who left a hotel apprenticeship because she disliked it in 1947, began work at Huntley and Palmer's factory after bumping into an old schoolfriend who worked there and encouraged her to ' "come and work with me!" '[42] Similarly, May Hobbs found one job while roaming Hoxton with her friend Jean 'not, in fact, looking too hard—when we bumped into another mate of ours . . . Well, Gladys said, why didn't we go along to the firm where she worked? . . . So along we went and they took us on to start work on the next Monday.'[43] Young women's increasing reliance on friends marked a slight diminishing in parental control over this aspect of their lives, prompted by changes in young women's employment choices and earning potential. Mediation between labour demand and youthful aspirations was an increasingly important role of young women's social networks.

As well as accelerating some longer term developments in young women's mobility patterns, the increase in demand for young women workers during the Second World War wrought some short-term, but significant, changes to their employment pathways. Occupational mobility was central to this. Studies by Mass-Observation concur with Jephcott that girls' voluntary occupational mobility rose as the conscription of

38 M. Hobbs, *Born to Struggle* (London: Quartet Books, 1973), 37–45.

39 Jephcott, *Rising Twenty*, 120.

40 NLSL, Making Ends Meet, A14/a/2, Eileen.

41 Wilkins, *Adolescent*, 31.

42 RMA, 1997.127.5b, interview with Midge Harris.

43 Hobbs, *Struggle*, 35.

young adults increased demand for juvenile labour in non-essential jobs.[44] The increase in involuntary mobility was, however, far more significant. The Blitz blew away the jobs of many women like Florence Rosenblatt, who worked as a shop assistant at Liverpool's Lewis's store until it was destroyed by bombs in 1941, when 'I stood outside, with hundreds of girls that worked there, and we just cried.'[45] However, most important in increasing involuntary mobility among young adult women was their conscription from 1941. The most significant effect of this was the collapse of domestic service as a major employer. For many servants, the war provided a means of escape from an occupation that, because of the deference demanded by employers, and the relative isolation of many servants from their peers, was still difficult to leave. Among my sample, the war was the most common reason given for leaving domestic service. Mass-Observation noted a large number of former servants among those war factory workers it studied. The story of 24-year-old Molly, who had previously worked at an isolated country house, was typical:

> Mrs B. [her former employer] was very angry, but she had to let me go. . . . So I wrote to her the other day, and I told her that for ruining my eyes, I do all my work here without looking at it. It was cleaning your silver, I said, ruined my eyes. . . . I told her I'm ever so happy, and my board is tiny, and . . . I'm putting away as much as I got altogether with her.[46]

By 1942 the Ministry of Labour was noting, with some consternation, that while servants' employers had been given the power to make special representations to keep their maid—as Molly's employer had done—many young women 'left of their own accord to take up war work'.[47] The continued expansion of industrial, retail, and clerical job opportunities through the 1940s confirmed this as a permanent shift in employment patterns. Jephcott noted in the mid-1940s that domestic service had ceased to be a large employer of young women in the northern communities she studied, because of the proliferation of retail and factory jobs.[48] General employment expansion, war work, and particularly conscription, thus dealt the final blow to the job that had occupied many thousands of working class girls for decades.

Young women who grew up in wartime shared many of the priorities that guided their predecessors' peacetime choices, but new considerations

[44] Jephcott, *Rising Twenty*, 69–74; M-OA: FR 1083, 'ATS Campaign', February 1942.

[45] LRO, NWSA, 2002.0531a, interview with Florence Rosenblatt.

[46] Mass-Observation, *War Factory* (London: Gollancz, 1942), 38.

[47] *Ministry of Labour Gazette* (March 1942), 98.

[48] Jephcott, *Rising Twenty*, 129.

also emerged. Although Summerfield has characterized women war workers as 'heroics' or 'stoics' according to their recollections of employment choices and experiences, the evidence presented here suggests that this is too crude a distinction to have much value—a number of Summerfield's own sample, in fact, move between the two.[49] Contextualizing women's wartime choices in a longer trajectory than the years between 1939 and 1945 highlights a complex interaction of long-standing priorities with wartime circumstances. A desire for interesting and sociable work was by 1941 combined with a widespread wish to help the war effort. In that year 17-year-old Evelyn Haythorne decided that

> I now wanted something different in the way of work, something for the war effort, but I couldn't go into the services because I was not eighteen nor was I old enough for munitions work. That Monday morning I was utterly fed up and said as much to my workmates. 'We can't do anything to help the war,' I complained, 'only sell flaming flags.'

She eventually left to take up industrial work, which allowed her to do her bit but also enabled her to continue living with her mother; she had no desire to leave home.[50] Lilian Airey, a skilled embroidery designer at a textile manufacturing firm, felt frustrated with her work, although it was a reserved occupation that involved making uniforms:

> there were people on munitions earnings £10.00 a week and we were earning £2.00. . . . we used to sort of think ooh, we'd sooner go on munitions than do this silly job you know, this isn't war work, I mean we wanted to be out driving ambulances and being with the RAF and all the lads you know [laughs].[51]

As Mass-Observation noted, many women viewed 'proper' war work as that which directly attacked the enemy. A survey of 1,031 women in 1941 found least opposition to conscription among young, manual workers, with 84 per cent of 17 to 20 year olds being willing to undertake war work. Patriotic reasons accounted for a significant proportion of female recruitment to the Forces.[52]

However, the accounts of women like Haythorne and Airey also point to a range of other considerations that tempered their 'heroic' discourse. A survey of attitudes to the Auxiliary Territorial Service (ATS) recorded

[49] Summerfield, *Reconstructing*, 77–114.

[50] E. Haythorne, *On Earth to Make the Numbers Up* (Castleford: Yorkshire Art Circus, 1991), 106 and 116.

[51] TLSL, Manchester Studies Collection, 1075, interview with Lilian Airey.

[52] M-OA, FR 1083, 'ATS', 15 and 30.

that many women, like these two, were reluctant to join the Forces, largely because of the infringements on their liberty this imposed.[53] Mass-Observation found that young women who took up full-time war jobs were influenced by their previous employment experiences, and 'do so either to get away from the dull routine of office or factory work'.[54] Many resented compulsion, particularly in areas with little tradition of women's industrial work. A large number of women who worked at Newton Aycliffe Royal Ordnance Factory, situated in County Durham, where few women had previously undertaken industrial work, were negative about their experiences. Kitty Burn's most positive comment in retrospect was that 'although I didn't realise it at the time I realise now it was something that had to be done, and someone had to do it.'[55] Young working class women, who had to work for economic reasons, juggled a desire to help the war effort with a number of practical considerations. Consequently, although they were central to wartime production, they were frequently treated as a social and moral problem by social investigators and policy makers when they refused to conform to a stereotype of self-sacrifice.

Occupational mobility was, then, a much overlooked characteristic of most women's working lives. Whereas government literature implied the existence of a minority of serial, unemployable job-changers, who lacked discernment and commitment, social surveys suggest that most young women held less than four jobs prior to marriage between the 1920s and the 1940s. A survey of Bristol's young people carried out in 1942 found that the average number of jobs ranged between 2 and 3 among girls and between 2 and 4 among boys in 1944.[56] As Thomas found in his study of the late 1940s, occupational mobility was experienced by the majority of workers, who changed jobs just once or twice during their working lives, moves that were particularly likely to happen in the first decade of their working lives.[57] The existence of occupational mobility testified, then, to the fact that most workers did not have a 'job for life'; many explored a number of employment options in their youth either involuntarily or, increasingly, voluntarily.

[53] Mass-Observation, *ATS*, 8.

[54] MO-A, FR 533, 'Women and the War Effort', December 1940, 5.

[55] IWM, 19686, interview with Anon.

[56] Fletcher et al., *Welfare of Youth*,14.

[57] G. Thomas, *Women in Industry*, Social Survey, New Series, Reports, 104 (1949), 10.

Overall, boys and girls experienced similar levels of occupational mobility but this differed according to local demand. In Birmingham in the early 1950s, girls were likely to experience greater mobility, probably because of the large number of apprenticeships open to boys in the motor industry.[58] Wilkins's study, by contrast, suggested that boys were likely to move jobs more frequently than girls, because of their established employment pathway of casual or temporary work until taking up an apprenticeship, or, in the 1940s, entering National Service. It took them a greater number of job changes to find a job with which they were satisfied,[59] unsurprising given that most expected to work until old age, unlike most young women. Despite these important differences, young women and young men clearly shared some important characteristics in their early employment, being likely to change jobs more than once as juveniles, before becoming more settled in their later teens, as young men sought to establish themselves in a trade, while young women made the best of limited employment prospects, and both began to save for marriage.

The social significance of occupational mobility was also restricted. Just as chapter 3 demonstrated the pervasive influence of family background on a young woman's choice of first job, so the subsequent amount of movement between socio-economic classes, or grades within the working class, was very limited. The employment pathways of my own sample suggest that domestic servants were most likely to enter other forms of service employment, or factory labour, than clerical or the more lucrative branches of retail work.[60] Contemporary investigations reached the same conclusion. A Mass-Observation survey of 2,609 woman war workers found that an increasing number of women had moved from office to factory work—a cause of dissatisfaction to many former clerks—but the converse was not true.[61] That the greatest expansion of young women's work occurred in unskilled and semiskilled jobs helps to explain why in the late 1940s Thomas found that most mobility occurred between occupations on the same level, a pattern supported by Wilkins's study.[62] Young women's voluntary mobility between jobs did not, then, equate with significant social mobility.

[58] B. H. Reed et al., *Eighty Thousand Adolescents* (London: Allen and Unwin, 1950), 34–5.

[59] Wilkins, *Adolescent*, 60.

[60] See Appendix.

[61] M-OA, FR 2117, 'Women at Work: The Attitudes of Working Women towards Postwar Employment and Some related Problems' (June 1944), 11.

[62] Wilkins, *Adolescent*, 10.

Geographic Mobility

The increasing independence that young women had over job choices as they grew older was one means by which familial control over them was weakened. Another was leaving home. Very few young working class women could afford to leave home voluntarily during these years, since, as chapter 1 discussed, their low wages were grounded in the assumption that they were dependants within the parental home. Nevertheless, young women's migration, primarily from rural to urban areas, but also from depressed to more prosperous towns, increased, particularly in the 1930s and 1940s. They constituted a significant, though greatly overlooked, proportion of the migrant workforce.

Young, female servants had long constituted a major proportion of migrants from rural areas to England's towns,[63] but this trend increased from 1911, largely because of increasing urban employment opportunities. Young women migrated at an earlier age than men, and the gender differential in outward migration from rural districts increased between 1918 and 1951. As Saville's data highlight, the female/male ratio in rural areas began to diverge from the national norm from the age of 15. In 1911 the ratio of females to every hundred males for 15 to 20 year olds in England and Wales stood at 102, but at 86 in rural districts. By 1951 the ratio was recorded as 105 for England and Wales, but 71 for rural areas.[64]

As chapters 2 and 3 made clear, most young servants had no choice over their migration; their families required them to go. However, the attractions of urban life were heightened by employment expansion and the growth of commercialized leisure during our period. By the mid-1930s, as Scott points out, migrating to work in urban households provided young women from rural or depressed areas with a transitional occupation while they searched for more lucrative employment in shop or café.[65] In Liverpool, for example, servants increasingly transferred to retail employment.[66] Servants were thus increasingly likely to settle permanently in large urban conurbations rather than return to their

[63] B. Hill, 'Rural-Urban Migration of Women and their Employment in Towns', *Rural History*, 5 (1994), 186.

[64] J. Saville, *Rural Depopulation in England and Wales, 1851–1951* (London: Routledge, 1957), 116.

[65] P. Scott, 'The State, Internal Migration, and the Growth of New Industrial Communities in Interwar Britain', *English Historical Review*, 115 (2000), 345.

[66] D. Caradog Jones, *The Social Survey of Merseyside*, 2 (Liverpool: Liverpool University Press), 302.

home communities to marry; this was Winifred Foley's experience in the 1930s.[67] Wartime conscription and increasing urban demand for young women's labour accelerated this trend and enabled increasing numbers of rural young women to bypass domestic service and move directly into factory or shop work. Young women's employment patterns thus fundamentally changed the composition of rural communities in the first half of the twentieth century.[68]

The long-standing pattern of rural to urban migration through domestic service helped to shape interwar unemployment policy. Successive governments attempted to solve a mismatch between the growing demand for labour in the midlands and south-east of England, and the large proportion of unemployed workers in northern regions, by encouraging the latter's migration to more prosperous areas. Young women were central to this strategy. Although many discussions of labour transference begin with the introduction of a government-sponsored labour transference scheme in 1928, this was in fact preceded and influenced by the work of the Central Committee of Women's Training and Employment (CCWTE), which was formed in 1915 with financial assistance from the Ministry of Labour. Its aim was to provide professional training for women 'whose earning capacities and opportunities were injured by conditions arising from the War'. By December 1924 the CCWTE had provided 4,506 women, mostly young and single, with a range of vocational training and clerical courses,[69] but the organization increasingly concentrated on providing domestic service training, following the granting of additional funding for this purpose by the Ministry of Labour in 1920. Over 10,000 women and girls were trained to be housewives or domestic servants in 1921–2;[70] similar proportions continued to be trained and placed in domestic service until the mid-1930s.

This scheme has often been viewed by historians as an attempt to encourage women to return to 'home and duty' following the First World War.[71] However, a longer view of interwar labour transference suggests that concern with women's unemployment did not only reflect anxiety over the effect of war on long-established gender roles.

67 Foley, *Child*, 245–7.

68 I have discussed changes in young women's migration from rural to urban areas in more depth in S. Todd, 'Young Women, Work and Family in Interwar Rural England', *Agricultural History Review*, 52/1 (2004).

69 Report of the Ministry of Labour for the years 1923–24, PP 1924–1925, xiv, Cmd 2481, 224–6.

70 Ministry of Labour, *Second Interim Report of the CCWTE*, 8.

71 D. Beddoe, *Back to Home and Duty: Women between the Wars* (London: Pandora, 1989).

Young, single workers remained the primary focus of the geographic transference scheme established by the Ministry of Labour in 1928, reflecting high demand for young, cheap workers. In most of the firms that used these migrant workers, they undercut existing wage rates, and were sometimes provided with weekly pocket money by the Ministry of Labour to facilitate further wage cuts.[72] As Table 6 shows, juveniles and women constituted over 54 per cent of transferees overall. Young women were particularly important, with more girls being transferred than boys because they could be used as domestic servants. Table 7 highlights that it was not until 1936 that demand for young women was sufficiently high in light manufacturing that more were transferred to industrial work than into residential service, demonstrating slow and uneven economic growth; even in 1936, 40 per cent of transferred women were placed in domestic service.[73] Transference exacerbated an existing migration trend from north to south, and from rural and semi-rural areas to urban conurbations.[74]

Parental opposition, homesickness, and the insecurity of the employment provided[75] proved strong obstacles to the development of the transference scheme, as the high rate of return—the Ministry of Labour estimated in 1937 that 35 per cent of juveniles and 27 per cent of adults returned home[76]—demonstrated. Parental concern about their daughters' welfare and the removal of their potential to make an economic contribution to the family economy was exacerbated by the introduction of the household means test in 1931, since a transferee's earnings could detrimentally affect the benefit entitlement of her parents' household.[77] One Liverpool woman explained her objection to the transference scheme thus:

> My girl is 22. She used to earn 22s and give me 16s. Now she is on the dole and gets 15s and I get 13s out of it. I couldn't let her go and have nothing, because if she goes I would have to give up my home here and where would I be? She does not eat 13s worth of food.[78]

[72] W. Hannington, *The Problem of the Distressed Areas* (London: Gollancz, 1937), 122, 126–7.

[73] Report of the Ministry of Labour for the year 1928: PP 1928–29, vii, Cmd 3333—Report of the Ministry of Labour for the Year 1938: PP 1938–39, xii, Cmd 6016; Ministry of Labour, *Annual Reports on Juvenile Employment*, 1933–1935 (London, 1934–6); A. D. K. Owen, 'The Social Consequences of Industrial Transference', *Sociological Review*, 29/4 (1937), 331–4.

[74] See also South Shields Advisory Committee for Juvenile Employment, *Annual Report for the Year 1929* (London: HMSO, 1930), 9.

[75] Modern Records Centre, University of Warwick (MRC), TUC Archive, MSS 292/132.6/5, unpublished MS: 'The Juvenile Transference Scheme', c. 1937.

[76] Scott, 'Migration', 339.

[77] Hannington, *Distressed Areas*, 118.

[78] Quoted in Pilgrim Trust, *Men without Work*, 262.

TABLE 6. Workers Transferred by the Ministry of Labour by Age and Gender, 1928–38

Year	Girls	Boys	Women	Men	Total individuals	Households	% Female	% Juvenile
1928	283	1,840	642	3,600	6,365	0	15	33
1929	1,994	2,622	2,239	36,843	43,698	2,850	10	10
1930	1,708	1,313	1,752	28,258	33,031	2,100	10	9
1931	1,986	868	2,631	17,889	23,374	1,680	20	12
1932	2,502	628	2,651	8,359	14,140	990	36	22
1933	3,055	1,117	4,038	5,333	13,443	605	53	31
1934	3,512	1,661	4,420	6,828	16,421	1,308	48	32
1935	4,648	4,880	6,350	13,379	29,753	3,718	37	32
1936	5,958	9,449	8,008	20,091	42,735	10,025	33	36
1937	6,450	7,675	6,416	17,585	38,126	7,673	34	37
1938	5,496	4,131	6,214	11,637	27,478	4,000	43	35
Total	37,592	36,184	45,361	169,802	288,564	34,949	29	26

Source: Ministry of Labour Gazette, various years; Ministry of Labour, *Annual Reports on Juvenile Employment*, 1933–1935.

TABLE 7. Destinations of Girls Transferred by Ministry of Labour, 1928–38

Year	% Girls placed in domestic service	% Girls placed in industrial work
1928	100	0
1929	100	0
1930	95	5
1931	99	1
1932	93	7
1933	86	14
1934	86	14
1935	75	25
1936	40	60
1937	24	76
1938	24	76
Total	60	40

Source: Ministry of Labour Gazette, various years; Report of the Ministry of Labour for the year 1928, vii (PP 1928–29), Cmd. 3333—Report of the Ministry of Labour for the Year 1938, xii (PP 1938–39), Cmd. 6016; Ministry of Labour, *Annual Reports on Juvenile Employment*, 1933–1935; A. D. K. Owen, 'The Social Consequences of Industrial Transference', *Sociological Review*, 29/4 (1937), 331–4.

Correspondence between the Ministry of Labour and the Unemployment Assistance Board indicates that family allowances were indeed often reduced if a son or daughter was transferred.[79] Government surveys and investigations by the Trades Union Congress (TUC) suggest that girls were more likely to leave employment than boys, a sign perhaps that parents were more receptive to daughters' grievances, given the value of their domestic help at home.[80] The reports of local Juvenile Employment Advisory Committees indicate that domestic servants, who experienced great isolation, were the most likely to return home.[81] The most important reason for return, however, was that dynamic sectors did not create jobs as fast as the declining sectors lost them. Consequently, as McKibbin

[79] TNA, LAB 19/93/1295/1935, Letter from Ministry of Labour Official to G. S. Owen at the Unemployment Assistance Board, March 1936.

[80] MRC, 292/132.6/5, 'Juvenile Transference Scheme'.

[81] Bristol Advisory Committee for Juvenile Employment, *Report for the Year 1930* (London: HMSO, 1931), 24; Oxford Advisory Committee for Juvenile Employment, *Report for the Year 1929* (London, 1930), 10.

points out, transference did not provide young workers with employment security.[82] A TUC investigation of the juvenile transference scheme found that many were in danger of being sacked once they qualified for wage increases in their late teens.[83] The transference scheme, then, was based solely on meeting the requirements of employers in the expanding sectors for young, cheap labour and, as such, upheld the very conditions that made adult employment so insecure.

The labour transference scheme ended when war began, but the scheme provided the basis for directing wartime labour. From April 1942, all single women were considered available for labour transfer, with women from Scotland, Wales, and northern and north-eastern England being transferred to the Midlands, where munitions industries and aircraft manufacturers were concentrated. Continuity was thus established with older patterns of migration. The extent of transference should not be exaggerated. The numbers of women involved are not available, but in the West Midlands engineering industry, in which the number of women workers increased by 150 per cent between 1939 and September 1942, just 10 per cent of new women workers had been transferred from other regions.[84] The swift and sometimes chaotic establishment of labour transference in the first two years of the war led to 'hardship, irritation, and . . . muddle'.[85] However, the return home of approximately one-third of male, transferred workers in the first year of the war led to some important concessions, including travelling grants, the organization of billets, and the opening of 155 workers' hostels.[86] These measures, together with wartime wage rises, meant that war work led a large proportion of young, working class women to live independently away from the parental home for the first time.

Young women's experiences of wartime transference were subject to greater documentation than those of interwar migrants, and are thus important for any reconstruction of migrants' perspectives and experiences. Migration provided a minority of young women with the opportunity to leave an unhappy home life; this was true of 2 per cent of 611 ATS members questioned in 1941 about why they had joined up.[87] However,

[82] McKibbin, *Classes and Cultures*, 126.

[83] MRC, 292/132.6/5, 'Juvenile Transference Scheme', 127.

[84] Scottish Trade Union Delegation to the Midlands, *Transfer of Scottish Girls. Report to Scottish Trades Union Congress General Council and the Organisation of Women Committee* (Glasgow: Scottish TUC, 1943), 8.

[85] Ibid., 7.

[86] H. M. D. Parker, *Manpower: A Study of Wartime Policy and Administration* (London: HMSO, 1957), 396 and 402; Scottish Trade Union Delegation, *Scottish Girls*, 6 and 20.

[87] Mass-Observation, *ATS*, 30.

leaving the family home was the primary reason for its more general unpopularity, this being the main objection expressed to war work by 27 per cent of the teenage girls who were among the 1,031 women questioned by the same study about their reluctance to join the ATS.[88] Many of the reasons that had provoked opposition to labour transference during the 1930s remained current: parents and daughters expressed concern over transferred workers' welfare and the limited economic contribution that they were able to make to the family home. Florence Rosenblatt was one of many women whose mothers would not let her take work away from home because she felt her daughter was, at 18, too young to live independently.[89] However, although Summerfield has attributed the reluctance of her 'stoical' sample to leave home to the obedience demanded of daughters,[90] the evidence presented here indicates that young women were also influenced by social considerations. Workers interviewed by Mass-Observation expressed great reluctance to leave home, some even fear.[91] Many women did not wish to leave family and friends, particularly when the future seemed so uncertain.

Migrant workers' experiences emphasize the continuing importance of regional identities. For many women, making friends from different social and geographical backgrounds was one of the most memorable aspects of the war. Mrs Andrews, a worker in the Army Pay Corps, believed that 'your horizons were broadened in the fact that you met people from all parts of the country'.[92] Some women found this a less positive experience. An investigation into the transference of young Scottish women to factories in the English Midlands found that one of the greatest causes of unhappiness was the isolation felt by those women who had no workmates from their home community.[93] The contrast between the urban areas from which war workers were often drawn and the rural districts in which many found themselves was a shock to many. Peggy Few, who joined the Women's Land Army to escape a stressful factory job in 1940, lodged with a country family just twenty miles from her home town of Reading, but vividly recalled differences from her urban home, such as the use of oil lamps and a well, and the cooking of lambs tail pies, which she was too squeamish to eat.[94] The Scottish

[88] Mass-Observation, *ATS*, 6.

[89] LRO, NWSA, 2002.0531a, Florence Rosenblatt.

[90] Summerfield, *Reconstructing*, 45–7, 80.

[91] Mass-Observation, *War Factory*, 80–1; M-OA, FR 433, 'The Human Factors in Employment Exchanges' (September 1940), 11; M-OA, TC 51/2/C, 'Attitudes to Jobs—Girls and Young Women', 4.

[92] TLSL, Tameside tapes, 60, interview with Mrs Andrews.

[93] Scottish Trade Union Delegation to the Midlands, *Scottish Girls*, 15.

[94] RMA, tape 1997.127.4, interview with Peggy Few.

TUC found that many young Scottish women employed in factories in semi-rural areas preferred billets to workers' hostels, because, although lacking amenities and entailing a long journey to work each day, the billets were in urban districts.[95] As this suggests, boredom could be an important feature of war work for women who were separated from family and social life. Many of them were, by the 1940s, used to a degree of commercial leisure consumption that was often impossible in rural districts.

Social background was also important in shaping responses to transference. Mass-Observation found that those women from middle class or skilled working class backgrounds often had poorer opinions of the billets or war workers' hostels in which they were housed.[96] Mass-Observers noted, as did the Scottish TUC, that those workers from unskilled backgrounds, who had lower expectations of food and welfare, were most contented.[97] Transference thus highlighted that important differences shaped by distinct regional cultures and even more importantly by income differentials continued to fracture working class lifestyles.

Employment, Poverty, and Aspiration

As well as being important in achieving familial aspirations, a young woman's wage-earning was also central to her own. Young women's own aspirations and identities were shaped by working class culture, transmitted through familial and wider social relations, and were closely bound up with their wage-earning. It is through the prism of working class culture that their employment aspirations and patterns are briefly scrutinized here. The impressionistic evidence cited cannot provide exhaustive explanations for occupational and social mobility, but the examples given do nonetheless provide insights into the 'subjective experience of mobility',[98] significant since, as Jerry White notes, it cannot be assumed that people's social and occupational aspirations conform to the Registrar General's classification system.[99]

[95] Scottish Trade Union Delegation to the Midlands, *Scottish Girls*, 15.

[96] Mass-Observation, *War Factory*, 14.

[97] Ibid., 97; Scottish Trade Union Delegation to the Midlands, *Scottish Girls*, 14.

[98] G. Payne and P. Abbott, 'Origins and Destinations', in ead. (eds.), *The Social Mobility of Women: Beyond Male Mobility Models* (London: Falmer, 1990), 11.

[99] J. White, *The Worst Street in North London: Campbell Bunk, Islington, between the Wars* (London: Routledge, 1986), 4, 188.

Mothers were often more influential than fathers in determining a daughter's occupational aspirations and experiences, just as they frequently shaped attitudes to schooling. The socially accepted hierarchy of women's work was in many areas based 'not on skill, but niceness',[100] and this was transmitted primarily by mothers, who made their daughters aware from an early age that social distinctions were denoted by cleanliness, appearance, and behaviour.[101] Dolly recognized that shopkeepers' daughters were treated favourably at school and 'seemed to be at the forefront of things' because 'they were just that little bit better dressed, and cleaner'.[102] Cleanliness implied that a family's poverty was not of their own making and many girls learnt from mothers to draw upon this as a source of self-esteem. Edna compared herself to 'the ragamuffins. . . . no-one could have been poorer than me but we was spotless'.[103] By the time they began work, many girls had already imbibed such values, and these were important in shaping limited job choices. A daughter's employment could reflect on her upbringing and affect the social status as well as the income of her household.[104] In this sense, the social backgrounds of workmates could be important. As McKibbin notes, friendship and workplace networks could reflect on one's own social status.[105] One 20-year-old Londoner from a skilled working class background told Mass-Observation that she wished to become a receptionist 'in a real good hotel', meaning one that was large and prospering, and served a wealthy clientele.[106]

As well as cleanliness, security was also of importance, particularly prior to the Second World War. The Ministry of Labour's investigation into vocational training highlighted that by the mid-1920s long-term security was often valued more than skill or wages,[107] because of unemployment. As Whitworth has suggested, a regular income in a safe job helped to guarantee the security of a household and enabled access to

[100] J. Castle, 'Factory Work for Women', in B. Lancaster and T. Mason, *Life and Labour in a Twentieth Century City: The Experience of Coventry* (Coventry: Cryfield Press, 1986), 149. See also McKibbin, *Classes and Cultures*, 135.

[101] R. Roberts, *The Classic Slum* (Harmondsworth: Penguin, 1971), 125–35; E. Ross, 'Survival Networks: Women's Neighbourhood Sharing in London before World War I', *History Workshop Journal*, 15 (1983), 14.

[102] Lifetimes, *Something in Common* (Manchester: Manchester Polytechnic), 27.

[103] NLSL, Making Ends Meet, A85/a/1, interview with Edna.

[104] Roberts, *Classic Slum*, 171; White, *Worst Street*, 191.

[105] McKibbin, *Classes and Cultures*, 135–7.

[106] MO-A: TC 51/2/C, 'Attitudes to Work—Young Women and Girls'.

[107] Ministry of Labour, *Report of an Enquiry into Apprenticeship*, 7 (London: HMSO, 1928), 166.

luxury and leisure consumption by the mid-1930s, and was an important signifier of respectability.[108] This began to change in the 1940s. As a consequence of post-war full employment, Young and Wilmottt found that Council work was diminishing in popularity because 'Security does not now matter enough to offset the low pay.'[109] Wages were thus clearly extremely important—Bobbie Gardiner was typical in her assessment that for Coventry girls, 'To work at Courtaulds was the top, you know, because they was the highest paying of all factories'[110]—but the wage packet was not the only factor that denoted a job's status.

Respectability, although an important consideration, varied in definition and value. During the interwar years respectability, the meaning of which varied according to local employment opportunities and a family's social status, was closely allied with escaping poverty, rather than with attaining middle class status—an important difference. Clerical work's good reputation partially rested on its social status—the first job of Margaret Forster's mother, as a clerk in Carlisle Public Health Department in 1917, 'was prestigious, people were in awe when told where Lily worked and for whom'[111]—but office work was also favoured because of the safety and security it offered. Other occupational distinctions were more ambiguous. Employment traditions were important. Marion Kent's mother sent her into domestic service because she considered local factories 'rough',[112] a typical rationale for such a choice.[113] In contrast, as Elizabeth Roberts has shown, mothers in areas offering relatively clean light manufacturing work, or non-manual employment, might favour this over residential service because it offered regular, relatively lucrative wages, enabled daughters to stay in the parental home, and did not have the connotations of social inferiority that many urban women associated with service, a feeling that Roberts's sample and my own suggest grew stronger after the First World War.[114]

[108] L. Whitworth, 'Men, Women, Shops and "Little Shiny Homes": The Consuming of Coventry, 1930–1939', Ph.D thesis (Warwick, 1997), 126–31.

[109] Young and Willmott, *Family and Kinship in East London* (Harmondsworth: Penguin, 1957), 96.

[110] MRC, Coventry Women's Work Collection, MSS 266/6/3, interview with Bobbie Gardiner. See also MRC, Coventry Women's Work Collection, MSS 266/6/5, interview with Elsie Lee; MSS 266/3/1/2, interview with Winifred Cotterill.

[111] M. Forster, *Hidden Lives* (Harmondsworth: Penguin, 1995), 61.

[112] LRO, NWSA, 1999.0060, interview with Marion Kent.

[113] TLSL, Manchester Studies, 36, interview with Edith Edwards; R. Roberts, *A Woman's Place: An Oral History of Working Class Women 1890–1940* (Oxford: Blackwell, 1984), 54.

[114] Roberts, *Woman's Place*, 62.

These changes meant that by the interwar years, domestic servants, particularly those from urban areas, had an ambiguous sense of their own status. Servants were more likely than other workers to associate respectability with middle class values, around which they structured their social and domestic aspirations. Edith Edwards grew up in Macclesfield and entered domestic service at the age of 14 in 1929 because her family could not afford for her to train to be a nurse or a clerk; her mother considered factory work rough. Her own views on service demonstrate that respectability was to some degree malleable. Edith, like most of the servants in my sample, felt that 'there was always a stigma about' domestic service, and she herself felt that it was socially inferior to many other occupations. Nevertheless, like many women prior to the Second World War, Edith concurred with her mother's opinion that

> it was a sort of a domestic science training, and also you saw another side of life—you heard—you see living with educated people—you, you were taught, you sort of self-taught—and of course there was always a good library in all the houses. . . . I mean I can tell people that have been in very good service . . . by the way they do things, and if they talk about cooking, and dishes.[115]

Edith emphasized the close relationship that domestic service offered her with middle class society, stressing the advantages of this for her own education and adult domestic life. Giles has shown that servants commonly cited these as benefits of the job.[116] These women often had an ambivalent relationship to respectability that rested in their familiarity with, and aspirations to imitate, middle class social mores, but also in their awareness that in middle class company, and in many working class communities, they were destined to be treated as socially inferior. Their expression of their own worth was centred on putting the skills and behaviour they learned as servants into practice as wives and mothers.

As alternative employment opportunities expanded, the sexual division of labour shaped notions of respectable work for women in different ways. By the 1940s, shop work was considered respectable in small northern towns where factory work had long been a male preserve, whereas the expansion of clean, light manufacturing work in the south-east heightened the attractions of such jobs for both daughters and their mothers.[117] Employers shaped their practices to the type of

[115] TLSL, Manchester Studies, 36, interview with Edith Edwards.

[116] J. Giles, *The Parlour and the Suburb: Domestic Identities, Class, Femininity and Modernity* (Oxford: Berg, 2004), 79–82.

[117] Jephcott, *Rising Twenty*, 128.

labour they wished to attract, as Castle's examination of Coventry's Courtaulds factory demonstrates. Courtaulds' appeal rested not solely on relatively high wages, but also on its strict division of the sexes and marriage bar, which enhanced its respectability. Elsie Lee, the daughter of a skilled car worker, explained that 'nice girls wouldn't go and work in a factory but Courtaulds was different, it was a woman's factory.'[118] Many women who grew up in Lancashire felt the same about the Tootals firm prior to the Second World War, which was, in Helen Drinkwater's words, 'concerned about the health and wellbeing of the girls' although, like Courtaulds, it enforced strict discipline and prohibited union membership.[119] This definition of respectability placed no value on contact with middle class society, instead being defined by high standards of hygiene, welfare, and morality. The social composition of the workforce was nonetheless important. The values upheld by Courtaulds, and the selection procedures operated by the firm, brought a high proportion of the daughters of skilled workers into the workforce, which in turn heightened the respectability of this type of factory work.

As Courtaulds' strategy suggests, a daughter's welfare—both physical and moral—was another important consideration for many women. Concern over this could in fact conflict with notions of respectability, which were just one of several factors that shaped employment choices. Janet, who grew up in a Nottinghamshire village in the 1920s, wanted to become a shop assistant in a city centre store. Such work was considered glamorous and ladylike, but was too far from home for her mother's liking: 'In fact when I was going to work in Nottingham she says, "I'm sure you're not, you're going to factory or else!" '[120] Mothers placed emphasis on their daughters' happiness when possible; Jephcott noted that by the 1940s many actively supported their daughters' desire to find any kind of alternative to domestic service because 'although (as in one case) the mother admits that it helped her to become [a] capable housewife . . . she had so little freedom and so few pleasures that she certainly would not like such a job for her own daughter.'[121] Such testimonies emphasize the youth of these wage-earners and the fact that decisions about employment involved a careful evaluation of the consequences of a job for a daughter's welfare and for her family's income, as well as for a household's social status, factors that were not always

118 Castle, 'Factory Work', 143–4.
119 LRO, NWSA, 1999.0283, interview with Helen Drinkwater.
120 NLSL, Making Ends Meet, A80/a/1, interview with Janet.
121 Jephcott, *Rising Twenty*, 43.

entirely compatible and that varied in importance according to local employment opportunity and household need.

A similar combination of factors shaped the social aspirations that mothers communicated to daughters, with marital aspirations being chief among them; mothers, Jephcott noted, 'have more definite aims about this than they have concerning [a daughter's] career'.[122] Maternal concern for a daughter's emotional and economic well-being in her adult life could be combined with the knowledge that an economically secure child might offer financial as well as emotional support to ageing parents. Working in an office heightened a young woman's opportunity to make middle class friends and marry into the middle class. Dolly Scannell's mother viewed her daughter's secure job in a council office as a 'wonderful opportunity' partly for this reason.[123] However, finding a middle class husband was not the only form a 'good match' could take. A household's standard of living depended on a woman's domestic management skills and a man's co-operation in contributing his earnings to the family economy.[124] In the 1920s many mothers in smaller or rural labour markets approved of domestic service because it curbed a daughter's liberty and thus protected her moral health, as well as teaching her domestic skills that might be attractive to a future spouse and would aid her financial well-being.[125] By the 1940s, however, more placed emphasis on finding a man who would be a good provider than on training in housewifery, a recognition that higher wages in non-manual and skilled industrial work could help to mitigate the domestic burden through the purchase of labour-saving appliances and perhaps a new house. One reason for the growing unpopularity of domestic service among young women was the isolation experienced by many workers and the lack of opportunity to meet men who were not poorly paid servants or delivery boys.[126] Jephcott recorded the aversion of many north country girls to courting miners, due to the dirty, risky, and insecure nature of their work, and—a factor that Jephcott noted with no emphasis, but which seems more important than she suggests—miners'

[122] Jephcott, *Rising Twenty*, 45.

[123] D. Scannell, *Mother Knew Best* (London: Macmillan, 1974), 163.

[124] Davies, *Leisure*, 48–54; Roberts, *Woman's Place*, 148–68.

[125] See for example LRO, NWSA, 1999.0060, interview with Marion Kent; Roberts, *Woman's Place*, 54.

[126] Butler, *Domestic Service*, repr. of 1916 edn. (London: Garland, 1980), 98; Ministry of Labour, *Report of the Committee Appointed to Enquire into the Present Conditions as to the Supply of Female Domestic Servants* (London: HMSO, 1923), 18–19; Young Women's Christian Association, *Household Employment* (London: YWCA, *c.*1933), 2.

lack of desire to 'get on' in life and 'make something more' of themselves. These considerations were taken very seriously by the young women's mothers;[127] they transmitted to their daughters not only the material disadvantages of being a miner's wife, but also the division between the desires of adult men rooted in a strong, parochial working class community and women who desired a different kind of life. A man's potential to better himself, his recognition that a different sort of life to that led by his father existed and might be his, was as important as his immediate material circumstances in structuring marital aspirations, then.

As this suggests, young women's relationship to employment, and to working class culture, differed from young men's. Whereas manual employment could reinforce working class masculinity, the relationship of femininity to the labour process was more problematic, raising the importance of social considerations. As White and Steedman have shown, women often engaged critically with working class family and community life, which held fewer consolations for them than for men.[128] Expanding employment opportunities meant that paid work became increasingly central to the realization of their aspiration to escape. Elsie's desire to improve her life was transformed into concrete aspiration by the expansion of clerical work:

> I'd rather have had a pen in my hand than a bloody machine on my knee. And this 'walking tall'. . . . I thought 'I'm going to hold my head up like anyone else, and nobody's better than me.' . . . If I'm dressed and I feel good, that's what I feel and I can hold my head up. . . . I did feel I wanted to be better.[129]

Elsie's words indicate that young women's aspirations were not focused upon having a career, although work was central to their fulfilment. Histories of youth have tended to divorce the worlds of work and commercial consumption, foregrounding the latter in analyses of identity formation. In reality, appearance, romance, and employment cannot easily be separated; putting her hair up and perhaps wearing long skirts or a uniform denoted a young woman's status as a worker.[130] Nellie Hilton, like an increasing number of mill girls in the 1920s, aspired to work in a textile mill 'a bit cleaner' than average, and where workers did not have to don

127 Jephcott, *Rising Twenty*, 78–9.

128 White, *Worst Street*, 188; C. Steedman, *Landscape for a Good Woman* (London: Virago, 1986), 6–8, 14–15, 106–9.

129 Lifetimes, *A Couple from Manchester* (Manchester: Manchester Polytechnic, 1975), 40.

130 Alexander, 'Becoming a Woman', 213–15.

the traditional clogs and shawl.[131] A survey of 1941 found that the uniform was the single most important reason given by those who wished to join the WAAF.[132] Evelyn Haythorne was attracted to joining the Land Army in wartime because a workmate suggested it offered independence and glamour: 'Have you seen their uniforms, they're ever so smart? My cousin's in them and she says it's a great life.'[133] Expanding, relatively well-paid employment opportunities, in themselves and in the opportunities for pocket money, fashionable clothes, and courtship they provided, were central to the development of a youthful, modern femininity that distinguished young women from the poverty of their mothers' lives.

Young women's aspirations were therefore ambiguous and sometimes nebulous, and cannot simply be characterized as the pursuit of respectability or middle class status. Alison Light has pointed to similarities in the material aspirations of middle class and working class women by the later 1930s, as labour-saving domestic appliances, wirelesses, and home ownership were promoted through women's magazines and literature and became increasingly attainable as wages rose.[134] However, as Sally Alexander notes, a young working class girl's 'imagined future was tempered by poverty'.[135] Daughters' aspirations were shaped by maternal hopes, but also by a critical evaluation of their mothers' lives and by a wish to escape from the poverty and domestic burden their mothers had experienced. However, they also articulated a realization of the limitations that social background placed upon them. Their social aspirations were defined more by a desire to avoid poverty, through the attainment of economic security, than by an aspiration to middle class status. Consequently, self-sufficiency, gained through secure employment, is a central theme of their narratives throughout the period. Elsie's desire to find secure work was partially inspired by her mother's struggle to make ends meet,[136] while Dolly, who was adamant that she would not enter a violent marriage like her mother's, saw being economically self-sufficient as a means of avoiding this.[137] This sentiment was echoed by White's respondents in North London[138] and Higgins's respondents in Birmingham and Hull.[139]

[131] LRO, NWSA, 1999.0340, interview with Nellie Hilton. See also LRO, NWSA, 1995.0125, interview with Ann Smith.

[132] Mass-Observation, *ATS*, 8.

[133] Haythorne, *Numbers*, 106.

[134] A. Light, *Forever England: Feminism, Literature and Conservatism between the Wars* (London: Routledge, 1991), 10–15 and 183–5.

[135] Alexander, 'Men's Fears', 416.

[136] Lifetimes, *Couple from Manchester*, 36–40.

[137] Lifetimes, *Something in Common*, 11.

[138] White, *Worst Street*, 188.

[139] N. Higgins, 'The Changing Expectations and Realities of Marriage in the English Working Class, 1920–1960', Ph.D. thesis (Cambridge, 2003), 93–6.

How successful these women were in achieving their aspirations depended not only on family background and local employment opportunities, but on when they entered work, pointing to an important generational shift often overlooked by studies that emphasize continuity, particularly across the 'long weekend'[140] between the wars. Many of those who began work in the 1920s found that their aspirations, raised by employment expansion during the First World War, were thwarted by a post-war contraction of opportunities and by poverty. A large number articulated disappointment that the family economy had had to take precedence over their ambitions. Many domestic servants, including Lavinia Swainbank and Mrs Cleary, recognized that their occupation was primarily determined by lack of alternative employment and household poverty.[141] Winifred Cotterill, who began work as a clerk but became a factory worker at Coventry's GEC firm in 1922 after a year's unemployment, was her household's sole breadwinner. She said,

> maybe you wonder why I never tried to get away from GEC. Well it was 'safe' and I had a mother to keep and although I always thought I was capable of doing a better job, the opportunity didn't come.[142]

Such testimonies highlight a mismatch between young women's aspirations, raised by the wartime experiences of mothers and older sisters, and the economic reality of the 1920s and early 1930s. Miss Cotterill's memories also highlight the mixture of obligation, affection, and resentment which characterized relations between daughters and parents.

Women who worked in the mid- and later 1930s were more likely to (partially) realize their aspirations, and their narratives often present their lifestyle as the result of successfully struggling against the odds, while rationalizing the compromises they made. Following a family row, Elsie was unable to enter the clerical job at her uncle's firm she had hoped for, and followed her mother into clothing work, where she emphasized that her hard work paid off eventually because she 'decided to learn the trade from beginning to end, which I did'[143] and became a valued, skilled worker who prized her economic independence with skills she was proud of in themselves, and in the self-sufficiency they gave her. In wartime, conscription could act for young women as a motif of

140 R. Graves and A. Hodge, *The Long Weekend*, 2nd edn. (Harmondsworth: Penguin, 1971).

141 TLSL, Manchester Studies, 28, interview with Mrs Cleary; L. Swainbank, 'Housemaid', in J. Burnett (ed.), *Useful Toil* (Harmondsworth: Penguin, 1974), 221.

142 MRC, Coventry Women's Work Collection, MSS 266/6/2, letter from Winifred Cotterill to J. Castle, 1982.

143 Lifetimes, *Couple from Manchester*, 38.

both freedom and restraint in employment choice and more general aspiration. A *Report on Youth Registration* in 1942 found that 'Young people have become interested in themselves partly because the Country has become interested in them.'[144] The plethora of local studies of young workers during wartime, and the expansion of clerical work, encouraged young women to feel that their aspirations should be realized. However, the most noticeable effect of war was in the growth of new, half-formed ambitions and aspirations for travel, independence, and variety, which tended to find expression in vague hopes for post-war life, which included unspecified, interesting jobs. The Bristol Survey suggested that although both boys' and girls' employment aspirations were raised by war, the latter's were aimed at transcending class and gender boundaries to a far greater extent: boys aspired to entering engineering, the Navy, or the RAF, whereas girls wanted to become dancers, nurses, dress designers, or—less frequently—writers, photographers, sportswomen, and journalists. The most popular and strongest aspiration, shared by girls and boys, was to travel.[145] Work was viewed as a potential passport to a different sort of life, but it was not one that could be simplified as 'middle class'.

Nevertheless, in the economic and political uncertainties of the immediate post-war years, young women's aspirations became more ambiguous, combining employment, romance, and materialism in their desires for a life different from their mothers' that included a larger degree of social independence. One young, unmarried factory worker, questioned by Mass-Observation on her post-war employment plans, responded, 'I don't want to stay on here myself. I wouldn't like to stay at home either—I'd get too bored. I'd really like a job that took you out of doors. I don't quite know what. I used to work in a leather factory, making handbags, so I was used to factory work before I came here. But it's very monotonous sitting all day at a bench: I'd like something with more variety.'[146] May Hobbs became a secretary when she left school in the early 1950s because 'I suppose I imagined myself being taken on by a dream boss and going travelling all over the world as his private secretary and marrying him.'[147] A gap continued to exist between reality and aspirations shaped by ambivalent and ambiguous notions of escape and independence, as well as by a desire for economic security.

[144] Ministry of Labour and National Service, *Report on Youth Registration* (London: HMSO, 1942), 6.

[145] Fletcher, *The Welfare of Youth*, 17.

[146] M-OA, FR 2059, 'Do the Factory Girls Want to Stay Put or Go Home?' (March 1944), 5.

[147] Hobbs, *Struggle*, 28–9.

Such ambiguity resulted from young women's own recognition that their class and gender severely limited their life choices, even in the post-war world. In 1948 Jephcott quoted one young woman who 'At 18 . . . still does not know what she fancies, "something interesting, not factory, not shop" ' but she also noted that girls' knowledge of career options remained very limited; they had not 'considered anything except shop, office or factory work',[148] probably because little else was available. Young women's awareness of their limited options grew with age. Thirty-four per cent of the 450 teenage girls questioned by Wilkins in 1950 had vocational ambitions (but only 27 per cent of those who had attended a non-selective secondary modern school), and another 6 per cent possessed 'nebulous' aspirations; among the unknown number of 25-year-old women who responded, however, these proportions dropped to 19 per cent and 1 per cent, respectively, whereas marriage, given as a major ambition by 4 per cent of the teenage sample, was cited by 42 per cent of this older sample.[149] In this sense, the growth of commercial youth culture in the 1950s can be understood as the creation of a space that offered at least a transient exploration of alternative realities in which glamour superceded the ongoing need to earn a living.

Conclusion

Mobility—occupational, geographic, and social—was central to young women's working lives and aspirations. Their employment histories demonstrate that few workers experienced 'a job for life', with most taking a series of relatively low-paid, unskilled or semiskilled positions. This type of intragenerational occupational mobility should be central, rather than peripheral, to our understanding of employment experience and class identity. Young women's limited choices were shaped by the demands of the family economy, and, later in the period, by their own desire for immediate financial and social independence. Young women's decisions were also informed by their awareness that their occupation influenced their status within the family and community. This relationship between occupation and social status was more nuanced and less straightforward for young women than for men.

Geographic mobility was central to young women's expectations and experiences of working life. In many rural communities, migration

[148] Jephcott, *Rising Twenty*, 131.

[149] Wilkins, *Adolescent*, 70–5.

patterns into domestic service were already well-established by the 1920s, and this trend extended to depressed urban areas and was exacerbated by wartime labour demand in the 1940s. A major aspect of state policy towards youth centred on young workers' use as migrant labour, an element often overlooked in Whiggish accounts of increased state surveillance and protection of young people.

Migration, like occupational mobility, shaped young women's aspirations and sense of identity. The critical perspective on aspects of working class life evident in many women's occupational and social aspirations was influenced, for some, by the sense of detachment from it that employment away from home provided. However, the women who stayed at home also viewed employment as a means of escaping the insecurity and domestic burden that characterized their mothers' lives. Young women's own employment aspirations were shaped as much by the common experience of poverty as by a desire to escape it. If the place of occupational and social mobility in working class life is to be fully understood, a sophisticated and nuanced conceptualization of class is required. It must recognize the importance of gender and generation as well as (rather than instead of) occupation in fracturing working class experience, and be flexible enough to incorporate thwarted aspiration as well as pride in one's work, and a desire to escape poverty co-existing with a sense of obligation to one's family, together with recognition of difference from outside groups. These elements interacted to create a distinctive, gendered, and generational identity for young working class women. The ways that this identity forged and was in turn shaped by workplace relations is explored in chapter 5.

5

Work Culture

In his journey around England in 1933, J. B. Priestley observed of young women factory workers that 'nine out of every ten of those girls working at the long rows of machines only see their factory life as a busy but dreamy interlude between childhood and marriage'.[1] Representations of young women workers in contemporary social surveys, government reports, and newspaper articles throughout the period also suggested that young women lacked engagement with their workplace or the labour process. These women were construed as apathetic with, as feminist Ray Strachey asserted, a 'meanwhile attitude to work',[2] attributed to their identification with domesticity and marital aspirations. Against this, but equally damning, young women were portrayed as potentially or actually delinquent, the 'boisterous workers' noted by the *Leicester Evening Mail*'s report on young women strikers in 1931.[3] These representations in fact posed a false dichotomy, for the young women strikers in Leicester were the very same workers Priestley found 'dreamy' and apathetic less than two years later. Clearly, both offered a one-dimensional view of young women in the workplace, arising from the assumption that work played only a minor role in the lives and identities of this group.

This chapter and the following one are directly concerned with refuting that assumption and with highlighting the complex relationship that young women forged with the workplace. While chapter 6 focuses on young women's engagement in workplace militancy, and their relationship with the labour movement, the present chapter is concerned with their daily work culture. It contends that it is true for young women as well as for men that, as Willis points out, 'work, and the massive experience of it, is right at the centre of our living culture. . . . It affects the general social

[1] J. B. Priestley, *English Journey* (London: Heinemann, 1934), 133.

[2] R. Strachey, *Careers and Openings for Women* (London: Faber, 1935), 52; see also J. Blainey, *The Woman Worker and Protective Legislation* (London: Arrowsmith, 1928), 48.

[3] *Leicester Evening Mail* (7 December 1931), 7.

nature of our lives in the most profound ways'.[4] Young women's workplace culture is analysed as a site of complex, historically specific, and changing generational, gender, and class relations. It is argued that coping with, circumventing, and at times resisting employers' demands were vital in forging a working class, youthful, feminine identity.

This chapter draws on but also challenges the models used by previous studies to explain young and women workers' workplace behaviour. The conflictual model, used by Humphries[5] and Willis,[6] suggests that work culture developed out of young workers' dissent from employers' aims. The domesticity model, common to labour historians, suggests that women workers failed to engage with workplace relations (for example, through low trade union participation) because they saw their futures as being outside the workplace.[7] One weakness of both models is that they collapse the discrete categories of workplace culture, resistance, organization, and militancy. As Whitston points out, ' "worker resistance" . . . has been used indiscriminately to refer to everything from a refusal to work overtime to participation in the general strike, and influences the struggles of reactionary craftsmen, revolutionary engineers, and pragmatic pieceworkers.'[8] To avoid doing so here, trade unionism and militancy are dealt with in the following chapter, whereas the present chapter is concerned more generally with workplace culture.

This division also enables a more nuanced approach than the previous models allow. The motivations of those who conform rather than rebel, or who act outside the parameters of the organized labour movement, have been neglected or generalized as 'passive' by historians seeking to identify class conscious resistance. The material presented here suggests that Stephen Humphries' compelling study overstates the amount of young workers' militant resistance to their employers. In doing so, he overlooks the reasons young women often conformed to their employers' wishes, as well as neglecting the fact that deference was itself a complex relationship mediated between workers and employers, enshrining some obligations

[4] P. Willis, 'Shop Floor Culture, Masculinity and the Wage Form', in J. Clarke, C. Critcher, and R. Johnson, *Working Class Culture: Studies in History and Theory* (London: Hutchinson, 1979), 186.

[5] S. Humphries, *Hooligans or Rebels? An Oral History of Working Class Childhood and Youth 1889–1939* (Oxford: Blackwell, 1981).

[6] P. Willis, *Learning to Labour* (Aldershot: Ashgate, 1977).

[7] S. Lewenhak, *Women and Trade Unions* (London: Ernest Benn, 1977), 206.

[8] K. Whitston, 'Worker Resistance and Taylorism in Britain', *International Review of Social History*, 42/1 (1997), 3.

for employers as well as limited rights for many workers. Nevertheless, Humphries' account is a salutary reminder that work culture was strongly shaped by class relations, a fact neglected by more recent studies such as Fowler's history of *The First Teenagers*, which suggests that a high degree of satisfaction with work existed among young workers and assumes that relations between young women and their employers were very good.[9] Langhamer's valuable study of the workplace as a leisure venue has highlighted the importance of workmates as friends during this period, but again, does not analyse the implications of this culture for class and labour relations within the workplace.[10] This chapter argues that tension between workers' and employers' interests was important in forging alliances between young women. Their responses to the workplace, individual and collective, were multifaceted, being strongly influenced by their family background as well as by the nature of their job.

Young women's experiences of employment, and their workplace relationships, underwent significant change in this period. As earlier chapters have shown, the young female workforce at the end of the First World War was concentrated largely in residential domestic service and, to a lesser extent, in the textile industry. By the late 1940s, the majority were employed in large factories, offices, and shops. The limited number of existing studies that reflect on women's attitudes to work and on their relations with workmates and employers are confined to single occupational groups, generally in the industrial sector. Sarsby's study of the pottery industry,[11] and Glucksmann's examination of assembly-line production,[12] are among the most valuable. Their methods and conclusions are drawn on in this chapter's examination of the importance of the family in structuring attitudes to work; gender relations within the workplace; and young women's methods of enduring or enjoying their jobs. However, this study's remit is deliberately broad, covering factory workers but also shop assistants and clerks, and the long-neglected domestic servants who constituted the largest group of young working women until the 1940s, and who have too often been dismissed as simply 'deferential' in their attitudes to work.

[9] D Fowler, *The First Teenagers: The Lifestyles of Young Wage-Earners in Interwar Britain* (London: Woburn Press, 1995), 65–6.

[10] C. Langhamer, *Women's Leisure in England 1920–1960* (Manchester: Manchester University Press, 2000), 92–3.

[11] J. Sarsby, *Missuses and Mouldrunners: An Oral History of Women Pottery Workers at Work and at Home* (Milton Keynes: Open University Press, 1988).

[12] M. Glucksmann, *Women Assemble: Women Workers in the New Industries of Inter-War Britain* (London: Routledge, 1993), 158–97.

Paternalism and Deference

Workplace relations varied according to sector. The benevolent employer, often heading a family-run firm, who encouraged the workers to feel that personal bonds existed between themselves and their managers, was still a common feature of British industry during the 1920s.[13] Although such paternalism declined in the 1930s, the demands of wartime production temporarily halted this trend. Summerfield has pointed out that women war workers were encouraged to feel that they and their employers were 'a family', facing hardship together and engaging in equal sacrifice.[14] As Mrs Somerville said of her chemical firm, 'everybody was a family and everybody would tell experiences [of the blitz]'.[15] Paternalism also characterized relations between clerks and their employers. Women who worked as secretaries were frequently in closer contact with their boss than with more junior workers and the work relations this forged, together with the relatively high social status of white collar work, meant that trade unionism remained low among clerks throughout this period.[16] However, paternalism was most characteristic of the older occupation of domestic service. The experience of living in a family's home, servants' limited social networks, and the strict hierarchy within such households encouraged the formation of strong bonds between a servant and her employers, characterized by deference. Winifred Foley was reluctant to leave her first domestic service position owing to her elderly employer's dependency on her, despite Foley's recognition that her mistress exploited her.[17] Such ambivalence is common in servants' accounts of relations with their masters and mistresses.[18]

Domestic service highlights the complexities of deference. Servants were generally obedient and compliant, but kindness and generosity on the part of employers were often essential in winning their servants' co-operation.[19] A fine balance was struck, and repercussions could follow if an employer

[13] J. Childs, 'Quaker Employers and Industrial Relations', *Sociological Review*, 12/2 (1964), 297–301; T. Griffiths, *The Lancashire Working Classes c. 1880–1930* (Oxford: Clarendon Press, 2001), 160–5.

[14] P. Summerfield, *Reconstructing Women's Wartime Lives* (Manchester: Manchester University Press, 1998), 167–8.

[15] Tameside Local Studies Library (TLSL), Manchester Studies collection, tape 1146, interview with Mrs Somerville.

[16] See chapter 6.

[17] W. Foley, *Child in the Forest* (London: BBC, 1974), 111.

[18] See for example, TLSL, Manchester Studies, 9, interview with Mrs Sandys.

[19] P. Taylor, 'Daughters and Mothers—Maids and Mistresses: Domestic Service between the Wars', in Clarke et al., *Working Class Culture*, 136.

transgressed this, demonstrating that stoicism or an acceptance of the status quo cannot be interpreted as an abnegation of dignity. Repercussions were likely to take the form of covert acts of individual resistance rather than a collective response. The most drastic was resigning from a post, a well-established pattern of negotiation by the interwar years as chapter 4 noted. Eileen Balderson, who worked as a servant after leaving school in 1931, believed that high labour demand was one of the most positive aspects of the job, stating, 'Domestic servants are said to have been exploited. I do not agree. Exploitation applied much more to other workers. . . . Girls sought advancement through domestic agencies, always asking for a bigger wage than they expected to get. There was no need for a girl to stay where conditions were poor.'[20]

More covert strategies were also used to challenge unacceptable behaviour on the part of employers, and to maintain servants' 'good character', essential in a sector where respectability was the main prerequisite of employment. After discovering that her aristocratic employers placed coins under the carpet to test the honesty of their maids, Jean Rennie glued the coins to the floor: they subsequently disappeared.[21] The frequency with which variations of this story appear in domestic servants' autobiographies and were passed between servants over this period[22] indicates that this was frequently an apocryphal, anecdotal signifier of discontent with employers. The story emphasizes the importance of trust in the relationship between employers and servants. To cast doubt on a servant's trustworthiness was not simply to suggest they were unfit for their job, but to slur their character. It was therefore bitterly resented. Mrs Hughson, for example, left her first job after being accused of stealing milk by the housekeeper and receiving no support from her employers: 'I said "I do not drink milk—and I do not steal—and I don't tell lies." '[23] However, other servants could not afford to cause a confrontation. Mrs Halliday was incensed when her employer locked up a cake so that she would not eat it; consequently 'I thought, "I will find that cake!" ' and determined to have a small slice, unknown to her employer.[24] The story about the coins juxtaposed employers' distrust with their servants' honesty and also their ingenuity; sticking the coins to the floor indicates that the servant

[20] E. Balderson with D. Goodlad, *Backstairs Life in a Country House* (Newton Abbott: David and Charles, 1982), 13.

[21] J. Rennie, *Every Other Sunday* (London: A. Barker, 1955), 51.

[22] See, for example, Lancashire Record Office (LRO), North West Sound Archive (NWSA), 1999.0017, interview with Mrs Halliday; Humphries, *Hooligans*, 171.

[23] TLSL, Manchester Studies, tape 26, interview with Mrs Hughson.

[24] LRO, NWSA, 1999.0017, interview with Mrs Halliday.

was wise to her employer's tricks—and was able to circumvent them. Moreover, the servant in the story gets the better of her employer within the bounds of the deferential relationship. She continues to do her job efficiently, and is, during both her work and her action, unseen and unheard—qualities demanded of the model servant, and which make it difficult for her employer to initiate confrontation. The anecdotal nature of the story does not detract from its significance. The oral tradition it highlights was itself a reaction to the subservience demanded by employers. Such anecdotes indicated to younger servants that certain transgressions were popularly condoned by other servants, and suggested means of negotiating the deferential relationship with their employers. The telling of and listening to such stories provided an outlet for discontent with aspects of the employer–servant relationship. This highlights the important interaction between women's personal employment experiences and their social networks in shaping their workplace behaviour.

The Family and Workplace Culture

Young women were socialized into work primarily by their family. Kinship recruitment networks were fostered by employers to strengthen workers' loyalty. Young workers were aware that misbehaviour might affect and be censured by their families, or by the worker, often an older sibling or friend, who had 'spoken for' them to their employer and secured them their job. Lucy Lees discovered this as a 14-year-old mill worker in Lancashire in the early 1920s, when her elder sister was censured for Lucy's practical joking and their father was informed.[25] Elsie Lee, a factory operative at Courtaulds, was sympathetic to attempts by the Transport and General Workers' Union (TGWU) to recruit workers there in the early 1930s, but, she recalled, '[you] muttered and mumbled amongst yourselves but—you hadn't got the confidence. You weren't brought up at school to be confident, not at home . . . seen but not heard.'[26] Obedience and deference were thus taught at an early age and subsequently reinforced by workplace relations.

The inculcation of obedience and deference did not reflect the full scope of parental influence, however. Gramsci offers a model for understanding the complexities of socialization. His 'man-in-the mass' was

25 LRO, NWSA, 1999.0335, interview with Lucy Lees.

26 Modern Records Centre, University of Warwick (MRC), Coventry Women's Work Collection, MSS 266/6/5, interview with Elsie Lee.

shaped by 'two theoretical consciousnesses (or one contradictory consciousness)': the economic imperative of conforming to the status quo, but also the 'common sense' that emerged from shared experiences with neighbours, family, and fellow workers, of oppression and exploitation, and which shaped dissent.[27] Many parents encouraged self-sufficiency and hard work, but also an ability to 'stand up for yourself'. Mrs Halliday, who had to take work as a domestic servant in the early 1930s, was continuously reminded by her mother that her employers 'have more money than us, but they're not better than you'.[28] Many daughters were directed by their parents to leave jobs at various times, despite the importance of their earnings.[29] Betty Ferry's mother advised her to 'liven up!' when she began her working life at a leather factory, but when Betty's supervisor made her work through the lunch hour, 'my mother came to the firm, asked to see the Boss, and told him what she thought of him. I remember her saying to him, "No wonder you can have posh cars outside here when you're working the girls in a lunch hour." ' Betty's employer assured her mother he would speak to the supervisor concerned.[30] Parental authority thus at times challenged the more oppressive aspects of workplace discipline. Employers' promotion of young workers' dependency on their parents, to justify low wages and paternalistic management techniques, meant that they had to pay at least lip service to such parental concern. Such encounters highlight what Smythe rightly calls 'the continuing strength of the child–parent relationship'[31] for young wage-earners.

Workplace Networks

Changing employment patterns also influenced workplace behaviour. An increasing proportion of young women found themselves employed in large, industrial workplaces, where networks of mutual support flourished. Middle class observers underrated their significance, concurring

[27] A. Gramsci, *Selections from the Prison Notebooks*, ed. Q. Hoare and G. Newell Smith (London: Lawrence and Wishart, 1971), 419–25.

[28] LRO, NWSA, 1999.0017, interview with Mrs Halliday.

[29] Foley, *Child*, 111; LRO, NWSA, 1999.0017, Mrs Halliday; TLSL, Manchester Studies, 9, Mrs Sandys.

[30] B. Ferry, 'Boot and Shoe Maker', in R. Gray (ed.), *Working Lives* (London: Centreprise, 1976), 108.

[31] J. Smythe, ' "Ye Never Got a Spell to Think aboot it." Young Women and Employment in the Inter-War Period: A Case Study of a Textile Village', in E. Gordon and E. Breitenbach (eds.), *The World is Ill Divided: Women's Work in Scotland in the Nineteenth and Early Twentieth Centuries* (Edinburgh: Edinburgh University Press, 1990), 109.

with Ray Strachey's disapproval of girls who gave their attention not to their work but 'instead to lipstick and the fashions, and the efficacy of a permanent wave.'[32] In fact, workplace socializing was an important means of developing an inclusive identity characterized by a set of shared values.[33] Moreover, as a Mass-Observation survey of 1943 astutely noted, 'Economic pressure is the greatest single factor making women work. The compensations are mainly company and experience which work gives'.[34] Olive Jones recalled that as 12-year-old half-time mill workers in 1918 she and her workmates played playground games in the lunch hour, emphasizing their youth.[35] Women also stressed the support offered by workmates. In many shops and factories, as at the shop where Marjorie Gardiner worked in interwar Brighton, women relied on their workmates covering for them while they took unauthorized breaks.[36] Many war workers negotiated shift work so that those with boyfriends on leave could take as much time off as possible.[37] An investigation into Scottish war workers transferred to England's Midlands highlighted a strong sense of solidarity and found that 'their desire to help each other' helped to overcome homesickness and sustain morale.[38]

Workplace culture should not be romanticized, however. An unofficial workplace hierarchy, based upon age, longevity of employment, and (in firms which employed married women) marital status, frequently existed. Initiation rites emphatically introduced young workers into this structure. They were particularly common in male-dominated trades and in those sectors in which women were likely to remain in employment in adult life, signifying the long-term importance of the workplace in these contexts. Linda Thew had her face scrubbed raw in her first days as a Co-op shop assistant in the early 1930s by male apprentices who had undergone similar rites. This custom had declined by the 1940s as her workplace began to employ more young women who, like her, expected to leave work on marrying and felt simply that 'we were there to do a job'.[39] Some women viewed such rites as a light-hearted introduction to the

[32] Strachey, *Careers*, 52.

[33] M. Tebbutt, *Women's Talk?: A Social History of 'Gossip' in Working Class Neighbourhoods, 1880–1960* (Aldershot: Scolar Press, 1995), 86–97.

[34] Mass-Observation Archive (M-OA): FR 2117, 'Women at Work', June 1944, 28.

[35] LRO, NWSA, 1999.0343, interview with Olive Jones.

[36] M. Gardiner, *The Other Side of the Counter: The Life of A Shop Girl 1925–45* (Brighton: Queenspark, 1985), 14.

[37] LRO, NWSA, 1995.0125, interview with Annie Olive.

[38] Scottish Trade Union Delegation to the Midlands, *Transfer of Scottish Girls. Report to Scottish Trades Union Congress General Council and the Organisation of Women Committee* (Glasgow, Scottish TUC, 1943), 11.

[39] L. M. Thew, *The Pit Village and the Store* (London: Pluto Press, 1985), 225.

world of work that emphasized a sense of belonging: Emily Money was determined not to be caught out by the 'laughs with new girls', which she knew to be characteristic of factory employment, and recalled with pride that when asked to fetch a bucket of steam, 'they didn't catch me'.[40] Other girls had less happy memories of the authority sometimes antagonistically wielded by older workers: Nellie Oldroyd's unhappiness at work was worsened by the 'very unfriendly' girl meant to instruct her in her duties.[41]

Initiation rites had multiple meanings. Willis has pointed out that they marked the progression from schoolboy to worker among men; emphasized a young worker's subordinate position in the workforce; and reflected the harsher side of the production process while simultaneously forging a loyalty with which to face, and possibly resist it.[42] An examination of young women's employment indicates that such customs were not simply a signifier of masculinity. The seniority conferred on older workers could conflict with the formal authority structure, but also reminded young workers of their subordinate position in the workforce, promoting deference and stoicism. Rites could signify worker solidarity, but also antagonism, based upon older workers' fears of being displaced by young women. Linda Thew experienced this as one of the first young women to be employed as a Co-op grocery assistant: 'most men saw my appointment as a threat to their jobs and livelihoods'.[43] The women questioned by Glucksmann recounted similar experiences from their interwar factory jobs, recalling that initiation rites could involve having tools or materials hidden, indicating a level of hostility amongst older workers, women as well as men.[44] Similarly, while some young pieceworkers benefited from workmates' support in helping them meet targets, others attracted antagonism when they were new, and slow, particularly if production bonuses were awarded collectively.[45]

Social divisions fractured relations between women workers. The problematic relationship between femininity and the workplace could reinforce divisions between the workforce, as women sought to distance

[40] E. Money, 'Liquorice', in R. Van Riel (ed.), *All in a Day's Work* (Pontefract: Yorkshire Art Circus, 1981), 31.

[41] N. Oldroyd, 'Sweetmaking', *All in a Day's Work*, 9.

[42] Willis, *Learning to Labour*, 193. See also R. Roberts, *A Ragged Schooling: Growing up in the Classic Slum* (Manchester: Manchester University Press, 1976), 186.

[43] Thew, *Pit Village*, 144.

[44] Glucksmann, *Women Assemble*, 109.

[45] MRC, Coventry Women's Work Collection, MSS 266/3/1/2, interview with Winifred Cotterill; J. Beauchamp, *Women Who Work* (London: Lawrence and Wishart, 1937), 30–1; Glucksmann, *Women Assemble*, 164–5.

themselves from the 'rough' reputation of factory workers. Mrs Mullis was among many of Courtaulds' Coventry employees who judged workers from Bedworth—a relatively poor area—'rougher' than those from Coventry.[46] A desire to distance themselves from the prevailing stereotypes of industrial work could lead to a degree of collusion between women workers and supervisors. Winifred Cotterill remembered fondly her foreman's compliment, 'Winnie, it's so nice to see clean underwear', which she felt distinguished her from 'crude and dirty'[47] workmates. During the Second World War, similar feelings could also fracture the sense of unity that employers and government sought to promote. Kitty Burn, a Durham munitions worker, got on with everyone at her factory apart from 'the girls from Middlesbrough. . . . Their language was a bit strong. . . . it was hard work, and it was hot work . . . but the Middlesbrough girls were always off skiving—running outside for smokes and so forth.'[48] Such testimonies demonstrate that localized identities continued to interact with class, gender, and generational relations.

Gender Relations

Gender relations within workplaces changed between the 1920s and the 1950s. The sexes were segregated in many interwar workplaces, either as a result of the sexual division of labour—typists, for example, were unlikely to meet men aside from managers—or because of a firm's strategy. Courtaulds and Rowntree were among those industrial firms to segregate women manual workers from male employees.[49] When this was eroded by wartime labour demand in the 1940s, Summerfield suggests that gender antagonism was experienced by many women workers, with adult men resenting the threat apparently posed by younger, female employees.[50] Harassment was certainly a feature of many workplaces. Arthur Excell recalled that the foreman at Morris Motors intimidated young women who worked there, insisting they go out with him.[51]

[46] MRC, Coventry Women's Work collection, MSS 266/6/5, interview with Mrs Mullis.

[47] MRC, Coventry Women's Work collection, MSS 266/3/1/2, interview with Winifred Cotterill.

[48] Imperial War Museum Sound Archive (IWM), tape 19686, interview with Anon.

[49] J. Castle, 'Factory Work for Women', in B. Lancaster and T. Mason (eds.), *Life and Labour in a Twentieth Century City: The Experience of Coventry* (Coventry: Cryfield Press, 1986), 139–40; R. Fitzgerald, *Rowntree and the Marketing Revolution, 1862–1969* (Cambridge: Cambridge University Press, 1995), 225.

[50] Summerfield, *Reconstructing*, 146–8.

[51] A. Excell, *The Politics of the Production Line: Autobiography of an Oxford Car Worker* (Southampton: History Workshop, 1981), 31.

However, personal testimonies suggest that such antagonism was only one facet of gender relations, albeit an extremely important and often overlooked one. Some young women, like Betty Ferry in the 1920s and May Hobbs in the 1950s, valued friendships with young male co-workers.[52] However, having a large female support group was also often important in mixed workplaces. For Betty Ferry, the companionship of other young female factory workers provided support and relief from the flirtatious and prank-playing relationships she established with her male peers.[53] Excell noted that the increased presence of women at Morris Motors during the Second World War, and the firm's need to maintain good relations with them, meant that harassment of women diminished during the 1940s.[54] The assertive image of the factory girl was thus partially explained by her strategies for dealing with male workmates or managers.

The workplace, particularly when it employed a large number of adult as well as younger women, was more often a venue for social education than the parental home. Elsie, a factory worker, was one among many who 'didn't know we were poor—until I started work.'[55] As well as raising women's consciousness of their class position, the oral culture of larger workplaces provided many with a rudimentary education in sex and courtship. Mary Welch, a leather worker, recalled of her London factory in the 1920s:

> The machinists were nearly all married and middle aged. They were over on the other side of the room and they'd all chat to each other. . . . I learned quite a lot about sex and marriage from the married women. But they were doing us a special favour. They wouldn't let you listen to them talking.[56]

This aspect of work could compound the culture shock experienced by many young entrants to employment, particularly those who only started work in their later teens, as became more common in wartime, when conscription brought young adult women into the workplace who had previously been kept at home. Kathleen Holland stayed at home helping her invalid mother until the age of 18 when she was conscripted into a war factory:'I thought it was dreadful, they made fun of me. They thought I was somebody posh because I'd stayed at home.'[57] *Woman's Own* magazine printed several letters from young women shocked and surprised at the

[52] Ferry, 'Boot and Shoe Maker', 110; M. Hobbs, *Born to Struggle* (London: Quartet Books, 1973), 37.

[53] Ferry, 'Boot and Shoe Maker', 110.

[54] Excell, *Production Line*, 31–2.

[55] Elsie, quoted in Lifetimes, *A Couple from Manchester* (Manchester: Manchester Polytechnic, 1976), 18.

[56] M. Welch, 'Leather Worker', *Working Lives*, 56.

[57] TLSL, Manchester Studies, 1075, interview with Kathleen Holland.

sex education they received from their war work, like the young factory girl who wrote: 'I am working among a lot of girls and am full of fears of all sorts. They talk about things that frighten me.'[58] However, others found it valuable. Evelyn Haythorne was confused by her first meeting with a gay man in a wartime British restaurant, but her mother refused to tell her what 'homosexual' meant. Consequently, 'Next day at work I asked a woman, who was a lot older than me. . . . She looked a little taken aback but took me and Betty to one side and told us'.[59] Gittins's suggestion that the transmission of information on reproduction and birth control partially explains the low birth rate among women employed in large industrial workplaces[60] is difficult to conclusively prove, but the material presented here and in studies by Humphries and Langhamer strongly supports her hypothesis.[61] As increasing numbers of women entered large retail and industrial workplaces, so their social education became more expansive than that of their mothers' generation, a process that possibly changed their own attitudes towards parenting. Kathleen Holland's experiences led her to decide that 'when I get married, if I have daughters, they'll never be like me. They won't be as green, won't be sheltered.'[62] Many of the 103 young women questioned by Jephcott in the mid-1940s expressed similar views; exposure to GIs led some to compare themselves unfavourably with young Americans, who were felt to be better informed.[63] The increase in large workplaces thus supplemented the social and sexual education given in the family home, and shaped young women's own ideas about sex and courtship, but also about the role of mother–daughter relationships, thus prompting greater willingness to transmit such information within families in the 1950s and 1960s.

The workplace became an increasingly important venue for courtship. As chapter 4 highlighted, the lack of opportunities to meet young men was one reason young women found domestic service unattractive, particularly as they entered their late teens. Sex segregation could also make relations difficult between women and men in some larger, industrial interwar workplaces. Women who worked at Coventry's Courtaulds firm,

[58] *Woman's Own* (April 3, 1942).

[59] E. Haythorne, *On Earth to Make the Numbers Up* (Castleford: Yorkshire Art Circus, 1991), 113.

[60] D. Gittins, *Fair Sex: Family Size and Structure, 1900–39* (London: Hutchinson, 1982), 89–93 and 157–80.

[61] S. Humphries, *A Secret World of Sex: Forbidden Fruit: The British Experience, 1900–1950* (London: Sidgwick and Jackson, 1988), 60–1; Langhamer, *Women's Leisure*, 123.

[62] TLSL, Manchester Studies, 1075, interview with Kathleen Holland.

[63] P. Jephcott, *Rising Twenty: Notes on Some Ordinary Girls* (London: Faber, 1948), 91–2.

for example, were segregated from men during breaks as well as on the factory floor. Elsie Lee rarely met men employed at Courtaulds due to these rules and also because 'you didn't want to go in where there was machinery and dirty work, you see.'[64] My own sample suggests that women were increasingly likely to meet husbands in the workplace during the 1940s, because of the erosion of sex segregation. Many women who worked nights had liaisons with male workers; Kitty Burn, who worked at Newton Aycliffe Royal Ordnance Factory, remembered that 'During break times—meal times, which was sometimes on night shift, early hours of the morning [other women workers] would disappear over the fields with these men.'[65] Elsie Bell courted her husband, who worked at the same factory as herself, on the train to and from work.[66] The workplace, particularly in larger factories, offices, and shops, could provide a degree of freedom to socialize with the opposite sex away from watchful parental eyes.

Despite the importance of the workplace in their daily lives, women workers, particularly in communities characterized by a strong sexual division of labour, identified themselves less with the workplace than many male workers did. Most young working class women continued to aspire to marry, and in so doing, to retire from full-time paid work. Bobbie Gardiner, who worked at Courtaulds, was given the option of staying on when she married in 1939 but refused; 'I thought, I've had enough, I'm getting married! [Laughs] I'm posh, I'm getting married.'[67] Her view reflects the importance of marriage as an initiation into adulthood for women, and the idealization of the male breadwinner model, but also emphasizes the unpleasantness of many paid jobs, which heightened the attraction of marriage for women in their late teens and twenties.

For this reason, rites surrounding a woman's marriage were far more common than initiations into the workplace. Brides-to-be were put in fancy dress and had balloons attached to them as they were leaving work on their last day,[68] or a woman's friends provided cakes and drinks.[69] The notion of marriage as an initiation into sexual independence and adulthood was also prominent. Joyce Shaw, a wartime munitions worker, was

64 MRC, Coventry Women's Work Collection, MSS 266/6/5, interview with Elsie Lee.

65 IWM, 19686, interview with Anon.

66 IWM, 19715, interview with Anon.

67 MRC, Coventry Women's Work Collection, MSS 266/6/3, interview with Bobbie Gardiner.

68 MRC, Coventry Women's Work Collection, MSS 266/6/4, interview with Mrs Johnson.

69 MRC, Coventry Women's Work Collection, MSS 266/6/3, interview with Bobbie Gardiner; LRO, NWSA, 1999.0020, interview with Joyce Shaw.

one of several factory workers who recalled having to

> ... go and climb up—you went up this ladder and at the top was an article. And you had to get that and bring it down before they'd give you your present. A jerry! [chamber-pot] I must tell you, because it made me laugh so much. . . . I had to climb up for the jerry! Oh dear me yes—shall I tell you what it said in it? Wash me out and keep me clean and I'll not tell what I have seen [laughs]. It was an artist what did that, what worked there.[70]

The interwar marriage bar, and the notion that full-time work was a 'temporary stay' for women, which survived the 1940s, were thus upheld with the minimum of disruption to the employers who this ideology directly benefited.

The meanings of this celebration of marriage were ambivalent. Marriage represented liberation from the subordinate role of daughter and worker for a young woman with several years' employment experience behind her, and a degree of social and sexual independence.[71] Elsie Lee's forewoman warned her when she left Courtaulds to marry in 1933 that she would wish she were back at work within the year, but 'I did not'.[72] Housewifery, at least in the first few, childless years, was preferable to full-time work for many women, as the overwhelming support for going back to the home noted by Mass-Observation during the war demonstrated.[73] Florence Rosenblatt, who enjoyed being a factory supervisor in wartime Liverpool, nevertheless suffered depression in the final year of the war because 'my whole life was work' and she was glad to finish when her husband returned from Burma because 'I was so tired. I didn't have a career after that, I had a baby instead [laughs]. And that was that. . . . I was so happy to have him [her husband] home.'[74] Although young women might idealize marriage, particularly in wartime, their marital aspirations also indicate that for many working class women, full-time paid work was endured, rather than fulfilling.

Ultimately, however, marriage was a contradictory state, an initiation into adulthood that simultaneously reduced the (limited) social and financial

70 LRO, NWSA, 1999.0020, Joyce Shaw.

71 N. Higgins, 'The Changing Expectations and Realities of Marriage in the English Working Class, 1920–1960', Ph.D. thesis (Cambridge, 2003), 124–6; S. Westwood, *All Day, Every Day: Factory and Family in the Making of Women's Lives* (London: Pluto Press, 1984), 102–3; J. White, *The Worst Street in North London: Campbell Bunk, Islington, between the Wars* (London: Routledge, 1986), 198.

72 MRC, Coventry Women's Work Collection, MSS 266/6/5, interview with Elsie Lee.

73 M-OA: FR 2059, 'Do Factory Girls Want to Stay Put or Go Home?', March 1944, 7; M-OA: FR 2117, 'Women at Work', June 1944, 14.

74 LRO, NWSA, 2002.0531a, interview with Florence Rosenblatt.

independence that waged work allowed young women, as Margery Spring Rice's 1939 survey of *Working Class Wives* indicated.[75] Moreover, the large number of married women who became part-time workers in the 1940s and 1950s emphasized that the male breadwinner model was a myth, demonstrating that many households continued to rely upon a married woman's wage. Nevertheless, the tenacity of such celebrations, which sociological studies have shown survived the lifting of the marriage bar and remained a pervasive element of women's industrial workplace culture into the late twentieth century,[76] demonstrates the continuing centrality of heterosexual romance and domesticity to the construction of femininity.

Attitudes to Work

As chapter 4 pointed out, many young women were concerned to find work that was intrinsically interesting, particularly as their employment opportunities—and aspirations—expanded during the 1930s and 1940s. For a minority of women, particularly those employed on tasks considered skilled, their work was a valued component of their identity, from which they derived a great deal of interest. Nora Holroyd, who began work as a weaver in Lancashire in the 1920s, commented, 'It was interesting, I enjoyed what I did, you know'.[77] Elsie Brown, who worked in a Manchester factory during wartime, 'loved it, every minute of it. . . . We riveted the Lancaster bombers, went on at 7 at night, till 7 in the morning. . . . Believe me, it was hard work.'[78] Although Summerfield does not highlight such a distinction between skilled and unskilled workers in her sample of war workers, their testimonies clearly offer similar examples.[79] As this indicates, pride in one's work was not the prerogative of men, but tended to be common to many workers employed on jobs that were varied or interesting, offered promotion prospects, and were defined as skilled.

Young women who were employed on more repetitive, monotonous work did not generally express such satisfaction. Nevertheless, many were capable of questioning their employers' definitions of skill, which, as Zeitlin

[75] M. Spring Rice, *Working Class Wives: Their Health and Conditions*, 2nd ed. (London: Virago, 1981), 13–20, 109–19.

[76] A. Pollert, *Girls, Wives, Factory Lives* (Basingstoke: Macmillan, 1981), 104–11; Westwood, *All Day Every Day*, 111–18.

[77] LRO, NWSA, 2000.0651A, interview with Nora Holroyd.

[78] TLSL, Manchester Studies, 1075, interview with Elsie Brown.

[79] Summerfield, *Reconstructing*, 85–6.

has shown, has always been a contested term.[80] Many women recognized that speed and dexterity were skills, rather than simply biological characteristics as employers often suggested. Emily Money recalled of her work in a liquorice factory that 'making Pontefract cakes was quick work, you needed nimble fingers . . . you had to cut off the sides like lightning'.[81] As Joan Harley found in the mid-1930s, young women employed in the clothing trade valued their opportunity to acquire dressmaking skills, which enabled them to make their own fashionable clothes.[82] Although these women did not generally express the same degree of interest in their jobs as those whose work was more varied and widely recognized as skilled, they demonstrate that in some important ways skilled and semiskilled workers' attitudes to their work did not necessarily differ markedly.

The majority of young women, however, were more concerned with simply enduring their work. The labour processes on which they were engaged differentiated workers' strategies to survive the working week. Unlike adult women, a large proportion of whom were paid by the piece, a sizeable majority of young women were time workers, like young men. Time workers had less control over the labour process and their earnings, but they could also take time to 'lark about', which pieceworkers could ill afford. Distracting themselves from the monotony of the labour process was the main aim of many young workers. Their talking, singing, and joking, disliked and often forbidden by employers, provided a distraction from tedious work, was a means of reappropriating work time, and undermined supervisors' authority. Many young women took unauthorized breaks by 'pretending you were going to the toilet, like', following a trend noted by Collier's First World War investigation.[83] Mrs Mullis worked at Coventry's Courtaulds factory in the 1920s, where young women were strictly supervised. Nevertheless, as time workers, she and her friends took as long as possible to deliver material from one room to another, giggling, whispering, and dancing the Charleston up the factory stairs.[84] During the Second World War Mass-Observers noted that factory afternoons were characterized by 'lavatory-mongering', when women 'drift out

[80] J. Zeitlin, 'Engineers and Compositors: A Comparison', in R. Harrison and J. Zeitlin (eds.), *Divisions of Labour: Skilled Workers and Technological Change in Nineteenth Century England* (Brighton: Harvester Wheatsheaf, 1985).

[81] Money, 'Liquorice', 28.

[82] J. L. Harley, 'Report of an Enquiry into the Occupations, Further Education and Leisure Interests of a Number of Girl Wage-Earners from Elementary and Central Schools in the Manchester District, with Special Reference to the Influence of School Training on Their Use of Leisure', M.Ed. dissertation (Manchester, 1937), 47–8.

[83] D. Collier and B. L. Hutchins, *The Girl In Industry* (London: Bell, 1918), 26.

[84] MRC, Coventry Women's Work Collection, MSS 266/6/5, interview with Mrs Mullis.

to the cloakroom, and stay there for half an hour or more, eating sandwiches, talking, reading, and often just doing nothing at all. . . . Anything is welcome, so long as it provides a change from sitting at the bench.'[85] Office workers frequently adopted similar strategies when they were able. Joyce Musgrove, a secretary in the Second World War recalled, 'It was routine most of it—the same thing every day. If I got an opportunity to get out of the office, to go to take a message to another section, I'd be "yes I'll do it, shall I go". '[86] Young women workers showed similarities with male colleagues, who used workplace lavatories as a place to escape for short breaks, a smoke, and a chat.[87] The desire of these young women to take short breaks from tiring or monotonous work was made subversive by the strictness of their employers, who permitted no, or very few, breaks from the job.

As well as attempting to make time go quicker, some, particularly manual workers, relished the limited opportunities for resistance to productivity objectives that this reappropriation of their time afforded them. Emily Money recalled that at her factory, 'There were seven of us girls round a table and we did have some laughs, chattered all day. Somebody would hiss "Sshh, Mr Baxter's coming!" and we'd all go right quiet then crack out giggling as soon as he'd gone.'[88] This could conceal real antagonism towards supervisors, as was the case at Courtaulds where Doris Addicott resented the fact that, 'All they wanted was your work out. . . . Nobody wanted to know if you'd got any problems.'[89] In 1937 the Factory Inspectorate disapprovingly noted that in large factories, 'the "herd" effect renders it more difficult to maintain discipline and attention to work.'[90] Music could also be important as a means of passing and wasting time. From the late 1930s an increasing number of firms introduced *Music While You Work* for industrial workers, as the link between workers' morale and raising productivity began to be noted. In the Second World War this trend and factory workers' own propensity for group singing at their benches when permitted were frequently noted in propaganda as signifying high morale; however, such singing was, as one Mass-Observer

[85] Mass-Observation, *War Factory* (London: Gollancz, 1942), 30.

[86] IWM, 19694, interview with Joyce Musgrove.

[87] B. Jackson, *Working Class Community* (Harmondsworth: Penguin, 1972), 71; F. Zweig, *The British Worker* (Harmondsworth: Pelican, 1952), 111.

[88] Money, 'Liquorice', 29–30.

[89] MRC, Coventry Women's Work Collection, MSS 266/6/1, interview with Doris Addicott.

[90] Report of the Chief Inspector of Factories and Workshops for the year 1937: x, (1937–38), Cmd 5802, 49.

noted, frequently 'a symptom of boredom more than exuberance'.[91] At Newton Aycliffe Royal Ordnance Factory, 'if the danger woman [supervisor] walked in we used to sing to let everybody know to calm down, you know, not to speak to each other and that, until they got away.'[92] Their employment as time workers meant that these young women had little negotiation power over production organization, a factor that was important in shaping pieceworkers' attitudes to changes in the labour process as the following chapter shows. However, their employment patterns also allowed time workers a degree of freedom to reappropriate work time and disrupt production, which was unknown to those who were paid by the piece. As Humphries has suggested, 'The common boast of working girls that factory work was "just a lark" was an expression of the victory of humour and devious tactics over the alienating effects of routine drudgery'.[93]

Absenteeism was another strategy used to reappropriate time. Prior to the 1938 Holidays with Pay Act, and throughout wartime, unauthorized absence was the only chance most women workers had of a day's holiday. Whereas married women's absenteeism has been noted as a strategy for balancing their domestic duties with their paid work, its prevalence among younger women, noted by Humphries's study of the pre-1940 decades,[94] demonstrates that it could also signify dislike of work or employers, fatigue, or simply a desire to exert control over time. Kitty Burn suffered heavy nosebleeds while working at Newton Aycliffe ROF, and began to use this as an excuse to miss work regularly:

> until one day I got this letter to go in front of this committee to explain the reason why I had been absent for so long. So off I went . . . and got the shock of my life—I was like a private standing in front of generals, captains, lieutenants, sergeants. . . . So I was really annoyed about this because I wasn't in the army, so I came home had a talk with my parents—went up to the doctor's and got a permanent sick note. So after that every time, whether I had a nose bleed or [not], I took the sick note in and there was nothing they could do about it [laughs].[95]

Large workplaces afforded scope for going missing, as May Hobbs found as a factory worker in London in the early 1950s. At one job with a particularly benign supervisor, she and her friend Jean would regularly clock into work each afternoon and then go home or shopping until it was time to return to work to clock out.[96] Although these examples are probably

[91] Mass-Observation, *War Factory*, 31. See also TLSL, Manchester Studies, 1075, interview with E. Beasley.

[92] IWM, 19688, interview with Violet Braithwaite.

[93] Humphries, *Hooligans*, 141.

[94] Ibid., 143–5.

[95] IWM, 19686, interview with Anon.

[96] Hobbs, *Born to Struggle*, 36.

extreme, many women occasionally took a day off to have a lie in or a day out. Testimonies suggest that this became increasingly common from the mid-1940s, when rising labour demand and wages meant that losing a day's pay was not the catastrophe that Josie Castle has shown it could be for young workers in the interwar years.[97]

More young adult women were pieceworkers, who were less able to appropriate time in this manner. Many evolved negotiation strategies with employers, explored in some depth in chapter 6. However, by the early 1940s, Mass-Observation found that rising wages, combined with a lack of luxury commodities on which to spend higher earnings, reduced pieceworkers' incentive to maximize production in order to qualify for additional wage bonuses, which gave them greater control over their time in the workplace.[98] Pieceworkers and timeworkers were both able to use clandestine means to appropriate materials and express dissent from employers' demands. Petty theft was an option for both pieceworkers and time workers who wished to appropriate workplace materials for personal use and to compensate for low wages. Humphries has argued that much of this pilfering was caused by familial need, citing examples of young workers who took food or saleable goods from their employers.[99] Many women recall being searched on their way out of work. Meg Powell, a munitions worker in the 1940s, remembered that 'people would take little bits, something you could use at home . . . one time a woman was found with a clock up her jumper, that was a laugh'.[100] Mary Gregory also claimed that thefts from her factory—'we put stuff under the boiler suits to walk out with it'—were due to workers' need to supplement their low wages, although her interview also suggests that general resentment towards an authoritarian management was an important provocation.[101] Young women also seem to have used workplace theft to increase their own personal affluence and ability to engage in leisure consumption. Jephcott deplored the large number of girls who regarded ' "lifting" from their works . . . as perfectly legitimate', and cited one example of a young woman who responded 'in reference to some useful material unlawfully acquired, that since she was "skint" she had to take the stuff of course'.[102] As commercial leisure consumption became increasingly important to youthful femininity in the 1930s and 1940s, so the pressure and desire

97 Castle, 'Factory Work', 153–4.
98 M-OA: FR 1157, 'What Workers Really Earn' (March 1942), 5.
99 Humphries, *Hooligans*, 169–71.
100 IWM, 19717, interview with Meg Powell.
101 NWSA, LRO, 1999.0292, interview with Mary Gregory.
102 Jephcott, *Rising Twenty*, 128.

to indulge in it grew among young women. Their use of theft to do so indicates that even by the late 1940s young women's earnings were often insufficient to provide personal affluence, and demonstrates how the demands of the family economy fractured access to leisure. It is difficult to ascertain whether McKibbin's conclusion that petty criminality was 'intrinsic to factory culture' can be applied to women workers, but it certainly played a part in the working lives not only of industrial workers but also of shop assistants and to a lesser extent office employees.[103] For many workers, then, enduring work involved the reappropriation of time or materials, a pattern that suggests many resented the demands that paid work placed on them, and sought to create support and survival strategies that included an alternative, collective identity to the homogeneous 'employee'.

Conclusion

Examining young women's culture without reference to their paid employment forces an artificial separation between culture and production, which divests an integral part of young women's lives of any meaning. Youthful femininity was fundamentally shaped by the workplace as well as by the family and by commercial leisure developments. Women's importance as reproducers of labour power differentiated their relationship to the labour process from that of men. They were aware that they might experience sexual harassment in the workplace, and many valued the support networks offered by the large, same-sex peer groups that were a feature of larger households, factories, shops, and offices. As the size of workplaces grew, and as the use of a marriage bar diminished in the late 1930s and 1940s, the ways in which work socialized young women into class and gender relations changed. In particular, workmates became an increasingly important source of social education, and particularly of advice on courtship, sex, and marriage.

Yet although most young working class women ultimately hoped to retire from full-time paid work upon marriage, close scrutiny of their workplace behaviour offers little support for contemporaries' conviction that this shaped a detached indifference towards their work. Young women's lives were clearly affected by relations with workmates and employers, which structured a large proportion of their time and shaped their social

[103] R. McKibbin, *Classes and Cultures in England, 1918–1951* (Oxford: Oxford University Press, 1998), 140.

identity. Moreover, an element of dissent from employers' objectives was central to developing work culture among young women. Some women engaged in deliberate acts of theft or sabotage, although they were a minority. More common, and often overlooked by historians, were the ambivalent attitudes of the majority towards the workplace. For many, enduring their work was their main objective. Their methods of doing so nevertheless brought them into conflict with employers, and belie contemporary and historiographical representations of them as apathetic or passive. Many women clearly attempted to negotiate relationships with employers, often in subtle and covert ways. Women's accounts point up the complexities of deference, and the ways in which relationships with family members and workmates developed shared values among young workers. The ways in which the methods of dissent that such values could help to develop interacted with formal labour relations, and developed at times into militancy, are examined in the following chapter.

6

'Frivolous' Workers?: Trade Unionism and Militancy

Women have never been backward in strikes. They are, on the contrary, more often accused by their officials of being too forward, so that they 'down tools' for frivolous reasons and drag out the men after them. It is a fact that the courage and loyalty of unorganised women in supporting organised men have been amongst the principal factors in deciding the latter to organise them.[1]

So Barbara Drake, as Chair of a Labour Research Department Enquiry into women's trade unionism, concluded in 1920. It is a representation at odds with that presented in many subsequent historical accounts of women's labour organization, which have frequently assumed that women's low trade union membership signified a lack of interest in labour relations. Until the mid-1980s, Hamilton's assertion of 1941, that women's domestic responsibilities led to a lack of engagement with the workplace,[2] was widely accepted, being reflected in Lewenhak's work.[3] More recently, Boston and others have identified gender antagonism in trade unions' relations with women workers as an impediment to women's workplace organization and militancy.[4] This concentration on why many women did *not* participate in the labour movement has failed to interrogate contemporary representations of young women who initiated workplace

[1] B. Drake, *Women in Trade Unions*, 2nd edn. (London: Virago, 1984), 201.

[2] M. A. Hamilton, *Women at Work: A Brief Introduction to Trade Unionism for Women* (London: Routledge, 1941); D. Beddoe, *Back to Home and Duty: Women between the Wars* (London: Pandora, 1989), 147. This view still is accepted by a number of labour and social historians; see T. Griffiths, *The Lancashire Working-Classes c. 1880–1930* (Oxford: Clarendon Press, 2001), 62.

[3] S. Lewenhak, *Women and Trade Unions* (London: Ernest Benn, 1977), 177–270.

[4] S. Boston, *Women Workers and the Trade Unions*, 2nd edn. (London: Lawrence and Wishart, 1987), 10–11, 155–84; S. Bruley, 'Gender, Class and Party: The Communist Party and the Crisis in the Cotton Industry in England between the Two World Wars', *Women's History Review*, 2/1 (1993); S. O. Rose, 'Gender Antagonism and Class Conflict: Exclusionary Strategies of Male Trade Unionists in Nineteenth Century Britain', *Social History*, 13/2 (1988).

militancy as 'frivolous', inspired by short-term self-interest or hedonism, rather than by political commitment. The prevailing focus on women's lack of engagement with labour relations has also neglected to examine the wider workplace interests of young women. Most studies have focused on equal pay, which was central to many official industrial disputes, but was often a more important priority for older women, who were more affected by a gender disparity in wages than younger workers.

This chapter examines the relationship between young women's workplace culture, the labour movement, and workplace militancy. The first section analyses young women's relationship with trade unionism, arguing that they were dissuaded from joining because of important differences between their own economic and political interests and those of the trade union leadership. As Drake emphasized,

> women's movement [towards trade union organization] has closely followed, if it has not kept pace with, that of semiskilled and unskilled men . . . . [difficulties in organizing them] do not . . . refer primarily to sex, but to the fact that women mostly belong to a class of semi-qualified and badly-paid workers. No obstacles, moreover, are really insuperable, but these tend, on the contrary, to disappear spontaneously with changes in economic and social conditions.[5]

This poses a challenge to the widespread use of 'patriarchy' in conceptualizing women's treatment by the labour movement.[6] Many of those historians who use the term choose not to define it, but Walby, whose sociological studies have been widely quoted in this respect, defines patriarchy as 'a system of interrelated social structures through which men exploit women', and asserts that 'gender relations can only be understood if [patriarchy] and [capitalism] are analytically separated'.[7] This definition lends support to Rowbotham's warning that patriarchy 'implies a structure which is fixed, rather than the kaleidoscope of forms within which women and men have encountered one another.'[8] As a static and ahistorical concept, it divorces gender ideology from the material circumstances that produce and revise it, evading the constant and changing interaction of class, gender, and generational relations that shaped young

[5] Drake, *Trade Unions*, 198, 202.

[6] H. Benenson, 'Patriarchal Constraints on Women Workers' Mobilization: The Lancashire Female Cotton Operatives 1842–1919', *British Journal of Sociology*, 44/4 (1993), 613–33; S. Blackburn, 'Gender, Work and Labour History: A Response to Carol Morgan', *Women's History Review*, 10/1 (2001), 121–35; Rose, 'Gender Antagonism', 191–208; S. Walby, *Patriarchy at Work* (Cambridge: Cambridge University Press, 1986), 100–1.

[7] Walby, *Patriarchy*, 69.

[8] S. Rowbotham, *Dreams and Dilemmas* (London: Virago, 1983), 208–9.

women's employment experiences. As Humphries suggests, trade unions' reluctance to organize women workers cannot be solely attributed to gender discrimination; rather, it was shaped by employers' use of women as a source of low-paid, low-skilled labour, a trend that also affected young workers of both sexes as chapter 1 of this study highlighted. Blocking the entry of women and young people to certain occupations could help to maintain their skilled status, preserve their wage rates, and thus protect the family economy.[9]

Nevertheless, this cannot be applied as a universal and exclusive explanation. Although this study does not view patriarchy as a social structure, it does pay attention to patriarchal attitudes and relationships where they arise in specific historical contexts. Humphries underestimates the part that defending male privilege also played in developing trade union strategies. As earlier chapters of this book have pointed out, breadwinning brought personal rewards in terms of financial independence and status in the family. For these reasons, close scrutiny of the historical context in which labour relations evolved is required. This chapter follows the approach pioneered by Bornat, investigating the influence of kinship and localized employment patterns upon young women's trade unionism,[10] as well as the changing relationship between the trade union movement, state, and employers.

The second section of the chapter examines young women's workplace militancy, defined as overt, collective contestations of control over the production process or profit margin. It demonstrates that low union membership does not necessarily signify a lack of collective consciousness or strength. Those methods of surviving and sometimes resisting employers' demands outlined in chapter 5 could be drawn upon when a catalyst for militant action appeared. The important shifts in occupational distribution traced in earlier chapters, from domestic service to factory and office work, were accompanied by the expansion of mass production methods, and by a transition from paternalistic to scientific management techniques. Young women's experiences of these changes offer an insight into how the large numbers of unskilled and semiskilled workers overlooked by most existing studies of these developments reacted to them and, in turn, influenced their course.

[9] J. Humphries, 'Class Struggle and the Persistence of the Working Class Family', *Cambridge Journal of Economics*, 1/3 (1977), 241–58.

[10] J. Bornat, 'Home and Work; a New Context for Trade Union History', *Oral History*, 5/2 (1977). See also M. Van Der Linden, 'Connecting Household History and Labour History', *International Review of Social History*, 38/1/supplement (1993), 163–73.

The examples offered here support Whitston's assertion that the militant actions of the rank and file workforce were often opposed to the reformist objectives of trade union leaders.[11] As Rose suggests, 'It is important to recognise that those who were marginal to . . . organizations and movements may actually have been central to the dynamics of labor's history.'[12] It is argued here that young women's expanding employment and earning opportunities, the extension of the franchise in 1928, and the discourse of the People's War increased both young women workers' awareness of their unequal political and social status at work and in wider society, and their recognition that they could wield political influence in the workplace. Moreover, although their marital aspirations and consequent expectations of a short working life offer a partial explanation for their low levels of trade unionism, these factors also led them to be more critical of aspects of the labour process, and less concerned to compromise with employers, than were many of those men who expected a far longer working life.

The Workers United? Trade Unions and Women's Representation

Women's trade union participation followed a similar course to men's between 1918 and 1943, but was consistently far lower, and declined in the latter half of the 1940s. However, both male and female union density varied significantly between sectors. In the shipbuilding, metal, and electrical industries, which employed relatively few women but many skilled men, male union density outstripped women's throughout the period, although the density of women as well as men increased dramatically during the Second World War: male density increased from 39 to 48 per cent in 1943, while women's increased from 2 to 11 per cent, a proportionately similar rise. Union density among female workers in the textile industry, a major employer of women in skilled as well as unskilled occupations, was similar to men's and was above 50 per cent throughout the period. In those growth industries heavily reliant upon unskilled and semiskilled workers, such as food and drink manufacture, and in the distributive trades, female and male union density remained comparatively low: in retail, union density never rose above 16 per cent for either women or

[11] K. Whitston, 'Worker Resistance and Taylorism in Britain', *International Review of Social History*, 42/1 (1997), 1–24.

[12] S. O. Rose, 'Gender and Labor History. The Nineteenth-Century legacy', *International Review of Social History*, 38/1/supplement (1993), 161.

men, while in the food, drink, and tobacco industries it peaked in 1948 at 6 per cent for women and 12 per cent for men.[13]

These gendered and sectoral distinctions point to four factors: the different approaches taken by craft and general unions towards women and young workers; the status of trade unionism in particular sectors; the relative proportions of skilled, semiskilled, and unskilled workers in different sectors; and changes in women's employment patterns. Craft unions were concerned to ensure that their skills remained the preserve of only a relatively small group of workers, in order to protect their bargaining rights with employers. Consequently, the Amalgamated Engineering Union (AEU) only admitted women in 1942, by which time they were employed in a large number of skilled engineering jobs. Between the 1920s and the 1950s general unions such as the Transport and General Workers' Union (TGWU) increased in importance concurrently with the expansion in semiskilled and unskilled work. Their bargaining power relied upon representing the largest possible proportion of their constituency, and they were consequently more concerned to recruit women and junior workers.

This contradicts the prevailing emphasis given to gender conflict in the existing historiography of the trade union movement. Historians are divided over the reasons for women's exclusion from trade unions. Some have argued that it represented a conservative attempt to preserve male jobs against the threat of cheap female or juvenile labour, fuelled by a patriarchal gender ideology.[14] Yet although Griffiths and Bruley have pointed to male opposition to female unionization in some textile districts of Lancashire,[15] about two-thirds of the membership of the Northern Counties Amalgamated Association of Cotton Weavers were women, mainly drawn from areas where women worked alongside men as weavers or dominated the weaving sections. In consequence, the union's pay claims were not differentiated by sex.[16] This supports Humphries's claim that the trade union movement's objectives in this period should be viewed through the prism of the working class family economy; the fight to retain a family wage, by preserving the monetary value attributed to skilled men's work, recognized the importance of men as breadwinners

[13] Membership figures taken from S. Lewenhak, 'Trade Union Membership among Women and Girls in the United Kingdom, 1920–1965', Ph.D. thesis (London, 1972), 32, 45. Density data taken from G. S. Bain and R. Price, *Profiles of Union Growth: A Comparative Statistical Portrait of Eight Countries* (Oxford: Blackwell, 1980), 37.

[14] Benenson, 'Patriarchal Constraints'; Blackburn, 'Gender'.

[15] Griffiths, *The Lancashire Working-Classes*, 62; Bruley, 'Gender, Class and Party'.

[16] Drake, *Trade Unions*, 119; Bruley, 'Gender, Class and Party'.

and women's domestic responsibilities.[17] Where the 'family wage' had little relevance, as in districts of Lancashire, trade union strategies differed. Craft unions' hostility to the organization of women workers on equal terms was thus the product of specific material circumstance rather than of a universal gender ideology. Gendered and generational antagonism certainly fuelled, and was in turn exacerbated by, such strategies but they were not the sole cause of craft unions' blinkered conservative exclusiveness, as the unions' opposition to the admittance of unskilled and semiskilled *men* prior to the Second World War demonstrates.[18]

Although age-disaggregated trade union membership figures are not available, the general trend highlights the importance of non-gendered factors in trade union recruitment and retention. The strength of trade unions and the related issue of the balance between labour demand and supply were crucial here. Women's trade union membership rose from 437,000 in 1914 to 1,342,000 in 1920, a rise of 207 per cent, and an increase in density from 9 to 25 per cent. Over the same period, male membership more than doubled from 3,708,000 to 7,006,000, and density rose from 32 to 58 per cent. This testifies to the importance of the war in mobilizing semiskilled and unskilled workers of both sexes as unions began to recognize the importance of this growing section of the workforce.

Trade unionism fell substantially between 1920 and 1933, largely because of unemployment. Also significant was the failure of the 1926 General Strike, and the TUC's subsequent strategy to secure a role in governance, an approach that was frequently less than receptive to active rank and file political participation. By 1933 membership stood at 3,661,000 men and 731,000 women, a proportionately very similar—and very significant—decline of over 50 per cent for both sexes since 1920. An increase in labour demand explained an increase in trade union membership from the mid-1930s, a trend markedly accelerated by the Second World War. In 1939 1,010,000 women were trade unionists, with female union density recorded at 16 per cent; the comparable male figures stood at 5,288,000 (39 per cent). By 1943, 1,716,000 women (27 per cent) and 6,151,000 men (45 per cent) were represented by the TUC. The increase in women's union density signified growth in labour demand; their movement into heavily unionized sectors, such as engineering; unions' growing realization

[17] Humphries, 'Class Struggle', 241–58.

[18] A. Davies, *Leisure, Gender and Poverty: Working Class Cultures in Salford and Manchester, 1900–1939* (Buckingham: Open University Press, 1992), 30–1; E. J. Hobsbawm, 'The Aristocracy of Labour Reconsidered', in id. (ed.), *Worlds of Labour: Further Studies in the History of Labour* (London: Weidenfeld and Nicolson, 1984), 238–9.

of the importance of recruiting unskilled and semiskilled workers; and the support for trade unionism given by Ernest Bevin, the former General Secretary of the TGWU who was appointed Minister of Labour in 1940.[19]

While women clearly became more significant in the trade union movement during the first years of the Second World War, 1943 represented a peak in their union membership and density. In the mid- and later 1940s their membership declined, although, importantly, not to pre-war levels. In 1951 female density still stood at 25 per cent, but by this stage male density had reached 56 per cent. This reflected the long-standing sexual division of labour; the growing importance of the unions in those heavy industries where many male manual workers were employed, some of which were nationalized in the late 1940s; and a decline in women's employment in strongly unionized sectors like engineering and textiles.

These general factors partially explain the pattern of women's trade union membership, but also of importance was trade unions' changing approach to young, female workers. As full-time junior workers experiencing relatively slight gender disparity in earnings, these women were unlikely to be strongly affected by the sexual division of labour or their union's attitude to equal pay or part-time workers. The TUC's treatment of young women was characterized by a patriarchal attitude towards workers considered too young for full political participation. This was, however, gradually challenged both by an awareness that these women were an increasingly important group of workers, and by an anxiety that left to their own devices, they had the potential to act in a militant fashion that could endanger the trade union leadership's attempts to carve out a central role in national governance.

In the 1920s, trade unions did not appear particularly inviting to young women. Historians have pointed to neglect of women's issues following the demise of the Women's Trade Union League (WTUL) and the National Federation of Women Workers (NFWW) following the First World War, and the neglect of issues like equal pay and the rights of part-time married workers, issues of increasing interest to women by the 1940s.[20] This should not be overstated, however. The increase in mixed unions following the First World War was supported by many female trade unionists and represented a recognition of common interests with

[19] On Bevin see H. A. Clegg, *A History of British Trade Unions since 1889*, 3 (Oxford: Oxford University Press, 1994), 257–8; H. K. Middlemas, *Politics in Industrial Society* (London: Andre Deutsch, 1979), 261–4.

[20] Lewenhak, *Women and Trade Unions*, 258–9; Boston, *Women Workers*, 211.

male unskilled and semiskilled workers in the post-war era.[21] Moreover, female representation did not disappear entirely: the Workers' Union, for example, employed Julia Varley, formerly of the NFWW, as its chief women's organizer throughout the 1920s.[22]

Of greater significance was the treatment of young women at grassroots level. In those few skilled unions to which women and young workers were admitted, they often paid only a proportion of the adult male trade union subscription rate, a practice that recognized their low earnings but also confined them to sections with fewer benefits and limited access to union office.[23] Even in areas where adult women's trade union participation was relatively high, as in cotton unions, entry was often blocked until employees graduated to skilled work in their late teens,[24] or was restricted to (generally male) apprentices.[25]

Patriarchal relations fuelled the approach of trade union leaders, but these were based on age- as well as gender-specific roles. In 1928 the TUC's annual Congress condemned the use of juveniles as cheap labour, but viewed the solution as lying not with the organization of young workers, but with parents, who were urged

> not to subsidise unfair employers . . . but to see that the wages paid are commensurate with the duties and responsibilities placed upon their children. . . . They should also assure themselves that the working hours are not such as to interfere with the physical and mental development of their children.[26]

Although the TUC urged trades councils to establish youth sections in the late 1920s, these were meant to have an educative rather than a politically active role.[27] Individual unions concurred with this: Mary Abbott, a Lancashire textile worker, met hostility in her local union branch when she and her young workmates requested their local union committee to raise the question of holidays with pay at the union's national conference in 1935. When she subsequently defied the local officials by sending a telegram to the national executive detailing their request, the secretary of the local committee summoned her: ' "That's not right," he says "they'll

[21] S. Alexander, 'The Women's Trade Union League: 1874–1921', in ead. (ed.), *Becoming a Woman and Other Essays in 19th and 20th Century Feminist History* (London: Virago, 1994).

[22] Boston, *Women Workers*, 132–54.

[23] Drake, *Trade Unions*, 210–11.

[24] Bornat, 'Home and Work', 93.

[25] Transport and General Workers' Union (TGWU), *Minutes and Record of the Biennial Delegate Conference of 1939* (London: TGWU, 1939), 34.

[26] Modern Records Centre, University of Warwick (MRC), TUC Archive, MSS 292/132/1, TUCGC, 'Memorandum to Trades Councils', 6 June 1928.

[27] MRC, TUC Archive, MSS 292/6/1, TUCGC, 'Memorandum to the Annual Conference of Trades Councils', 1929.

think we've got a lot of militants in this area now." And er I said "Well," I said, "we could probably do with some." ' Her determination was fuelled by the support of her father, an active trade unionist.[28] Young workers were frequently treated, by trade unions as well as by employers, as subordinate dependants. This approach neglected young women's own grievances and their instrumental role in the family economy.

An awareness that young women were a distinctive group of workers and citizens emerged as a result of their increased prominence as factory, shop, and office workers, and of the campaign leading up to their enfranchisement in 1928. Targeted recruitment drives occurred sporadically from the late 1920s. These embodied a recognition of young women's interest in social as well as political events, while simultaneously using this as evidence that they were inherently disinterested in trade unionism. One delegate from the National Union of Distributive and Allied Workers (NUDAW) at the 1925 TUC women's conference, for example, supported the provision of social and educational activities, because ' "The great majority of women employed in industry were between 16 and 25 years of age and it was much more difficult to deal with them than it was to deal with adult men" '.[29] This emphasis on social and educational activities continued throughout the 1930s and 1940s.

The increasing employment of young women as semiskilled industrial workers in light manufacturing encouraged general unions to target them in the 1930s. Under Bevin's leadership, the TGWU recognized that young women represented a significant proportion of the unskilled and semiskilled industrial workforce it was attempting to represent. A women's page appeared in the union's magazine and publicity was given to the recruitment campaigns launched by and on behalf of women. It expanded the range of union activities, believing that 'enthusiasm for dancing, cycling, rambling, football, gymnastics, and other organised sports and pastimes can usefully be diverted into trade union channels.'[30] Although this recognized the inaccessibility of union bureaucracy to many young women, it also suggested that they were not viewed as potentially active participants in the more political aspects of trade unionism. Nevertheless, by 1939 the TGWU and the General and Municipal Workers' Union (GMWU) were the two largest unions and continued to dominate in the following decade. They represented a growing number of women,

[28] Tameside Local Studies Library (TLSL), Manchester Studies Collection (MSC), tape 671, interview with Mary Abbott.

[29] Quoted in TUC Women's Conference, *Annual Report for 1925* (London: TUC, 1926), 6.

[30] TGWU, *Delegate Conference*, 7–9.

whose opportunities for employment in light engineering and munitions manufacture increased with rearmament in the late 1930s and still further in the 1940s.[31]

Despite the general unions' strategies, the central concern of the TUC remained skilled, adult men. The recruitment of young women was initially inspired by a fear that these older, male workers might be replaced with cheaper, unskilled or semiskilled labour in the depressed late 1920s and early 1930s. In 1932 London Trades Council expressed anxiety that 'The progress of science is evolving machines which can be handled by female labour in their teens. . . . this raises a problem of tremendous import to male workers.'[32] The implication was that women workers would threaten male livelihoods and impair the progress of trade unionism. This continued to shape the craft unions' perspectives into the 1940s. While skilled unions like the AEU began to open their doors to women as they lost large numbers of their male members to the Forces, attitudes to these female members remained ambivalent. Edith Hough felt that at the wartime factory where she worked, 'most of the men . . . thought they were superior to the women' because of their skilled status. Yet, as she pointed out, male attitudes were important in shaping women's own attitudes to their work and to trade unionism: 'A lot of women, unfortunately, didn't think about trade unions or what have you. I think they were brainwashed generally by men. Because a lot of women could only see themselves as—girls saw themselves as married women and nothing else.'[33]

This focus on skilled men, and the relatively short working lives of most women, led the TUC and many individual unions to emphasize in their recruitment campaigns the benefits that membership might bring for the rest of the family. In the early 1930s one recruitment leaflet argued that 'If you are a member of a Union you are assisting to maintain and improve the standard of life for all workers—men and women—including the man you hope to marry, whose wages will determine YOUR standard of comfort.'[34] Paradoxically, the TUC's attempt to include women and young workers in the trade union movement was built upon the assumption that their gender- and age-specific interests were irreconcilable with active participation. In negating their importance as workers, such propaganda undermined the very argument for young women's union membership it sought to promote. Yet simultaneously, it presented

[31] R. Croucher, *Engineers at War* (London: Merlin Press, 1982), 24–8.

[32] London Trades Council, *Annual Report for the Year 1932* (London: London Trades Council, 1933), 9.

[33] LRO, NWSA, 1992.0062, interview with Edith Hough.

[34] TUC, *Many a Miss Mrs Marriage*, pamphlet (London: TUC, 1931), 2.

women's activism as potentially a selfless crusade for social justice. This discourse was appropriated by many young women to articulate and rationalize their own activism both within and outside the organized labour movement, as the second section of this chapter will show.

Localized political traditions were also important. Bornat has pointed out the importance of kinship networks in recruiting young women into trade unions in those areas where they entered the same trades as their parents. This was particularly strong in the Lancashire cotton industry, where one union barred men from serving in union office unless their working wives and daughters were also members.[35] In areas characterized by a strong sexual division of labour, Savage has demonstrated that regular contact between junior and more senior workers could also facilitate trade union recruitment. This tended not to occur in many of the growing, light manufacturing industries, where unskilled and semiskilled workers, particularly women, were segregated from the skilled workforce.[36] Women were also more likely to join trade unions in areas where they would continue working after marriage, recognizing it as a beneficial investment.[37] Union density thus continued to be high in textile communities, but lower in light manufacture, which was concentrated in regions where women tended to give up full-time work upon marriage. Trade union hierarchies and protective strategies, changes in the division of labour, and employers' hostility to union organization thus coalesced to obstruct the recruitment of young women.

Outside the industrial sector very few women were unionized. The slight increase in retail membership over the period was concentrated in larger firms, particularly in the Co-op, whose employees were 100 per cent unionized. Domestic servants and clerks were more difficult to organize. The paternalistic relations and isolation from other workers that characterized domestic service hampered organization, and the TUC's efforts in this sector were weak and sporadic. TUC support for young unemployed women's transference into domestic service from the early 1920s[38] demonstrated a failure on the part of a movement dominated by skilled unions to recognize that semiskilled and unskilled industrial and retail work offered status and benefits unknown to domestic servants. Although trade unionism was higher in the clerical sector, it remained relatively

[35] Bornat, 'Home and Work'; see also Drake, *Trade Unions*, 119.

[36] M. Savage, *The Dynamics of Working Class Politics. The Labour Movement in Preston, 1880–1940* (Cambridge: Cambridge University Press, 1987), 43–4.

[37] Ibid., 54.

[38] MRC, TUC Archive, MSS 292/132/1, Letter from the Secretary of the TUC General Council (TUCGC), to International Federation of Trade Unions, 1928.

low: 24 per cent in 1921, when density stood at 40 per cent in the manual trades, and 31 per cent in 1950 when manual density was 49 per cent.[39] The Trade Disputes Act of 1927, passed in response to the General Strike of the previous year, hindered alliances between industrial and clerical unions by prohibiting public service unions such as the National Association of Local Government Officers (NALGO) from joining the TUC. In addition, many small, private firms were able to prevent unionization as clerical labour supply outstripped demand throughout the interwar years. Also important was clerks' social background; many were drawn from families that lacked either employment experience in the clerical sector or a tradition of trade unionism.

The position of young women in the trade union movement remained paradoxical between the end of the First World War and the early 1950s. Their union membership increased, and as a constituency they gained political significance, both because of their enfranchisement in 1928 and because of the increasing importance of unskilled and semiskilled workers for trade unions. Despite this, women remained under-represented at senior level, and many of their specific interests were clearly neglected. This has led Lewenhak to argue that in many unions, by the outbreak of the Second World War, women and girls constituted 'an apathetic, silent majority, acquiescing in the men's monopoly of policy-making.'[40] However, this representation is at odds with the militancy hinted at by Barbara Drake. The remainder of this chapter argues that in fact young women's workplace militancy was widespread between the 1920s and the 1950s, but took place largely outside the control of trade union leaders.

Workplace Militancy

There were relatively few industrial disputes between 1918 and 1950. The number of official strikes fell from 1,607 in 1920 to a low of 302 in 1928, after which a slow and stumbling rise began, to peak once more in 1937 at 1,129 strikes.[41] During the Second World War the number of official strikes was small, in part because of employers' willingness to settle wage disputes with unions and due to Government Order 1305, introduced

[39] G. S. Bain and R. Price, *Profiles of Union Growth: A Comparative Statistical Portrait of Eight Countries* (Oxford: Oxford University Press, 1980), 41, Table 2.3.

[40] Lewenhak, *Women and Trade Unions*, 210.

[41] Department of Employment, *British Labour Statistics: Historical Abstract 1886–1968* (London: HMSO, 1971), 396, Table 197.

in 1940, which made strikes illegal and remained in force until 1951.[42] However, as Rose points out, a large number of brief walkouts and illegal, unofficial disputes did occur and merit investigation, not least because striking, particularly when made illegal, was a last resort for workers and could signify widespread discontent.[43] The available data do not allow a quantitative assessment of young women's involvement in these. Nevertheless, a study of their participation, available through the brief snapshots offered by trade unions' records and those of employers, press reports, and personal testimonies, is possible and worthwhile.

Existing studies of women's involvement in strikes over these years have been largely confined to examinations of equal pay disputes during the Second World War. This has helped to create a historiographical consensus that gender fractured workplace interests, with Lewenhak claiming that many unofficial strikes occurred 'in defiance of men union officials'.[44] Certainly, equal pay was an important issue for many war workers, as Summerfield and Rose have highlighted.[45] However, this prevailing focus overlooks other grievances expressed by young women workers, who, although participatants in equal pay disputes, were not usually among the main protagonists. It also ignores those disputes that highlight a level of shared interest between female and male workers, and which illuminate tensions between the shop floor and union officials that could be at least as divisive as gender. This emphasizes the importance of examining labour relations 'from below' as well as by assessing the inclusiveness of the trade union bureaucracy.

Two types of dispute are examined here, through case studies of three strikes: the unofficial strike at the Rego clothing firm in East London in 1928 over the introduction of the conveyor belt system; the official strike at the Wolsey hosiery company in Leicester between 1931 and 1932, caused by the introduction of time-study management; and the illegal walkout at the Bath Co-operative Society in 1941 over juniors' pay rates. These have been chosen to illustrate the ability of unskilled and semiskilled young workers to engage in militancy and their reasons for doing so.

The first two disputes were, like many strikes between the 1920s and the 1940s, responses to the introduction of scientific production management

[42] R. McKibbin, *Classes and Cultures in England 1918–51* (Oxford: Oxford University Press, 1998), 145.

[43] S. Rose, *Which People's War?: National Identity and Citizenship in Britain 1939–1945* (Oxford: Oxford University Press, 2003), 69.

[44] Lewenhak, *Women and Trade Unions*, 240.

[45] P. Summerfield, *Reconstructing Women's Wartime Lives* (Manchester: Manchester University Press, 1998), 71–4; Rose, *Which People's War*, 106–8.

techniques. Production rationalization was not new to the interwar years but it was in this period that Taylorism gained popularity among employers across a range of sectors.[46] This strategy aimed to increase productivity and cut production costs by fragmenting work tasks into simplified processes that could be undertaken by cheap, unskilled workers.

Two rationalization strategies associated with Taylorism are of particular relevance to the present discussion. One was flow line organization. This frequently used the conveyor belt pioneered by Ford, and was based on the principle of subdividing tasks and minimizing skill requirements. It was this that incited the Rego dispute. The second was the time-study system, which was responsible for the Wolsey strike. The Bedaux firm's name had become synonymous with time-study by the early 1930s. Bedaux engineers were hired by firms to 'scientifically' streamline production and assess the time it should take a worker to undertake a particular task. The main aim was to increase labour productivity without raising wages. These two strategies were often used in combination. Such rationalization techniques frequently affected the working patterns of semiskilled and unskilled workers, particularly in the vehicle, food, drink and tobacco, light metal, and clothing industries.[47]

The Bath dispute has been chosen as an example of an unofficial, illegal wartime dispute over pay rates, the focus of almost half of all wartime strikes.[48] Unlike the disputes highlighted by existing studies, this was not concerned with equal pay for women, but with the maintenance of wartime bonuses for young adult women employed as shop and clerical workers, and with preventing the firm's simultaneous attempt to cut costs by employing more juvenile workers. The dispute highlights the threat that cheap, juvenile labour posed to young adult women in various sectors of the labour market. Whereas historians have frequently considered the threat that women's labour posed to men's, chapter 1 made clear that competition for jobs was more likely to occur between young adult women and cheaper juvenile girls than between the sexes. The dispute was also an attempt by semiskilled workers to consolidate wartime gains in their pay and conditions, a trend traced by Croucher and Clegg.[49] Many industrial workers' grievances over the introduction of Bedaux were connected to anxieties over the rate of pay such work offered. Thus a dispute

[46] There is more discussion of this in C. R. Littler, *The Development of the Labour Process in Capitalist Societies* (London: Heinemann, 1982), 99–117.

[47] Ibid., 114, 118–21.

[48] M. Davis, 'The Labour Movement and World War Two', TUC History Online, http://www.unionhistory.info/timeline/1939_1945.php (19 April 2004).

[49] Clegg, *British Trade Unions*, 3, 201; Croucher, *Engineers*, 290–5, 367.

involving women workers at Guest, Keen, and Nettlefolds' Smethwick works in 1942, which Summerfield has claimed was an equal pay dispute, was in fact partially prompted by the women workers' dissatisfaction at their rates of pay compared with those offered by aircraft work, and the detrimental effect that they believed the introduction of Bedaux would have on their pay rates, despite their union's acceptance of its imposition.[50] Strikes such as that at Bath strongly suggest that the battle for equal pay fought by women war workers was part of a wider struggle to improve and consolidate unskilled and semiskilled pay rates.

It is not claimed that these disputes reflect the entire spectrum of young women's workplace militancy, but this microstudy approach does enable an assessment of how gender and age influenced attitudes to workplace, trade unionism, and wider labour relations. It also demonstrates the importance of localized employment patterns and political traditions. The contrasting labour markets focused upon here help to explain differences in workers' grievances and the ways they sought to address these, and the varying outcomes of disputes.

Rego's young workers were drawn from Jewish households in the East End of London, a community characterized by adult women's employment and a high degree of trade unionism and political activism. The firm itself had some history of trade unionism, and the dispute there was partially provoked by the firm's refusal to institute a closed shop.

Many of the Wolsey strikers, by contrast, came from rural Leicestershire, an area characterized by a sexual division of labour stronger than that of East London. They were drawn from skilled working class households that had less need of supplementary earnings than the Rego workers' families. They worked in a sector characterized by close relations between employers and trade union officials, but the East Midlands textile firms lacked the strong history of women's active participation in trade unionism that many of the Lancashire textile towns possessed.

The Bath strikers differed again. They were shop and office workers, from predominantly skilled working class homes. Many of these relied heavily on daughters' wages during wartime, but these workers were also able to retain a large portion of their earnings for their personal expenditure because of wartime bonuses. They worked at the Co-op, which had strong trade union relations, and were members of the National Union of Distributive and Allied Workers (NUDAW) prior to the strike. All of the disputes occurred at firms that introduced changes in pay or production

[50] The National Archives (TNA), LAB 76/29, E. C. Bailey, unpublished MS: 'Strikes and Lockouts. Accounts of Individual Lockouts', 1946, 53–6.

processes to an established workforce, a factor that will be shown to have been important in explaining the young workers' militant response. The fact that young women from diverse backgrounds engaged in workplace militancy indicates that no one model can explain their actions, although these differences will be shown to have significantly affected their responses, their relationship with trade unions, and the outcomes of the disputes.

The introduction of flow line organization and the limited response of the Tailors' and Garment Workers' Union (hereafter Tailors' Union) to this provide the background for the Rego strike of 1928. The Rego firm's Edmonton factory paid a low average wage, a cause of dissatisfaction among the young women who constituted the majority of the factory's six-hundred-strong workforce, many of whom were important breadwinners in London East End Jewish households. This led many of the young women working at the firm to join the Tailors' Union in 1927 and 1928. Dissatisfaction was heightened among the skilled and semiskilled pieceworkers when trouser production was rationalized, through the introduction of the conveyor belt system, thus reducing the number of women pieceworkers employed to make one pair from three to one. After a stay-in strike in the trouser section on 11 September, a London official of the Tailors' Union, Sam Elsbury, negotiated a small increase in piece rates. Many more young Rego workers consequently joined the union and 500 were members by the beginning of October. However, the firm's management made it clear that this increase was to be temporary and hinted that future recognition of the Tailors' Union was also in doubt. The catalyst for a strike came when a female worker refused to pay her union dues and union members consequently refused to work with her. A strike was called for 8 October, primarily to force Rego management to accept a closed shop, but, as a meeting on 2 October made clear, with the combined aims of resisting rationalization and contesting the firm's definition of a fair day's pay. Relations between the London branches of the Tailors' Union and the Union's Headquarters were already undermined by resentment at the Headquarters' distant Leeds location, particularly since clothing workers in London had faced rationalization attempts throughout the 1920s. The unofficial dispute, which began on 8 October, lasted until 21 December when the firm agreed to recognize the Tailors' Union and to reinstate the strikers.[51] Rationalization was not prevented, but the long-term consequence of the strike was the formation of a breakaway union, the United Clothing Workers' Union (UCWU), established

[51] S. Elsbury and D. Cohen, *The Rego Revolt: How the United Clothing Workers' Trade Union was Formed* (London: Dorrit Press, 1929).

in 1930 by several of the London officials of the Tailors' Union, actively supported by the Rego workers, and, unlike the Tailors' Union, vehemently opposed to rationalization.[52]

The collapse of the UCWU in 1935 demonstrated the weaknesses of localized unions reliant on a small section of a specific trade and thus a narrow membership base. Yet the Rego dispute should not be viewed as one of abject failure for the workers. Many London workers actively supported the strike, and local residents contributed generously to financial appeals for the strikers, who were without strike pay.[53] For the workers themselves, the strike forced some modifications in the extent of rationalization and strengthened union recognition at Rego. The establishment of a union concerned with control over the labour process rather than primarily with wage bargaining at national level, brought rationalization to the forefront of the TUC's agenda, but the UCWU's relatively swift demise demonstrated the inability of one small union to radically revise the agenda of industrial relations.

The dispute at Wolsey had a different outcome. The Wolsey Company was a major employer of young women in Leicester. Its attempts to introduce the Bedaux system to some of its eight factories, between September 1930 and December 1931, were met with hostility by many workers, expressed through short stoppages and go slow practices. When Wolsey imposed Bedaux at their Coalville factory, 340 young women workers at the factory struck on 7 December 1931, earning themselves the disapproving title of 'Boisterous Workers' from the local press. This was a spontaneous walkout on which the Leicester Hosiery Union (LHU), recognized by Wolsey, was not consulted. It was not until 10 December, 3 days after the Coalville walkout, that the LHU formally agreed to support the dispute, the Union's secretary, Horace Moulden, admitting that, ' "as a result of the dispute at Coalville over the introduction of the Bedaux system, the Union has been compelled to face up to the issue of whether or not it is prepared to accept the principle of Bedaux as a wage-payment scheme." '[54] By 15 December the strike had spread to other Wolsey workers, although some skilled male workers opposed it. The LHU's support led many workers to join the union, and they eventually reluctantly returned to work on 11 February 1932, when negotiations between the LHU and management concluded in a settlement that resulted in a modified

[52] A history of the United Clothing Workers' Union is given in S. W. Lerner, *Breakaway Unions and the Small Trade Union* (London: Ruskin House, 1961), 85–143.

[53] Ibid., 108.

[54] Quoted in *Leicester Evening Mail* (10 December 1931).

time-study system.[55] The Wolsey dispute demonstrated that young women were often willing to join trade unions, but that their aims as well as their preferred means were frequently at odds with those of the trade union leadership, because of their unskilled and semiskilled status.

The Bath strikers were primarily concerned with rates of pay. In 1940 the Bath Co-operative Society had increased young women's wages to attract female labour, but in December 1941 it was decided to reduce this bonus for all young women except those aged 14 and 15, in order to cut costs and simultaneously attract very young, cheap workers. On December 6 a 'sit down strike' resulted among the Society's young female office workers, aged between 16 and 19, following the managing secretary's refusal to discuss the withdrawal of the bonus with these women. The young women informed NUDAW, and the union organized a meeting for junior employees on 11 December. Concurrently, the increase in bonuses to very young juniors prompted branch managers to press for a rise in their own wages. The management's refusal to discuss either this or the grievances of the young women resulted in a meeting, called by the workers, but clearly countenanced by the local NUDAW official, on 22 December, which voted to undertake an illegal strike on the following day. The proximity to Christmas and the importance of the Co-operative Society, as sole provider of food rations to many local consumers, ensured national as well as local publicity for the stoppage, which took place on 23 December and caused the Co-op shop to close. This resulted in management capitulating to the workers' demands on the same day.[56]

Despite the differences between these disputes, contemporary trade unionists', employers', and press accounts ascribed all of them to young women's political naïveté and a frivolity born of short working lives. Employers frequently blamed trade union leaders for the strikes; at Wolsey, where relations between management and the LHU had been excellent prior to the dispute, the firm's managing director contended that 'our girls are apt to get excited and it is very easy for the Union by the attitude they adopt to get them more excited and out of control',[57] although it is clear that the LHU only became involved in the dispute days after the workers walked out. Similarly in Bath, management blamed

55 Leicestershire Records Office (Leics RO), DE 4823, Internal Wolsey management report on meeting of workers and the trade union, 8 February 1932.

56 TNA, LAB 10/164, W. Hamilton Whyte, MS: 'Report of Enquiry into the Bath Co-operative Society Strike', 1942.

57 Leics RO, DE 4823, unpublished MS: 'Notes of Meeting Called by Conciliation Officer between Directors of Wolsey Ltd and Officials of LHU', 18 December, 13.

NUDAW's divisional officer, but a government inquiry into the dispute found that the junior workers who instigated the strike would have gone ahead regardless of the union's opinion.[58]

Union leaders themselves tended to blame the Communist Party (CP) for young women's alleged uncharacteristic militancy.[59] The CP was happy to take the credit, but in none of these cases was its involvement decisive. Although CP members were involved in the Rego dispute, there is little evidence that they were entirely responsible for it. Moreover, when the UCWU was subjected to overt CP control in the mid-1930s, most of the Rego workers returned to the Tailors' Union in protest.[60] There is no evidence of Communist influence in the other disputes. Mabel Morrison, a munitions worker during the Second World War, summed up the views of many working women on the CP's attempts to infiltrate workplaces. She was in her early twenties at the time, and a member of the TGWU, but she did not view herself as particularly politically active, having joined the union 'because you all did then', and she held no union position. Nevertheless, she was instrumental in organizing one of a number of brief walkouts by the women at her Manchester factory to demand higher pay:

> and we'd just got outside the gate and . . . there was this woman jumped on we had kind of a platform thing . . . and this woman came from nowhere and she was a Communist. And we said get off the bloody platform we've got nowt to do with you. . . . Russia wasn't in the war then. . . . The Communists did try and wheedle their way into the unions. We wouldn't have 'em. . . . You don't need someone coming from outside telling you to work faster when, er, a few weeks beforehand they were trying to er nobble the war effort.[61]

Other women recalled CP influence more positively. Edith Hough, a Labour Party member, recalled that at her factory, full employment in the Second World War enabled union organization. She attributed the success of unionization largely to 'some of the older people, members of the trade union', one of whom was active in the CP. Nevertheless, it was she and her young workmates, none of whom were CP members, who pushed for militancy in order to achieve a forty-hour week. In Edith's view it 'was the younger element who hoped that there was something to be gained and you hoped for better conditions, everything was going to be better after the war and you believed that you were fighting for that

[58] TNA, LAB 10/164, 'Bath Co-operative Society Strike', 5–6.

[59] See, for example, *Tailor and Garment Worker* (January 1929) on the Rego dispute; and Leics RO, DE 4823, internal management report on LHU meeting with Wolsey workers, 25 January 1931.

[60] Lerner, *Breakaway Unions*, 136, 140.

[61] LRO, NWSA, 1992.0103, interview with Mabel Morrison.

sort of thing.'[62] Young women were, then, frequently more politically astute than either their employers or union officials gave them credit for.

In fact, the disputes in which young women were involved clearly drew upon the workplace culture that the preceding chapter showed they themselves evolved. Women's workplace networks could be turned to political purposes. In the early 1920s, Olive Jones was pressurized not to work overtime for non-union rates—termed 'knobsticking', also the local name for strike-breaking—by other workers, who would gather outside the mill, shouting 'come out, stop knobsticking!'[63] Young women strikers recalled the importance of gossip and song in increasing support for strikes and maintaining morale on the picket line. A songbook was produced after the Rego strike that reflects a shared identity among the young women involved and is fused with anger and excitement.[64] Word of mouth proved important during all the disputes. Mabel Morrison recalled, 'We went through all the different departments trying to get the women to come out',[65] while Wolsey workers who walked out streamed across the city to alert the firm's workers at other mills.[66] Tolliday noted that this approach was also important in strikes he studied among young women factory workers in the 1930s.[67] A support network outside the trade union was in existence in each case; young women recalled the excitement of taking control of their workplace by singing, walking out, and picketing.

It was these aspects of young women's workplace militancy—the singing and gossiping—that led to charges of frivolity. Certainly, young workers frequently viewed strikes as, in one woman's words, 'a bit of fun'[68] when labour demand was relatively high and obtaining another job would not be very difficult. May Hobbs recalled that when she encouraged her factory workmates to call an unofficial strike to secure a pay rise in the early 1950s, 'I expected [my foster mother] to hit the roof at the idea, but I remember I said to her, "What'll happen if they give us the sack? I'll be out of work again." "There's plenty more jobs around," she replied, "so why are you worrying?" '[69] Mabel Morrison, like many of the Wolsey

62 LRO, NWSA, 1992.0062, interview with Edith Hough.

63 LRO, NWSA, 1999.0343, interview with Olive Jones.

64 UCWU, *Rego and Polikoff Strike Songs* (London: UCWU, 1929).

65 LRO, NWSA, 1992.0103, interview with Mabel Morrison.

66 *Leicester Evening Mail* (21 December 1931).

67 S. Tolliday, 'Militancy and Organisation, Women Workers and Trade Unions in the Motor Trades in the 1930s', *Oral History*, 11/2 (1983), 52–3.

68 LRO, NWSA, 1992.0103, interview with Mabel Morrison.

69 M. Hobbs, *Born to Struggle* (London: Quartet Books, 1973), 37.

workers, attracted the disapproval of her union by choosing not to spend the extended leisure time that striking offered attending official meetings: 'you'd go down to get your strike pay, they'd say "don't forget your meeting" we'd say "oh aye" and then I'd get on the bus, go into town, go to the Ritz. Go dancing.'[70] However, this should not be interpreted as apathy. Young women's recognition that striking, like gossiping, singing, and lavatory breaks, could break the monotonous working routine, and determination to make the most of this, signified a conscious opposition to employers' demands as well as alienation from trade union bureaucracy.

Recognition of the short-term personal benefits that striking could bring was constantly combined with a sense of economic responsibility. Choosing to strike signified commitment to one's job, since moving to a different post was often easier, but incurred the risk of unemployment or a wage cut. The importance of their contribution to the family economy often made young women determined to protect their earnings when production rationalization or pay cuts threatened them. As May Hobbs's previous comments illustrate, family support was often crucial to a young woman's decision to strike. AEU organizer Jim Crump, speaking of young strikers at the Lucas motor factory in Birmingham in 1932, recalled that ' "Most of the workers were . . . young girls whose fathers and brothers couldn't get a job. They were the breadwinners and you can understand they needed some nerve to come out on strike." '[71] In wartime, the illegality of striking was an additional pressure against 'frivolous' action. Striking, then, was a serious undertaking, designed to protect jobs and pay rates, which affected not only young women workers but also their families.

Boston's representation of such strikers as poorly paid girls with little employment or political experience[72] is extremely partial. Glenn has highlighted the skilled status of those young female textile workers who instigated strikes in New York over this period;[73] the same was true of the young women who initiated the disputes cited here. Most were in their late teens and early twenties with some years of employment experience behind them. They were clearly aware that the imposition of a time-study or conveyor belt system directly threatened negotiation practices previously established. This was particularly true of pieceworkers:the cutters

[70] LRO, NWSA, 1992.0103, interview with Mabel Morrison.

[71] Quoted in Tolliday, 'Militancy and Organisation', 52. See also L. Grant, 'Women in a Car Town: Coventry, 1920–45', in P. Hudson and W. R. Lee, (eds.), *Women's Work and the Family Economy in Historical Perspective* (Manchester: Manchester University Press, 1990), 221.

[72] Boston, *Women Workers*, 176.

[73] S. Glenn, *Daughters of the Schtetl* (Ithaca, New York: Cornell University Press, 1990), 185.

at Rego[74] and the weavers at Wolsey, who had managed to acquire a limited degree of control over the labour process threatened by rationalization strategies. The Wolsey workers justified their strike by declaring that, ' "Britons never shall be slaves" '.[75] This recurrent image signifies overwork but also a lack of control over the labour process.

The Bath workers also felt that they were entitled to a certain degree of pay and negotiation by virtue of their age, experience, and skills. One striker responded to criticisms in the local newspaper by stressing 'we were not on strike for a rise in wages. . . . We, junior staff, wanted the cancellation of the new wage scale, which tended to be a flattering attraction to new juniors coming into the Society's employment, but an insult to those who had served three or four years. . . . [we] just wanted them [*sic*] readjusted to their former rate'.[76] At the subsequent government investigation into the dispute, the strikers' representatives quoted the example of a 19-year-old worker who faced having no bonuses for two years because of the proposed pay cut.[77] Their skills and experience, and the fact that it was not easy to find comparable employment elsewhere, encouraged young women workers, including those who assumed that they would leave their jobs upon marriage, to be more engaged with workplace relations than is sometimes presumed.

Although localized sexual divisions of labour and political traditions did not determine or preclude militancy, they did shape different motivations and outcomes. The responses of the Rego workers to their employers and to the Tailors' Union were shaped by their politicized, East End Jewish upbringing. Their families had a tradition of clothing employment; older generations had fought earlier attempts at rationalization and, like Elsbury, were often committed to communism or socialism.[78] The young female cutters engaged with the organized labour movement, but proposed a more militant agenda than it would accept, establishing a union concerned with control over the labour process rather than conforming to the TUC's more limited aim of establishing wage bargaining at national level.

[74] E. Mofshovitz, quoted in R. A. Leeson, *Strike: A Live History, 1887–1971* (London: Allen and Unwin, 1973), 116–17.

[75] *Leicester Evening Mail* (13 May, 1931). See also Alice Roach, quoted in Tolliday, 'Militancy and Organisation', 52.

[76] Letter from 'Bath Co-op Employee', *Bath and Wiltshire Chronicle and Herald* (29 December 1941), 5.

[77] TNA, LAB 10/164, NUDAW, MS: 'Statement of Circumstances Leading to Dispute between the Staff and the Management Committee of the Bath Co-operative Society Limited', 11 February 1942, 1.

[78] Lerner, *Breakaway Unions*, 89–91. See also J. White, *Rothschild Buildings* (London: Routledge, 1980), 151, 209–10, 252–5.

At Wolsey there was no history of union representation, partly because of young women's employment patterns. The LHU recognized that many Wolsey workers came from skilled working class and lower middle class families and, increasingly, from rural backgrounds; their fathers worked in different trades, and their mothers were employed as clothing home-workers if at all; they themselves did not expect to remain in full-time employment after marriage.[79] During the late 1920s and early 1930s, trade unions' relative weakness did not make membership a priority for such workers. The existing relations between workers and management at Wolsey also helped to ensure that militancy did not develop into a concerted struggle for control over the labour process. The lack of the political tradition evident at Rego meant that the Wolsey strikers' protests concentrated on the immediate implementation of Bedaux, rather than developing the wide-ranging critique of the relationship between labour and capital posed by the UCWU. One Wolsey worker echoed the sentiments of many when she claimed,' "We have no quarrel with the firm at all—it is only the Bedaux system that we protest against. . . . It is inhuman." '[80] The workers' lack of active trade union participation after the strike did not imply content with the settlement; other minor walk-outs dogged Wolsey as it introduced a modified form of the Bedaux system, but the firm's presentation of the new time and motion study system as adapted to workers' needs, and the LHU's lack of opposition to it, prevented any long-term opposition to it being initiated. As Tolliday has suggested, the renaming of the Bedaux system weakened opposition to its introduction in such workplaces, by presenting it as a home-grown scheme rather than an outside intrusion.[81]

The fact that disputes like that at Wolsey did not increase women's active union participation was largely due to a division between the long-term objectives of trade union leaders, aimed at securing national bargaining rights and possibly a greater role in governance, and the more short-term, militant aims of many young female industrial workers who in the longer term aspired to marry and leave paid employment. However, it would be inaccurate to suggest that marital expectations alone were responsible for this division. The senior ranks of the LHU, like those of many unions, were not greatly concerned with building up an active rank and file membership, being far more preoccupied with establishing a good relationship with senior management that often, as at Wolsey,

[79] Littler, *Labour Process*, 119; *Leicester Evening Mail* (4 June 1931).

[80] *Leicester Evening Mail* (12 December 1931).

[81] *Daily Worker* (30 January 1932), 5; Tolliday, 'Militancy and Organisation', 50.

focused on male skilled workers' interests and overlooked the specific grievances of unskilled or junior workers. The close relationship that existed between the LHU and the employers prior to the Wolsey dispute—Moulden had previously been called in by management to sort out shop floor disagreements for them—did not help to overcome the economic objections to trade union membership posed by employment insecurity in the late 1920s and early 1930s.[82] Lewenhak has suggested that disputes over production changes, including a sit-down strike at Nottingham's Players' factory in 1943 over the introduction of Bedaux, indicate that workplace interests were fractured by gender, with male union officials opposed to the demands of the female workforce.[83] However, the disputes cited here point up a division between the political interests of union officials and those of the unskilled and semiskilled workforce. The militancy of the latter, as Tolliday and Whitston have suggested, threatened to undermine the trade union leadership's attempts to build a working relationship with government and employers that allowed for negotiation on wage rates and conditions but did not contest employers' control of production.[84]

The dispute at Wolsey demonstrates that opposition to management could be very strong but rather nebulous. McKibbin has suggested that this was particularly prevalent in non-unionized workplaces,[85] but it is more accurate to regard this attitude as arising from those social, economic, and cultural factors that also preclude unionization. It was common among workforces dominated by young women employed on unskilled or semiskilled work, with no expectation of working into adulthood, who lived in communities characterized by a strong sexual division of labour, and who were not brought up in any kind of politicized tradition. Such a workforce existed in the assembly shop of the *War Factory* reported on by Mass-Observation in 1942, where frequent complaints about specific working conditions were also accompanied by grumbling towards ' "them"; but the "them" does not refer exactly to the staff; it refers to a sort of hazy mixture of office girls, Mr Bevin, a lot of typed notices, and a row of people who sit at the far end of the canteen.'[86] As Tolliday suggests, the paternalistic working practices fostered by employers encouraged these workers not to focus grievances specifically at their managers.[87] This

82 Drake, *Trade Unions*, 132.

83 Lewenhak, *Women and Trade Unions*, 240–1.

84 S. Tolliday, 'Militancy and Organisation', 53; Whitston, 'Worker Resistance', 3, 20–1.

85 McKibbin, *Classes and Cultures*, 137.

86 Mass-Observation, *War Factory* (London: Gollancz, 1942), 71.

87 Tolliday, 'Militancy and Organisation', 50–3.

was testified to by the general confidence expressed by Wolsey's workers towards senior management.

However, workers were capable of manipulating such relationships in their own interests. Many male supervisors at Mass-Obsevation's war factory treated women's backchat, lateness, and refusal to take on extra work with a paternalistic 'amused tolerance', encouraged by the women themselves.[88] This enabled women to retain a degree of control over their working practices, evolving informal negotiation with their managers, as Tolliday found was the case among women workers at some interwar car factories.[89] This exercise of limited control helped young women to find the courage to walk out when grievances were not resolved; the Bath workers, in fact, used their managers' refusal to enter informal negotiation as a justification for their dispute.[90] The type of paternalism established at Wolsey and, to a lesser extent, at Bath discouraged women from making the sustained critique of labour relations that arose at Rego, but it did not prevent workplace militancy.

The Co-operative Movement had a tradition of strong union representation, and most if not all of the young women involved in the Bath dispute were union members. However, as at Rego, a division existed between local NUDAW representatives and the national executive. The support offered to the dispute by local officials was noted disapprovingly by the subsequent government investigation into the strike. The report accepted that the officials had not initiated the walkout, but revealed the government's view of how unions were meant to operate in concluding that 'the workers *unrestrained by their Union* [my emphasis] took advantage of Christmas Week to "teach the Management Committee a lesson" '.[91] At national level NUDAW was keen to distance itself from the dispute, subsequently dismissing Bath's divisional officer, despite the government investigation concluding that no such sanctions should take place. The union's leadership accepted that restraining militancy was a duty, not only in the interests of the war effort, but to forge a co-operative relationship with employers and government.

The case of Bath indicates how young women workers were affected by and contributed to the rhetoric and reality of the People's War. The notion that such disputes were divisive and damaging to the war effort was drawn on by the strikers' employers and critics. As Morgan and Evans

88 Mass-Observation, *War Factory*, 63.
89 Tolliday, 'Militancy and Organisation', 63.
90 *Bath and Wiltshire Chronicle and Herald* (23 December 1941), 1.
91 TNA, LAB 10/164, 'Bath Co-operative Society Strike', 3.

point out 'doing your bit', central to the government's representation of active citizenship, meant ' "putting up with things" without complaint'; this was particularly true for those on the Home Front, including young women.[92] Articulating discontent contravened this. However, the Bath strikers constructed a response that used the same discourse, laying particular emphasis on their entitlement as workers and citizens to negotiate with their employers. One letter from a young female striker to the unsympathetic *Bath and Wiltshire Chronicle and Herald* retorted, 'Surely we, as human beings living in a free country, are at least entitled to a hearing by the people who employ us?' The subsequent government enquiry partially accepted this, criticizing management's intransigence by concluding that 'The worst feature of the whole affair, in our considered view, is that the workers would not have secured the advantageous result obtained had they not acted as they did and held up the Management Committee to ransom.'[93] These workers, then, appropriated the emphasis placed in contemporary political rhetoric on compromise and consensus between employers, unions, and the state.

Such strikes developed a potentially radical conception of active citizenship. The Bath strikers sought to justify their action on terms similar to those used by male workers, emphasizing their value to the war effort. In doing so they drew on the argument that fair wages promoted active citizenship, through economic inclusion in society, on which some trade unions had increasingly drawn throughout the interwar years. In 1930, for example, the National Union of Clerks had argued that girl typists, were 'an essential element in business', and as such deserved not 'pin money' but 'a salary upon which she can hold her own as a citizen and a potential home maker.'[94] This quote highlights the problematic relationship between women and citizenship, not helped by the unskilled and semi-skilled status attributed to much of their work. In the war years this was exacerbated by the emphasis placed on military participation as the exemplary form of citizenship. The Bath strikers recognized their ambiguous position, and partially defended themselves by emphasizing their status as daughters and sisters of soldiers. In response to criticisms from a writer signing himself 'Serving Soldier', one striker retorted, 'My father was also a serving soldier in France during the last war'. Simultaneously, they sought to defend themselves in non-gendered terms, emphasizing

[92] D. Morgan and M. Evans, *The Battle for Britain: Citizenship and Ideology in the Second World War* (London: Routledge, 1993), 83.

[93] TNA, LAB 10/164, 'Bath Co-operative Society Strike', 4.

[94] *The Clerk* (March 1930), 43.

the 'extra responsibility' that the war placed upon them as workers in a firm responsible for distributing rationed goods.[95] The crucial nature of their work was highlighted by the disruption their strike caused, particularly two days before Christmas. The demands made by the strike focused solely on pay, but the context in which they were made, and the way in which they were articulated, strengthened these young workers' claim to a more active form of citizenship.

Overall, the results of the disputes were mixed. Neither the Rego nor the Wolsey strikers achieved their objective of preventing rationalization, and this is representative of the wider wave of strikes and walkouts over this issue, whether involving male or female workers.[96] However, as Whitston claims, disputes such as these 'humanised'[97] scientific management to some extent, forcing minimum wage guarantees and the preservation of negotiation rights over productivity rates.[98] As correspondence between the Wolsey firm and Bedaux engineers shows, employers were forced to reduce their productivity goals to gain workers' acceptance of the scheme.[99] When the state began to take a direct interest in increasing productivity during the Second World War, these interwar struggles were partially responsible for the ensuing productivity drive being managed by Bevin, and for the fact that this did not result in the reduction, but rather in the formalization and extension of semiskilled workers' rights and privileges.[100] In forcing modifications in the implementation of time-study schemes, they demonstrated the impossibility of implementing fully 'scientific' management over workers. Examining their actions emphasizes the ahistorical nature of Braverman's Whiggish deskilling thesis, which does not pay due attention, as Zeitlin's more historically sensitive account does, to workers' continuous attempts to preserve their interests by engaging in conflict over the definition and value of their work.[101] Even when employment was insecure and workers lacked a tradition of trade unionism, the productivity gains of labour intensification could be reduced by worker resistance.

[95] *Bath and Wiltshire Chronicle and Herald* (29 December 1941).

[96] Whitston, 'Worker Resistance'. [97] Ibid., 21.

[98] That this was also true in the textile industry, where older women were instrumental in the 'more looms' dispute of the early 1930s, is demonstrated by S. Bowden and D. M. Higgins, ' "Productivity on the Cheap"? The "More Looms" Experiment and the Lancashire Weaving Industry during the Inter-War Years', *Business History*, 41/3 (1999), 21–41.

[99] Leics RO, DE 4823, Letter from Bedaux Ltd to Wolsey firm's directors, 25 January 1932.

[100] Whitston, 'Worker Resistance', 24.

[101] J. Zeitlin, 'Engineers and Compositors: A Comparison', in R. Harrison and J. Zeitlin (eds.), *Divisions of Labour: Skilled Workers and Technological Change in Nineteenth Century England* (Brighton: Harvester Wheatsheaf, 1985); H. Braverman, *Labour and Monopoly Capital* (New York: Monthly Review Press, 1974).

The formalization of workers' rights during the Second World War was aided by the continuing militancy of young workers. Those at Bath Co-op were able to retain their wartime bonuses. Such disputes helped to ensure that the pre-war practice of dismissing young workers when they became eligible for higher wage rates at the age of 18, highlighted in chapter 1, was not simply replaced by the lowering of young adults' earnings as labour demand rose in wartime; they in fact rose relative to adult pay rates. The Bath strikers avoided prosecution, in part because of the unity they exhibited and the support they gained; as in many such cases, the Ministry of Labour concluded that 'the effect upon the future of industrial relations and the war effort generally might prove disastrous.'[102] The need to formalize and extend negotiation rights was emphasized by these workers' ability to halt trade.

Like many such disputes, those cited here brought more members into the relevant trade unions, but this was often a short-term result. The divergence between the interests of the workers and the less radical objectives of the union leadership meant that women's workplace militancy was not usually translated into active trade union participation.[103] This was explained by the divergence between the workers' aims, which were frequently short term and often contested control of the labour process, the wage structure, or negotiation procedures, and those of the union leadership. Although the trade union movement became increasingly concerned to represent unskilled and semiskilled labour, union leaders' lack of attention to rank and file workers as they sought to establish national wage bargaining rights, as occurred at national level in the Rego and Co-operative Society strikes and at local level in the Wolsey dispute, offered little incentive for young women to remain active members of trade unions after disputes were settled.

Conclusion

The years between 1918 and 1950 saw young women become increasingly important as worker-citizens. The interaction of gender and age with labour demand, regional sexual divisions of labour, and local cultural and political traditions shaped young women's relations with employers and

[102] TNA, LAB 10/164, 'Bath Co-operative Society Strike', 8.

[103] Croucher, *Engineers*, 28–30; K. Middlemas, *Politics in Industrial Society: The Experience of the British System since 1911* (London: Andre Deutsch, 1979), 209–10, 218–19; Tolliday, 'Militancy and Organisation'.

the labour movement. The way that these women sought remedies for their grievances were shaped by their status as unskilled and semiskilled workers, and frequently by their expectation of retirement from full-time paid work upon marriage. These factors did not, however, preclude militancy, nor did they determine disinterest in the organized labour movement. The level of young women's trade union membership was affected by many of the same economic and political factors that influenced levels of male membership. A worker's age, status, and their own and their household's socio-economic circumstances were frequently as influential as their gender in shaping their labour relations.

Young women's activism had significant results. In particular, it helped to bring about the modification of some mass production techniques and to preserve the narrowing of the age differential in wages during and after the Second World War. Workplace disputes also led some young women to contest, and renegotiate, the social and political roles ascribed to young people and women in the evolving social democratic state. These women emphasized their entitlement to active political participation, at a time when their enfranchisement was relatively recent. In doing so, they suggested a more proactive notion of citizenship to that offered by the ballot box or by the organized labour movement. Yet young women also used their grievances to simultaneously suggest that a set of shared values and concerns connected them with male workers. In doing so, they sought to negotiate a form of citizenship distinct from the 'gendered citizenship' that Innes has shown was central to the contemporary women's movement.[104] Young working class women's attempts to establish themselves as agents of change within the workplace thus illustrate that in order to understand the social and political dimensions of their lives, the established parameters of women's and labour history must be widened.

104 S. Innes, 'Love and Work: Feminism, Family and Ideas of Equality and Citizenship, Britain, 1900–39', Ph.D. thesis (Edinburgh, 1998), 5, 234.

7

Beyond the Workplace: Leisure and Courtship

Young women spent much of their time in the workplace; however, they were increasingly prominent as leisure consumers. Social histories have highlighted that much of the expanding commercial leisure provision of the interwar years was aimed at 16 to 24 year olds,[1] and regional case studies by Roberts and Alexander support Langhamer's conclusion that young working class women were prominent consumers of such new forms of leisure as dance halls, cinemas, and magazines.[2] Davies's groundbreaking study is a reminder that commercialization should not be the only prism through which working class leisure is viewed, highlighting the enduring significance of informal, communal activities in shaping youthful leisure and social identity in the first half of the twentieth century.[3] However, only Langhamer provides a comprehensive, national study of young women's leisure, and her focus neglects the importance of paid work in structuring and changing young women's social and financial independence. In particular, although existing studies suggest that gender bias shaped access to leisure and spending money, with young men receiving preferential treatment, the reasons for this have not been fully interrogated, implying that it was due to 'custom' or 'tradition'.[4] As a consequence, the reasons for the emergence of the young, female leisure consumer between 1918 and 1950 have not been

[1] For an overview of these developments and their impact upon young people see A. Davies, *Leisure, Gender and Poverty* (Buckingham: Open University Press, 1992), 83–96; C. Langhamer, *Women's Leisure in England c. 1920–1960* (Manchester: Manchester University Press, 2000), ch. 3.

[2] S. Alexander, 'Becoming a Woman in London in the 1920s and 1930s', in ead. (ed.), *Becoming a Woman and Other Essays in 19th and 20th century Feminist History* (London:Virago, 1994); Langhamer, *Women's Leisure*; E. Roberts, *A Woman's Place: An Oral History of Working Class Women, 1890–1940* (Oxford: Blackwell, 1984), 39–80.

[3] Davies, *Leisure*, 96–108.

[4] Davies, *Leisure*, 86–8, 97; Langhamer, *Women's Leisure*, 50, 89–90.

fully examined. The focus of this chapter, which traces in greater depth the ways in which daughters' changing working patterns, and role in the family economy, shaped changes in their social lives, argues that gendered and generational divisions in access to spending money and leisure time were largely attributable to households' economic circumstances, and to individuals' economic roles, which were shaped in specific historical contexts.

The focus and chronology of this study also means that this chapter can fill a second gap in the historiography: the nature of the transition that occurred in youthful lifestyles between the 1920s and the 1950s. Whereas Fowler argues that the interwar years witnessed the emergence of the working class youthful leisure consumer,[5] Osgerby and Langhamer have demonstrated that the teenagers of the 1950s enjoyed a considerably greater degree of affluence than their parents' generation.[6] However, the reasons for this change have not yet been interrogated. As earlier chapters of this book have suggested, a general rise in the working class standard of living was partially responsible for this. However, personal testimonies indicate that a complex combination of mutual emotional support, obligation and affection, and economic need, structured relationships between parents and daughters, and assisted the latter in extending their social independence. It is argued here that young women's increased earning opportunities expanded their social and financial independence, making them at times more prominent consumers of leisure than young men, and pioneers in the development of working class youth culture. This had profound effects on their relations with parents and, as the final section of the chapter shows, on their courtship patterns and expectations.

Young women workers' leisure consumption was not new to the 1920s. Young working class people began to become prominent consumers in large, industrial towns in the late nineteenth century as their employment patterns became increasingly distinguished from those of adult workers and as earning opportunities increased for young women.[7] The 'New Woman' of that period was epitomized by young, middle class women,

[5] D. Fowler, *The First Teenagers: The Lifestyles of Young Wage-Earners in Interwar Britain* (London: Woburn Press, 1995), 105–11.

[6] Langhamer, *Women's Leisure*, 55–7; B. Osgerby, *Youth in Britain since 1945* (Oxford: Blackwell, 1998), 5.

[7] R. Roberts, *The Classic Slum* (Harmondsworth: Penguin, 1973), 155–6; Davies, *Leisure*, 85, 96–104. For an extensive account of this development with regard to young men, see H. Hendrick, *Images of Youth: Age, Class, and the Male Youth Problem 1880–1920* (Oxford: Clarendon Press, 1990).

whose opportunities for independent living expanded in late Victorian and Edwardian England.[8] However, groups of young working class women were also identified as prominent consumers of leisure—and as labour activists—such as Lancashire textile workers and Manchester factory girls.[9] Young working class women's ability to find relatively well-paid work that allowed them to engage in conspicuous leisure consumption rose during the First World War as Thom and Wollacott have shown.[10]

Despite this, it was not until the period between the 1920s and early 1950s that leisure, and a degree of financial autonomy, became a general characteristic of young women's lifestyles. As domestic service, characterized by long hours and poor pay, declined, and shop, office, and factory employment expanded, so leisure, structured around the industrialized working day, became integral to young women workers' lives. Joan Harley's study of 169 young women workers in Manchester in the mid-1930s found that most, excluding servants, finished work by 7pm on weekdays, and, despite the claims placed on their time by domestic duties, most enjoyed at least four hours of leisure each evening.[11] A rising standard of living, contributed to by young women's increasing earning potential, led to a concurrent rise in their financial independence. In 1936 Rowntree calculated that in relatively affluent York, supplementary wage-earners aged over 15 accounted for about 15 per cent of the working class population and retained 12.5 per cent of working class income, only about half of which was essential for personal expenditure.[12] The changes in young women's family relations and leisure consumption that this testifies to are the focus of the first sections of this chapter, which are followed by consideration of how their increasingly conspicuous social and financial independence structured political and press representations of them.

[8] C. Dyhouse, *Girls Growing Up in Late Victorian and Edwardian England* (London: Routledge, 1981), 113, 131.

[9] E. Roberts, *Woman's Place*, 68–72; L. A. Tilly and J. W Scott, *Women, Work and Family* (London: Methuen, 1987), 189–90.

[10] D. Thom, *Nice Girls and Rude Girls: Women Workers in World War I* (London: I. B. Tauris, 1998), 155; A. Woollacott, *On Her Their Lives Depend: Munitions Workers in the Great War* (London: University of California Press, 1994), 134–61.

[11] J. L. Harley, 'Report of an Enquiry into the Occupations, Further Education and Leisure Interests of a Number of Girl Wage-Earners from Elementary and Central Schools in the Manchester District, with Special Reference to the Influence of School Training on Their Use of Leisure', M.Ed. thesis (Manchester, 1937), 60–3.

[12] B. S. Rowntree, *Poverty and Progress: A Second Social Survey of York* (London: Longmans, 1941), 125.

The contrast between young women's leisure consumption before and after the First World War, and between the leisure habits of young women in our period and those of other social groups, emphasizes the distinctiveness of the generations under study here, and of youth as a life stage. Throughout the years between 1918 and 1950, young women clearly experienced more leisure than their mothers. This was due not only to a reduction in their working hours, but to an acceptance of their entitlement, as wage-earners, to leisure. Although an increase in working hours during the first years of the Second World War diminished young women's leisure time, studies by Mass-Observation and Jephcott demonstrate that parents continued to allow young workers of both sexes to enjoy a relatively large amount of leisure time, particularly compared to their mothers.[13] Although young men were also prominent leisure consumers, interwar unemployment and wartime conscription constrained their leisure consumption as young women's grew. These factors, together with young women's expanding earning opportunities, meant that their leisure patterns underwent more significant change than those of young men during these years, and that they were increasingly prominent as leisure consumers.

Work and Leisure

The transition from schoolgirl to wage-earner was marked by an increase in young women's social and financial independence. Changes in appearance were increasingly common. Studies of Lancashire highlight that changes in dress and hairstyle were common among nineteenth-century mill girls when they first began work, and the same was true of other relatively well-paid groups like London clerks.[14] However, it was only with the post-1918 expansion of employment opportunities more lucrative than domestic service that this type of transition became a national trend. Grace Foakes, who became a waitress in 1920s London, recalled that 'When young ladies left school they were expected to put their hair up and let their dresses down',[15] just as young men often received their

[13] Mass-Observation Archive: FR1780, 'Youth Questionnaire', May 1943, 15–17; P. Jephcott, *Rising Twenty: Notes on Some Ordinary Girls* (London: Faber, 1948), 83–4, 104. See also Langhamer, *Women's Leisure*, 138–42.

[14] L. A. Tilly and J. W. Scott, *Women, Work and Family* (London: Holt, Rinehart and Winston, 1978), 186–8.

[15] G. Foakes, *Between High Walls: A London Childhood* (London: Shepeard-Walwyn, 1972), 72.

first pair of long trousers. By the 1930s, many juveniles first visited the hairdresser when they started work, or had new clothes bought for them.[16] Such customs persisted during the Second World War, despite the shortage of clothes and cosmetics, indicating the importance of employment as an initiation into a new stage of life. Dorothy King witnessed this as a schoolgirl in Ashton during the early 1940s: 'older girls as soon as they started work changed their hairstyles and took on quite a different appearance overnight.'[17] A degree of social and financial independence was integral to the identity of the young worker, as well as the adult male breadwinner, distinguishing them from non-earners in the household.

This type of transition was common to many regional labour markets, differing little between communities where women worked after marriage, as in many textile towns, and those where women expected to give up full-time employment when they married, as in many prospering light manufacturing towns like Coventry. It varied markedly, however, for those young women who entered residential domestic service. The long hours and low pay of servants meant that they were unable to make a very significant contribution to the family economy, although they commonly sent most of their wages home. They did not benefit from spending money or experience the increasing amount of leisure enjoyed by young office, shop, and factory workers, who, by the mid-1930s, were benefiting from reductions in working hours, rising wages, and the proliferation of cinemas and dance halls.

Young women's shared employment experiences and earnings distinguished them from older women, giving rise to a distinctively youthful leisure culture. As rising numbers of young women worked in larger factories, shops, and offices, so workplaces increasingly became a venue for friendship and for disseminating information on fashion and appearance. Mary Welch recalled that in her factory in 1920s London:

> if [the married women workers] were to see the girls making up too much, they used to say to them, 'You'll have a lot of pimples on your face, if you don't stop doing this and that.' .... They would give us that sort of advice, but they couldn't go too far because us little up and buddings weren't going to be spoken to like that. [18]

[16] L. M. Thew, *A Tune for Bears to Dance to* (Berwick-upon-Tweed: Bridge Studies, 1992), 212.

[17] Tameside Local Studies Library (TLSL), Tameside tapes collection, 6, interview with Dorothy King.

[18] M. Welch, 'Leather Worker', in R. Gray (ed.), *Working Lives* (London: Centreprise, 1976), 56.

Modish hairstyles, adaptations to work clothes, and cosmetics for older girls were important in asserting an identity distinct from the homogeneous, anonymous workforce demanded by employers. Emily Money remembered that 'We used to tuck and sew [work hats] at the back and add a bit of trimming to make ourselves look beautiful. Otherwise the hats stuck up all round and looked awful.'[19] Ann Smith was one of many mill girls who gloried in 'dressing up' for work, rejecting the traditional workplace garb of clogs and shawls.[20] For young men, by contrast, the overalls of the manual worker could be a badge of pride,[21] demonstrating a difference in the cultural significance of work in their lives. Women's fashions were in part an attempt to reject the identity imposed by the workplace. In the 1940s, women war workers shared scarce cosmetics, and objected to wearing safety caps, which flattened glamorous hairstyles,[22] although some also appreciated the fact that war relaxed some of the demands that feminine identity made on a young woman's budget and time. Kathleen Holland liked the fact that munitions workers 'were so natural . . . that hairstyle, the one that you bound round and turned over an old stocking to make it stay. . . . No hairspray or anything.'[23] The growth of larger workplaces thus enabled social networks to develop and was central to disseminating and developing the fashionable image of the modern young woman.

The strong social bonds forged in the workplace increasingly shaped young women's leisure time. A number of them participated in work-based sports and social activities,[24] to indulge in hobbies at low cost, or, like Winifred Cotterill, to fulfil a social aspiration to mix with white-collar workers of higher social standing than workmates on the factory floor.[25] Such participation was already declining by the 1920s, since firms were increasingly concerned to improve welfare facilities

[19] E. Money, 'Liquorice', in R. Van Riel (ed.), *All in a Day's Work* (Pontefract: Yorkshire Art Circus, 1981), 31.

[20] Lancashire Records Office (LRO), North West Sound Archive (NWSA), 1999.0125, interview with Ann Smith.

[21] W. Greenwood, *Love on the Dole* (London: Jonathan Cape, 1931), 55–60.

[22] Factory Inspectorate, Annual Report, 1944, xii (1945–46), Cmd. 6698, 8; LRO, NWSA, 2002.0531a, interview with Florence Rosenblatt.

[23] TLSL, Manchester Studies collection, tape 1075, interview with Kathleen Holland.

[24] TLSL, Manchester Studies, 638, interview with Louise Pace; D. Scannell, *Mother Knew Best: An East End Childhood* (London: Macmillan, 1974), 160–2. See also L. Oliver, ' "No Hard-Brimmed Hats or Hat-Pins Please": Bolton Women Cotton Workers and the Game of Rounders, 1911–39', *Oral History*, 25/1 (1997).

[25] Modern Records Centre, University of Warwick (MRC), Coventry Women's Work Collection, MSS 266/3/1/2, interview with Winifred Cotterill.

rather than to provide recreational activities.[26] This type of provision was most dramatically eroded by the institution of paid holidays in 1938, and concurrent expansion in access to commercial leisure activities, facilitated by rising wages. However, the lengthening of working hours during the Second World War meant that the workplace once more became the focus of many young women's social lives. Irma Smith remembered that 'It was my 21st birthday when the Manchester blitz was on, everybody had brought food [to work], we ended up in the shelter finishing it off.'[27]

More important was the role workmates played in informal leisure. Lily recalled of her time as a hospital maid in the mid-1920s:

> Say in a hospital there was quite a lot of girls you see working, and the girls . . . that, where there were nights off you used to pal on with them. And you used to just walk up and down the town.[28]

By the mid-1930s, the effects of this were evident in most towns and cities, and were strengthened by further reductions in working hours and the Holidays with Pay Act. Mrs Johnson stressed the importance of her female GEC workmates as her social life expanded in her late teens, during the mid-1930s:'We used to be friends, meet at one another's houses, go to a dance, something like that'.[29] During the Second World War, the National Association of Girls' Clubs noted that the prevalence of shift work broke down normal family routines, raising the significance of friendship groups; many young women workers took meals out together at cafés and British restaurants, for example.[30] Chapman's study of Middlesbrough in 1944–5 found that working women, like men, generally listed their workmates as their closest friends, emphasizing the significance of the workplace in shaping their social networks and a collective identity.[31]

[26] J. Crump, 'Recreation in Coventry between the Wars', in B. Lancaster and T. Mason (eds.), *Labour and Life in a Twentieth Century City: The Experience of Coventry* (Coventry: Cryfield Press, 1986), 273–4.

[27] TLSL, Manchester Studies, 1075, interview with Irma Smith.

[28] Nottingham Local Studies Library (NLSL), Making Ends Meet Collection, A50/a, interview with Lily.

[29] MRC, Coventry Women's Work Collection, MSS 266/6/1, interview with Mrs Johnson.

[30] Mass-Observation Archive (M-OA): FR1353, 'The Service of Youth', July 1942, appendix, xiii.

[31] D. Chapman, *A Social Survey of Middlesbrough*, Social Survey, Report, New Series, 50 (1945), 9.

Leisure and the Family

Chapter 2 pointed out that entering employment marked the beginning of a reciprocal financial relationship between parents and children. Social historians have demonstrated that most young wage-earners 'tipped up' their weekly earnings to their mothers, receiving a proportion back as spending money, a process recalled by all of my own sample.[32] Spending money enabled young women to participate in and thus shape commercial leisure developments, but was also important as a motif of youth, which distinguished this life stage from childhood in a period when few school-children received regular pocket money. Harley found that levels of spending money ranged from 6d to 6s among her sample,[33] and other surveys recorded similar results for the interwar years.[34] In the post-Second World War years, wages rose faster than prices, increasing young workers' affluence. A survey of Birmingham's young wage-earners in 1950 was typical in calculating average weekly pocket money as about 11s 4d for teenagers. Variance in the amounts received was partly explained by difference in age; as young workers' wages rose, so did their pocket money.[35] In the Birmingham study, 14-year-old girls retained 3s 3d per week, while 19-year-old girls had 26s 10d.[36] Consequently, as Davies has judged, those in their late teens and early twenties were 'relatively privileged as consumers of leisure.'[37]

Earnings clearly had an impact on the amount of spending money received. Mass-Observation studies of Worktown (Bolton) in the late 1930s found that uniform levels of pocket money tended to be established in those communities where a large number of young workers entered the same employment; localized historical studies corroborate this.[38] This points to a strong correlation between earnings and spending money, and also the importance of the local community in defining an accepted

[32] Davies, *Leisure*, 84–7; Langhamer, *Women's Leisure*, 101–2.

[33] J. L. Harley, 'Report of an Enquiry into the Occupations, Further Education and Leisure Interests of a Number of Girl Wage-Earners from Elementary and Central Schools in the Manchester District, with Special Reference to the Influence of School Training on Their Use of Leisure', M.Ed. dissertation (Manchester, 1937), 56–7.

[34] Rowntree, *Poverty and Progress*, 27, 78–81, 83–95, 127–42; M-OA: Worktown Collection, 28/B, Household Budgets, ms: untitled budget of family of six, n.d., *c.* 1938, and ms: untitled family budget, ms, 9 May 1938; Langhamer, *Women's Leisure*, 100–3.

[35] Ibid.

[36] B. H. Reed et al., *Eighty Thousand Adolescents* (London: Allen and Unwin, 1950), 38.

[37] Davies, *Leisure*, 81.

[38] M-OA, Worktown Collection, 28/D, unpublished ms: 'Motives for Saving: Preliminary Report', n.d., *c.*1938, 8. See also Davies, *Leisure*, 85; Roberts, *Woman's Place*, 43; J. Smyth, ' "Ye Never Got a Spell to Think aboot It." Young Women and Employment in the Inter-War

level of financial independence for young people that could influence individual households' practices. Consequently, while young servants received little pocket money—Eileen Balderson, who entered service in 1931, kept 6d of her 7s 6d weekly wage and sent the rest home, and this was typical[39]—the expansion of clerical, retail, and factory employment increased young women's financial independence.

The family economy and family size shaped the amount of leisure and spending money that young workers received. Rowntree unsurprisingly found that young workers in poor households were given significantly less pocket money than those above the poverty line.[40] The granting of spending money, and the amount received, was irregular when the family economy was affected by a breadwinner's unemployment or underemployment.[41] Edna, who lived alone with her mother, a clothing pieceworker whose earnings were erratic, earned 7s per week in her first job as an errand girl in Nottingham's lace market in the late 1920s. She received 6d pocket money out of this from her mother, but their economic circumstances meant that 'she'd take another three pence back off me for half a pint before the time had gone. We was really poor, you know.'[42] Family composition was important: younger siblings benefited from the contributions of older brothers and sisters and often enjoyed a relatively large amount of pocket money.[43]

Gender also fractured leisure access. Contemporary social surveys demonstrate that daughters, particularly oldest daughters, enjoyed less leisure time than their brothers, because of a maternal need for domestic help.[44] Chapter 2 noted that in circumstances where young women's earning potential was not great, particularly prior to the 1940s, daughters might be kept out of the labour force to aid a mother in the home.

Period: A Case Study of a Textile Village', in E. Gordon and E. Breitenbach (eds.), *The World is Ill Divided: Women's Work in Scotland in the Nineteenth and Early Twentieth Centuries* (Edinburgh: Edinburgh University Press, 1990), 106–7.

39 E. Balderson with D. Goodlad, *Backstairs Life in a Country House* (Newton Abbott: David and Charles, 1982), 9.

40 Rowntree, *Poverty and Progress*, chs. 3 and 5.

41 See, for example, East Sussex Records Office (ESRO), Archive of the University of the Third Age: Lewes and District Branch, Lewes in Living Memory collection, AMS 6416/1/7/45, interview with Frances Fuller; J. White, *The Worst Street in North London: Campbell Bunk, Islington, between the Wars* (London: Routledge, 1986), 204–6.

42 NLSL, Making Ends Meet, A85/b/1, interview with Edna.

43 M-OA, 28/B, Household Budgets; Rowntree, *Poverty and Progress*, 78–93, 127–42; Davies, *Leisure*, 84–5; Smyth, 'Young Women and Employment', 106.

44 D. Caradog Jones, *The Social Survey of Merseyside*, 3 (Liverpool: University of Liverpool, 1934), 219; Harley, 'Girl Wage-Earners', 96; Rowntree, *Poverty and Progress*, 436–40; J. Beauchamp, *Women who Work* (London: Lawrence and Wishart, 1937), 39–40; M. Paneth, *Branch Street* (London: Allen and Unwin, 1944), 38–9; Roberts, *Woman's Place*, 23–5; J. Sarsby, *Missuses*

However, it was more common for daughters to share domestic responsibilities while holding down a full-time job. Their domestic assistance clearly continued to be highly valued into the 1950s, particularly, as Mass-Observation found, in large households or those in which the wife and mother went out to work. A report compiled on young people's leisure in 1943 highlighted this clearly. The mother of one 14 year old responded:

> She doesn't get much time; I've a big family and I need her help at home in the evenings, help with the children. . . . Then Saturdays she does shopping for me, and needlework, and perhaps if my husband go [*sic*] out she minds the children.[45]

This comment emphasizes that whereas male access to leisure was unquestioningly accepted by many families, the same was not true for women. In 1942, a report by the Ministry of Education on the registration of 16 and 17 year olds concluded that girls were less likely than boys to join youth organizations, mainly because 'war conditions are laying an increasingly heavy burden on many girls' because of the war work of other family members, including mothers. One 'typical letter' from parents to their Local Education Authority was quoted:

> Dear Sir, I wish to apply for exemption of my daughter as she is the one we depend on for our food here. There are five of us—all on war work, including my wife. We all work from 8 am until 7.45 pm each day. We have no one but my daughter to cook us a meal and to keep the house clean for when we come home; also she has to run the messages and is on war work herself from 8 am to 5.30 pm.[46]

War, then, could increase young women's responsibilities, but the concern caused by married women's work also brought to light the type of domestic burden many young women carried in peacetime. One 14 year old in Bolton, who worked as a shop assistant between 9 and 6, told Mass-Observation in 1943 that 'My mother's on night shift, so I have to stay in and do the work.'[47] New housing developments, ownership of labour-saving devices, the extension of free health care to all in 1948, and falling family size diminished domestic demands on daughters—but it must be remembered that most working class homes were situated

and Mouldrunners: An Oral History of Women Pottery Workers at Work and at Home (Milton Keynes: Open University Press, 1988), 38; Smyth, 'Young Women and Employment', 107.

45 M-OA: FR 1567, 'Report on Girls between School-Leaving and Registration Age' (January 1943), 3–4. See also Roberts, *Woman's Place*, 81–2.

46 The National Archive (TNA), ED 124/47, MS: Note on the Reports by LEAs of the Registration of Young People in March 1943, 10.

47 M-OA: FR 1567, 'Girls between School Leaving and Registration', 3.

in older houses and did not possess domestic appliances prior to the mid-1960s.[48] Young women's access to leisure thus remained uncertain, conditional on their mothers' ability to shoulder a large degree of domestic responsibility.

Parental authority remained important in determining leisure access into the 1950s. Although this was frequently exerted over the leisure activities and finances of both sons and daughters, the latter tended to be subject to less generous allocation and greater regulation, as Davies and Langhamer have documented.[49] Eileen was typical in feeling that when she started work in the 1920s,

> I as a girl still came under the same restrictions as I did at school, and I wasn't allowed out at night unless they knew where I was going. By that I meant I was allowed to go round to a friend's house just round the corner, but no, no, there was very strong discipline and restriction on girls . . . oh I was terrified if I was a few minutes late.[50]

In 1950 Pearl Jephcott's study of several hundred young people found that this remained the case in both towns and rural districts.[51] Young women also frequently received less spending money than their brothers. In many more affluent households young men were allowed to substitute paying board for tipping up their entire earnings in their late teens. Women, conversely, more frequently had to wait until they were engaged to be married before they were permitted this degree of autonomy.[52] Mass-Observation's surveys of London's Paddington district in 1941 and 1943 demonstrate that although young wage-earners of both sexes had more spending money in the latter year as a result of rising wages, young women spent a larger portion of their money on 'essentials', such as clothing, lunches, and soap. The implication of this was that parents bought such goods for their sons, suggesting that a rise in household affluence benefited sons more than daughters.[53]

The reasons for this parental bias have not been fully examined by existing studies, implying that this was due to 'custom'. Yet historians of eighteenth-century England have pointed out that young women and

[48] S. Bowden, 'The New Consumerism', in P. Johnson (ed.), *Twentieth Century Britain: Economic, Social, and Cultural Change* (London: Longman, 1994).

[49] Davies, *Leisure*, 88; Langhamer, *Women's Leisure*, 103.

[50] NLSL, Making Ends Meet, A14/a/1, interview with Eileen.

[51] P. Jephcott, *Some Young People* (London: Faber, 1954), 55–6.

[52] Langhamer, *Women's Leisure*, 102–3; Sarsby, *Missuses and Mouldrunners*, 58. See also NLSL, Making Ends Meet, A23/a-b/1, interview with Mrs Mead.

[53] M-OA: FR 1780, 'Youth Questionnaire', May 1943, 6.

young men were prominent consumers in early industrialization because of their earning power,[54] indicating that the gender bias identified by studies of leisure access in interwar England was the result of historically specific circumstance rather than of 'tradition'. One reason for this was the sexual division of paid labour, which differentiated the cultural significance of work for young women and young men. For boys, entering employment marked the beginning of manhood, as they began to adopt the roles of worker and breadwinner that would be expected of them throughout their adult lives. However, for girls, as Alexander has noted, marriage, not employment, denoted womanhood.[55] This helps to explain parental concern to protect the respectability of their household and the welfare of their daughters; unsupervised young women, particularly on night-time streets, could denote vice or vulnerability. It was also partially responsible for a sometimes tacit acceptance that young men required a greater degree of leisure access and expenditure than their sisters.

As this indicates, economic factors alone did not determine family relationships. By the mid-1940s, social commentators expressed a growing recognition that daughters' leisure was limited by their mothers' view of older girls as a source of emotional as well as domestic support. A survey of young people in wartime Bristol found several cases of 'mothers who, sometimes for help with work, but often purely for companionship, monopolize their daughters' leisure'.[56] Many of these women lacked regular adult company, with husbands conscripted or working long hours. However, in many instances when a husband was present, adult women still valued the companionship of an older daughter, who might empathize with her mother rather more than a husband whose daily life was often so different from his wife's. Some young women enjoyed the companionship. In the mid-1930s, many of Joan Harley's respondents spoke with enjoyment of 'Amami night' or 'bucket night' when discussing their leisure; usually taking place on a Friday evening, this involved daughters, sisters, and mothers washing their hair and generally preparing for the weekend and was clearly valued for its companionship.[57] Ten years later, Jephcott found that many young women in her study spent much of their leisure time talking to their mothers who were often considered,

[54] N. McKendrick, 'The Consumer Revolution of Eighteenth-Century England', in N. McKendrick, J. Brewer, and J. Plumb (eds.), *The Birth of a Consumer Society* (London: Hutchinson, 1983).

[55] Alexander, 'Becoming', 215.

[56] B. A. Fletcher et al., *The Welfare of Youth: A City Survey* (Bristol: University of Bristol, 1945), 10.

[57] Harley, 'Girl Wage Earners', 96; Langhamer, *Women's Leisure*, 95–6.

in the words of one 18-year-old respondent, 'the best friends anyone can have'.[58] However, such companionship could also be experienced as a heavy obligation, an expectation of daughters that distinguished them from their brothers and fathers. Carolyn Steedman recalled that her mother's reliance on her eldest daughter for emotional support in the 1950s stemmed partly from her father's inadequacy as both companion and breadwinner, as well as from her wish for assistance with domestic work:

> I stayed at school late once, without telling her. . . . She was waiting on the doorstep: I withered, there was nothing I could say. She'd wanted me to go down the road to fetch a bunch of watercress for tea, and I ought to have known she couldn't go, couldn't leave my sister. I feel into the dark place of her displeasure, the sinking feeling of descent. She. . . . didn't go out enjoying herself; neither should I.[59]

In similar terms, Lorna Sage spoke of the 'domestic claustrophobia' of her 1950s childhood.[60] A theme that has run through this study is that mothers' relationships with their daughters were a complex combination of affection and obligation, aspiration and constraint, love and resentment. By the early 1950s, maternal hopes of having their own aspirations met by their daughters were strong, but their desire to give their daughters a better life was often combined with a wish to maintain emotional bonds with their children. As the need for children to pay their parents back in financial terms diminished, and smaller family size meant that working class mothers were able—and, increasingly in the post-Second World War years, expected—to give their children greater individual attention, so maternal expectations of companionship—and daughters' sense of obligation—may have grown. Many daughters clearly continued to shoulder significant familial responsibilities, and though these were increasingly emotional rather than material, they could still limit leisure time and independence.

Few women appear to have been aggrieved at the greater amount of leisure allotted to their brothers. None in my sample articulated discontent, reflecting the views of most of Langhamer's interviewees,[61] although none expressed agreement with this double standard either. An investigation of young people undertaken in wartime Bristol found that 'Sometimes the daughter resents parental domination: more often she

58 Jephcott, *Rising Twenty*, 44.
59 C. Steedman, *Landscape for a Good Woman* (London: Virago, 1986), 104–5.
60 L. Sage, *Bad Blood* (London: Fourth Estate, 2001), 186.
61 Langhamer, *Women's Leisure*, 103.

seems resigned and apathetic'.[62] Certainly, as Roberts suggests, many young women accepted the legitimacy of parental authority.[63] However, this may better be attributed to a sense of indebtedness than to apathy; this study has made clear that daughters recognized the economic and emotional responsibilities they could place upon parents.

Young women's ambivalent silence is also partially explained by their own ability to circumvent some parental regulation. Young adults in particular clearly attended dances and monkey parades or bunny runs without parental knowledge. All of these were courtship venues, the latter referring to streets along which young men and women paraded with friends, meeting, flirting with, and courting members of the opposite sex. Mrs Savage and her future husband, whose courtship in the 1930s consisted of walking the streets because 'We had no money, we couldn't go anywhere', took care to avoid her mother, who knew nothing of their relationship.[64] Similarly, Davies cites examples of young women who went dancing without their parents' knowledge.[65] Eileen was careful to be home before her curfew, but she recalled using forbidden cosmetics:'we used to put it on and wipe it off before we went home so father couldn't see it.'[66] As this suggests, young women's own wishes for greater social independence were instrumental in changing the experience of youth.

Another important reason many young women accepted parental authority over their leisure, albeit sometimes with reluctance, was their awareness that leisure allocation was based on established bread-winning strategies and gender roles, the material basis of which was hard to challenge. A strong correlation existed between levels of spending money and earnings variance between the sexes. In those families living above the poverty line in Rowntree's survey, girls received an average of 2s 8d per week, compared with 3s 6d per week for boys of the same age.[67] This reflected the far lower earnings variance among juveniles compared with that which characterized adult rates of pay. Studies of juveniles in the early 1950s concluded that boys and girls received roughly equal amounts of spending money.[68] One study of Birmingham in fact found that girls aged between 16 and 18 received on average more pocket money than boys, probably explained by the fact that many of the city's boys

[62] Fletcher et al., *Welfare of Youth*, 11. [63] Roberts, *Woman's Place*, 42–3.
[64] TLSL, Manchester Studies, 477, interview with Mrs Savage.
[65] Davies, *Leisure*, 90. [66] NLSL, Making Ends Meet, A14/a, interview with Eileen.
[67] Rowntree, *Poverty and Progress*, 78–93, 127–42.
[68] Jephcott, *Young People*, 56; Reed et al., *Adolescents*, 38.

of this age were apprentices, while girls were likely to be occupied in more lucrative semiskilled work.[69] The gap widened significantly among those aged 18 and over, reflecting the widening gendered earnings differential. In Rowntree's study young adult women had on average 7s 5d weekly spending money, while young adult men enjoyed 24s 11d per week. However, a large-scale 1950 study found that women aged 19 had on average 26s 10d, whereas 19-year-old men were granted 28s.[70] As this suggests, an increase in young women's earning opportunities, together with rising working class affluence, narrowed the gender differential in spending money for these workers in the post-Second World War years. This should not be overstated; the continuing practice of young men 'treating' their girlfriends points to the gender disparity in earnings and spending money that remained evident in the post-war era. Recent studies highlight a continuing bias towards sons in the granting of pocket money in the late twentieth century.[71] Gender relations were shaped within an economic context, but social and cultural factors were powerful influences upon them.

Maternal 'Indulgence'?: Co-operation and Conflict in Leisure Allocation

Despite the constraints placed upon young women's access to leisure, the period between the ages of 16 or 18 and their early twenties was considered by many to be 'the best time of their lives', a maxim constantly repeated by their elders.[72] Previous examinations of youthful consumption have not satisfactorily explained why working class households, many of which had no surplus income, allocated a relatively large degree of leisure and spending money to sons and daughters, implying that this was one effect of a rising standard of living. However, parents'—particularly mothers'—attempts to mitigate the effect of low household income or young workers' unemployment upon their children's leisure, documented by contemporaries,[73] demonstrate that their acceptance of youth as a period of relative affluence cannot be entirely attributed to increasing

69 Reed et al., *Adolescents*, 38. 70 Ibid.

71 A. Furnham, 'The Saving and Spending Habits of Young People', *Journal of Economic Psychology*, 20/6 (1999). 72 Thew, *Tune for Bears*, 146.

73 Rowntree, *Poverty and Progress*, 80; M-OA: Worktown Collection, 28/B, Household Budgets.

prosperity, and led Margery Spring Rice to disapprovingly categorize it as unwise maternal 'indulgence'.[74]

Closer scrutiny of the evidence suggests that the allocation of leisure and money was shaped by a more considered strategy than Spring Rice implies. Horrell and Oxley point out that in late nineteenth-century England, forging a reciprocal relationship with children allowed parents to benefit from young wage-earners' continued presence in and contribution to the household. Bias towards males in intrahousehold resource allocation was largely explained by their greater earning potential, and was less significant in those households where daughters earned relatively high wages.[75] Young wage-earners' contributions clearly continued to constitute a large proportion of household income between 1918 and 1950. Sons were still usually a more important long-term financial asset to households than daughters, explaining the restricted leisure of unoccupied daughters and the limited domestic work expected of sons, particularly in areas characterized by a strong sexual division of labour. However, between the late nineteenth century and the 1930s, an expansion in young women's employment opportunities, juxtaposed with the insecurity of adult males' employment, together with declining family size, and improved housing, raised the value of a young woman's paid work. Benninghaus has suggested with reference to Weimar Germany that maternal allocation of leisure to wage-earning daughters reflected the increasing value of young women workers' financial contribution to the household.[76] This pattern was also clearly discernible in England by the end of the interwar years.

Personal testimonies illustrate the importance of daughters' leisure access in forging intergenerational economic reciprocity. They suggest that although women rarely appeared to resent bias towards brothers in the allocation of leisure time or spending money, unfavourable comparisons with friends or siblings of the same sex did provoke feelings of injustice. A lack of social and financial independence was recognized as exploitation if a daughter felt her family could afford to grant it. Lily ran away from home at the age of 15 because 'I was absolutely fed up with

[74] M. Spring Rice, *Working-Class Wives: Their Health and Conditions*, 2nd edn. (London: Virago, 1981), 105.

[75] S. Horrell and D. Oxley, 'Breadwinning, Family Employment and Household Resource Allocation', in C. E. Nunez (ed.), *The Microeconomic Analysis of the Household and the Labour Market, 1880–1939* (Seville: University of Seville, 1998), 63–5.

[76] C. Benninghaus, 'Mothers' Toil and Daughters' Leisure: Working-Class Girls and Time in 1920s Germany', *History Workshop Journal*, 50 (2000), 23–44.

the conditions under which I was living. I mean I never used to get any spending money or anything.'[77] Emotional relationships between daughters and their mothers were thus influenced by the latter's balancing of household need, and in some cases her own desire for companionship, with a daughter's desires. Daughters looked to their mothers to grant them some independence, because of their mother's role as household manager, together with the connections between mothers' and daughters' lives, recognition of which was heightened by maternal attempts to raise or realize daughters' aspirations or to forge companionship with an older girl. Consequently, daughters frequently expected greater justice and consideration from their mothers than from fathers. As a young domestic servant in the 1930s, Mrs Hevness bought a bicycle on hire purchase, sending her parents money to make the payments on her behalf, only to discover months later that her father had used the money to bet on horses. Her bitterness was, however, directed mostly towards her mother, who, as household manager, received Mrs Hevness's financial contribution at the end of each week. Her use of this to fund her own and her husband's gambling were viewed by Mrs Hevness as evidence of mismanagement and unjust treatment:'my mother saw that she got her little bit. I'll say she did. She used to get the lot. I didn't used to get any.'[78] Mrs Hevness continued to send money home only because she knew it was essential to the maintenance of her younger siblings. As young women's importance as household breadwinners rose, so did their assertion of their right to social and financial independence, echoing the claims made by their wage-earning fathers who justified their leisure time and expenditure in a similar manner, as Alexander and Davies have shown.[79] The Council of the National Association of Girls' Clubs suggested that while older schoolgirls' domestic workload increased during the Second World War because of their mothers undertaking more paid work, this was less true of young working women who contended 'that they have already done their share by contributing to the family purse'.[80]

Generally, working class mothers appear to have agreed with their daughters. Mass-Observation reports indicate that mothers who did not urgently require domestic help, such as those who did not work outside the home, or whose families were of average size or smaller, were

[77] NLSL, Making Ends Meet, A50/a/2, interview with Lily.

[78] NLSL, Making Ends Meet, A78/a/1, interview with Mrs Hevness.

[79] Davies, *Leisure*, 49; S. Alexander, 'Men's Fears and Women's Work: Responses to Unemployment in London between the Wars', *Gender and History*, 12/2 (2000), 413.

[80] M-OA: FR1353, 'The Service of Youth', July 1942, 8.

very sympathetic to their daughters' desire for leisure. The mother of one 15-year-old office worker was typical of those Hampshire villagers questioned about their children's leisure by Mass-Observation in 1942. The household was headed by a male, unskilled worker, suggesting that the daughter's wages were of great importance to the family economy. Her mother commented:

She doesn't really do any [housework] except on Sundays, she might sweep up a bit, or wipe up. She doesn't have much time, and she's only a child after all. She has a long day, and I don't want to put too much on her. She might do a bit of knitting in the evenings, or in the summer she goes out on her bicycle or for a walk.[81]

That paid work marked a watershed in this regard was noted by many women, including Eileen, who found that the level of housework expected of her fell when she entered employment in the early 1920s,[82] and Dolly,[83] who had a similar experience when she began work 16 years later. Ferdynand Zweig found in the late 1940s that young adults were allowed significant financial autonomy partly because parents feared that 'the children, if overcharged, would leave them', with detrimental consequences for the family economy.[84] Although the amount of spending money given to young workers by their mothers was not the source of generational conflict that studies of post-1950 youth culture suggest it later became,[85] the extension of the industrialized working day and a rise in living standards increased youthful expectations of economic independence and had repercussions for intergenerational relationships within working class households.

The allocation of leisure was not simply shaped by economic considerations, however. Many mothers wished their children to enjoy youth more than they had. The strength of this aspiration is demonstrated by the numerous economies made in order to allocate leisure and spending money to children. In 1937 Mass-Observation asked Bolton adults how their households would economize should the need arise; none of their respondents considered reducing their children's spending money.[86] In Northumberland, characterized by a strong sexual division of labour that

[81] M-OA: FR1567, 'Girls between School-Leaving and Registration', 5.

[82] NLSL, Making Ends Meet, A14/a, interview with Eileen.

[83] Lifetimes Group, *Something in Common* (Manchester: Manchester University Press, 1975), 14.

[84] F. Zweig, *Labour, Life and Poverty* (London: Gollancz, 1948), 16.

[85] Osgerby, *Youth in Britain*, 30–49.

[86] M-OA: Worktown collection, Box 34: South Lancashire Savings Survey, 34/A, 7 point questionnaire, 43 replies, 'South Lancashire Savings Survey', 1938.

reduced young women's importance as wage-earners, similar 'indulgence' was nevertheless evident. Linda Thew recalled,

> In this interval between leaving school and getting married, some mothers indulged their daughters, urging them to have a good time before they settled down. Experience had taught the mothers they (the daughters) were unlikely to get it afterwards.[87]

Mothers in particular viewed youth as a period of compensation for the burden of responsibility that their daughters would shoulder in adulthood.

That youth was treated indulgently even in interwar Northumberland demonstrates the truth of Horrell and Oxley's assertion that 'Parents cannot be seen to be simplistically linking resource allocation to expected revenue'.[88] Scrutinizing the interaction of economic and emotional ties between mothers and daughters offers a more complete view of household relations than has been given by studies that overemphasize economic calculation in shaping parental allocation of leisure to children.[89] However, analysis of the mother–daughter relationship also tempers Roberts's argument that relations between parents and children were essentially deferential, with the latter acquiescing to parental authority.[90] Greater reciprocity clearly characterized relationships between mothers and their daughters than this suggests. Long-term social and economic considerations both shaped and limited gender bias in the allocation of such resources as money and leisure in many working class households. Forging emotional and economic bonds with daughters was one means of encouraging them to marry late and/or close to home, and to maintain a mutually supportive relationship with their mothers. This could be very important in areas like the north-east coalfield where a sexual division of labour was reflected in segregated leisure activities, and a married daughter was consequently a valuable source of companionship.[91] Moreover, numerous working class Mass-Observation respondents expected to be reliant upon their own savings and their children in old age[92] and as late as 1951 Rowntree and Lavers found a significant correlation between old

[87] Thew, *Tune for Bears*, 146.

[88] S. Horrell and D. Oxley, 'Crust or Crumb?: Intrahousehold Resource Allocation and Male Breadwinning in Late Victorian Britain', *Economic History Review*, 52/3 (1999), 517–18.

[89] S. Meacham, *A Life Apart: The English Working Class 1890–1914* (London: Thames and Hudson, 1977), 181–2.

[90] Roberts, *Woman's Place*, 42–3.

[91] N. Dennis, F. Henriques, and C. Slaughter, *Coal Is Our Life: An Analysis of a Yorkshire Mining Community*, 2nd edn. (London: Tavistock Publications, 1969), 201–7.

[92] M-OA: Worktown collection, 28/D, ms: 'Motives for Saving: Preliminary Report', 1939, 1–7.

age and poverty.[93] Such material supports Thane's argument that adult children, particularly daughters, remained an extremely important source of economic and emotional support for older parents.[94] It thus remained in parents' interests to develop a reciprocal relationship based on mutual support with their children. A short-term maternal need for domestic help in the home was often tempered by recognition of this, and could have benefits for daughters in terms of social and financial freedom.

Visions of the Modern Young Woman: The Street, the State, and the Press

The strong collective identity of young women workers that their work culture and leisure consumption forged was reflected in representations of them in the press and in political and popular discourse. Many historians have suggested that the emergence of this relatively independent young working class woman caused popular concern, contradicting the idealization of a domestic femininity and, in the Second World War, selfless citizenship.[95] Certainly, in both formal politics and street life, young working class women faced charges of delinquency or promiscuity. Women workers in exclusively or largely female workplaces or departments were frequently referred to as 'virgins' or 'angels', connotations of purity that were sometimes ironic and always sexualized.[96] Mrs Mead, who was a 'Player's Angel' at the firm's Nottingham factory from 1927 until the mid 1930s, recalled,

> we had great times and they were a grand lot of girls, course Players' Angels in those days were known as the Shockers y'know, they were ladies of doubtful integrity, as they were some of them let's be honest, but if you worked at Players, they [young men] used to look at you and think you were a bit of alright sort of thing [laughs] its true . . . the girls I knew, the women were very nice, there was the odd one that was er, racy but . . . in the main they were all very nice.[97]

[93] B. S. Rowntree and G. R. Lavers, *Poverty and the Welfare State* (London: Longmans, 1951), 35.

[94] P. Thane, *Old Age in English History: Past Experiences, Present Issues* (Oxford: Oxford University Press, 2000), 299–301.

[95] D. Beddoe, *Back to Home and Duty: Women between the Wars* (London: Pandora, 1989), 22–4; B. Melman, *Flappers and Nymphs* (Basingstoke: Macmillan, 1988), 10–21; S. Rose, *Which People's War?: National Identity and Citizenship in Britain 1939–1945* (Oxford: Oxford University Press, 2003), 135.

[96] See, for example, NWSA, LRO, 1992.0062, interview with Edith Hough, on factory 'virgins'. Newton Aycliffe Royal Ordnance Factory workers were 'Aycliffe Angels'.

[97] NLSL, Making Ends Meet, A23/a/1, interview with Mrs Mead.

As this suggests, the widespread reputation of factory girls as 'rough' was largely a misrepresentation based upon the very assertive collective identity created by these young women in the workplace as well as in their shared leisure activities. In the Second World War the Ministries of Labour and Education exerted pressure on young people to join voluntary service organizations in their free time in part because of concern over delinquency and promiscuity. The Youth Advisory Committees, under the auspices of the Ministry of Labour, believed that there was a 'grave necessity' for youth service, disapprovingly noting that 'Large numbers think they have done their share by working long hours.'[98] When 16 and 17 year olds were registered by LEAs from 1941, with a view to encouraging their participation in youth organizations, young women's reluctance to join was frequently ascribed to their lack of moral fibre, one Ministry of Education report commenting that 'if these young women had been interviewed when they were 14 and a half or 15 years of age they might have formed decent habits, instead of hanging about the streets' and concluded that 'they lack any sense of service'.[99] Youthful independence was treated with some suspicion by politicians and educationalists largely because of the social class of young workers, but age and gender mediated the anxiety expressed; whereas young men were portrayed as potential delinquents, young women's particular unwillingness to engage in organized leisure was interpreted as selfish and potentially immoral.

Yet, as Langhamer has pointed out, young women's leisure inspired optimism as well as fear.[100] From the 1920s onwards, and particularly during and after the successful campaign for young and all working class women's political enfranchisement, which was granted in 1928, the popular press and the growing number of studies of leisure frequently represented the modern, young working class woman as a sign of modernity and affluence.[101] From the 1920s, the young working class woman's increased employment opportunities, leisure consumption, political participation, and, later, her war service, emphasized the growing social, economic, and political importance of this group. In 1931 the *Manchester Evening News* concluded approvingly that 'the mill girl'

[98] TNA, LAB 19/99, Lt.-Col. the Hon. A. Lytton-Milbanke, Note on Youth Advisory Council Paper 1, 1941.

[99] TNA, ED 124/47, Y.W., MS: Notes of the Reports by LEAs of the Registration of Young People in March 1943, 5, 14.

[100] Langhamer, *Women's Leisure*, 53–4.

[101] A. Bingham, ' "Stop the Flapper Vote Folly": Lord Rothermere, the Daily Mail, and the Equalization of the Franchise 1927–28', *Twentieth Century British History*, 13/1 (2002), 17–37; C. D. Burns, *Leisure in the Modern World* (London: Allen and Unwin, 1932), 190–200.

deserved her conspicuous leisure consumption because she 'has worked hard for her living, and at the same time helped to "rear" her younger brothers and sisters' causing her to be 'shrewd and capable and very self-reliant'. Her work and sensible economizing legitimated her clothing expenditure and week in Blackpool; 'She has all the money saved during the year for this annual holiday, and she *does* have a good time'.[102] Similarly, during the Second World War, the government decided not to make membership of a youth organization compulsory, in part to distinguish Britain from fascist regimes, as well as because of a desire to protect the sanctity of family life,[103] but also because of a recognition that young workers' 'enthusiasm and endurance' in their work entitled them to leisure.[104] Using age as well as gender as an analytical category highlights that positive representations of womanhood were not simply confined to the domestic sphere as studies by Alison Light and Deirdre Beddoe suggest.[105] Young women's independence was used to suggest that leisure offered an adequate outlet for creativity in a society where work was increasingly shaped around monotonous, mechanized labour processes.

In fact, as Bingham has highlighted, it was the development of young women's potentially political collective identity as workers, rather than their prominence as leisure consumers, that caused greatest anxiety within the press and among politicians and many middle class social commentators. That their increasing employment in factories and shops would cause them to identify with the Labour Party was the main focus for pre-1928 opposition to the extension of the vote to women aged under 30,[106] a concern based on class as well as age. Liberal and left-wing feminists were unsurprisingly more sympathetic to young women's citizenship, among them Winifred Holtby, who noted in the early 1930s that the continued concern over these young women's political potential fuelled charges that adolescent girls were lazy, 'rude and disrespectful'—suggestive of apathy or antagonism towards society's political and class structures—and 'neglect their duty', which was ambiguously defined but widely viewed as residing outside political engagement.[107] The wartime juxtaposition of a celebration of young women's war work with anxiety

102 *Manchester Evening News* (14 May 1930), 3.

103 TNA, ED 124/81, ms: Partnership in the Service of Youth—Second Statement, 1945.

104 Board of Education, *The Youth Service after the War* (London: HMSO, 1943), 5.

105 A. Light, *Forever England: Feminism, Literature and Conservatism between the Wars* (London: Routledge, 1991), 10–15, 183–5; Beddoe, *Home and Duty*, 22–4, 89–90.

106 Bingham, ' "Flapper Vote" ', 24–6.

107 W. Holtby, *Women and a Changing Civilization* (London: John Lane, 1934), 118.

over their reluctance to join organized youth activities reflected an ongoing unease about the public presence of groups of assertive working class young people who did not respect the social order, as the government reports cited earlier suggest. As Davies has noted, young people who socialized in the streets were subject to police harassment in working class communities.[108] Similar unease prompted one middle class commentator's complaint about his experience as a train passenger in 1944:

> a horde of young, noisy, cat-calling factory girls and lads came crowding into the first class compartments, and refused to move to the empty third class carriages. . . . They loudly declared that they had as much right to the first class carriages.[109]

The identification of such behaviour with the factory highlights that the importance of the workplace as a site of socialization was a major cause of the concern that surrounded the decline of (deferential) domestic service and increase in industrial employment.

Courtship and Marriage

Courtship was an important part of young adult women's lives. It occupied a large degree of their leisure time; as earlier sections of this chapter have noted, many leisure venues were centred around courtship opportunities, such as the monkey parade and the dance hall. Chapter 5 highlighted the increasing importance of the workplace as a courtship venue. The final section of this chapter briefly considers how young women's attitudes to courtship and married life altered, in the context of their increasing employment opportunities and their growing social independence.

Young women wage-earners' leisure consumption distinguished them not only from their mothers and fathers but also, at times, from young men. Gender disparity in leisure access narrowed, largely because of the growth in young women's employment opportunities and the demise of domestic service. Leisure expenditure increasingly depended not upon great affluence, but upon a regular income. This distinguished young adult women, whose employment opportunities were expanding, from young adult men, who were more likely to experience unemployment in

108 Davies, *Leisure*, 99–102.

109 S. P. B. Mais, *Youth after the War* (London: Macdonald and Co., 1944), 16–17.

the interwar years[110] and were subject to wartime military conscription and post-war National Service. Young women themselves were aware of the consequences of this. In the interwar years, a boyfriend could expand a young woman's leisure access, as Langhamer has shown, providing her with an escort to dances and a financial passport to other forms of commercial leisure. Unemployment in the 1930s, however, hampered young men's access to commercial leisure and to courtship.[111] On Tyneside in the 1930s, where Hilda Ashby worked as a cinema usherette—a position that enabled her to indulge in a limited amount of leisure consumption—her parents and friends stressed to her that 'you had to look for a man that was working'.[112] The implication was that being single was better than courting, or being married to, an unemployed man, an attitude that emphasized young women's increasing financial independence.

As Hilda Ashby's attitude highlights, changes in young women's and young men's earning and employment patterns altered young women's courtship experiences and expectations. Whitworth has suggested that by the late 1930s in Coventry, male unemployment and an increase in women's earning power prompted a reassessment in gender relations; women were more likely to look for a boyfriend who had the determination to make something of himself, rather than one who was highly paid.[113] Mrs Hughson's experience supports this. She was a servant in Manchester when she got engaged in the 1930s. Her employer disapproved of her match, partly because Mrs Hughson's fiancé had had a series of casual jobs. This did not deter Mrs Hughson, but she clearly felt it was important to help her fiancé establish himself in a steady post that could support them both:

> He was a packer—and—he's had to leave that—it finished . . . then he had different jobs in the building trade—but when I was getting ready to marry him, I persuaded him to buy an insurance book—because there was money in those days in building up an insurance book.[114]

[110] C. Cameron, A. Lush, and G. Meara, *Disinherited Youth: A Report on the 18+ Age Group Enquiry Prepared for the Trustees of the Carnegie United Kingdom Trust* (Edinburgh: University of Edinburgh, 1943), 104.

[111] Langhamer, *Women's Leisure*, 126; See also Davies, *Leisure*, 43.

[112] H. Ashby, 'Wait 'Til The Banner Comes Home!', in K. Armstrong and H. Benyon (eds.), *Hello, Are You Working? Memories of the Thirties in the North-East of England* (Whitley Bay: Strong Words, 1983), 41–2.

[113] L. Whitworth, 'Men, Women, Shops and "Little Shiny Homes": The Consuming of Coventry, 1930–39', Ph.D. thesis (Warwick, 1997), 74–6.

[114] TLSL, Manchester Studies, 26, interview with Mrs E. Hughson.

Following this, Mrs Hughson left her full-time job and took a part-time cleaning post to allow her time to look for a flat to move into after her wedding. However, her fiancé's lack of similar initiative now caused her to have doubts and she briefly courted another man:

I was feeling a bit disappointed that my husband to be wasn't making a more business—like a method of going about this flat—so of course when I told my mother about it, she said well you've been going with him long enough—I said, 'look—I've been living in I didn't have much chance—I'm coming to think he's a bit slow, . . . and I told her about this young chap you see . . . and she said 'now—don't do anything silly, you don't know anything about him.'

Mrs Hughson subsequently discovered that her second suitor was married, which 'made up my mind to get married—so when I saw my young man . . . I told him,—"now I've been friendly with this chap . . . so it's up to you to fix the date—otherwise I'm going back in service." He said "alright—we'll have the fifteenth of August." ' As this suggests, young women adapted to male unemployment and their own expanding earning power by using the ingenuity and initiative that their mothers relied on to make ends meet, as well as their own income, to shape a courtship that offered a life a little better than their mothers had experienced. Their own financial contribution to marital preparations, together with the uncertain earnings of many young men, encouraged them to demand an investment of emotion and energy from fiancés who could not guarantee to be regular economic providers. These women's determination to make their courtship work testified to the attractions of marriage vis à vis a single, working life as an adult, working class woman, and possibly also to an awareness of the 'surplus women' debate that pervaded the interwar press and political discourse;[115] finding a man who had potential was better than no man at all.

By the 1940s, the relationship between courtship and leisure was undergoing further change, with young women increasingly looking to wage-earning, rather than a boyfriend, as a means of establishing a social life. Mrs Halten was well aware that she earned more than her fiancé while both of them worked at a Lancashire aircraft factory, and was consequently able to enjoy a greater variety of leisure activities than him.[116] As well as being attributable to the effect of rising wages and increased employment opportunities, this change was also due to the

[115] B. Melman, *Women and the Popular Imagination in the Twenties: Flappers and Nymphs* (Basingstoke: Macmillan, 1988).

[116] TLSL, Tameside tapes collection, tape 71, interview with Mrs Halten.

appearance of relatively affluent American GIs, which forced a reassessment of the limited income and leisure consumption of English boyfriends. Kathleen Holland recalled that the American soldiers she met at dances, and her own increasing awareness of herself as an attractive and independent young woman, made her question her courtship with the man who eventually became her husband. American soldiers

> were beautiful, they were fantastic. . . . in khaki [my boyfriend] never looked clean. I'd spent all my coupons on a new coat and hat. On the Sunday I was upstairs and my mother said 'Kathleen, here's Norman', he looked as if he'd fallen off a truck. . . . I thought 'I'm not walking out with you', I compared him with the Americans. . . . We had our dinner and then my mother said 'You'd better go for a walk.' I had this new coat. I said 'we'll go down Reddish Vale so none of my friends can see him.'[117]

The testimonies cited here highlight a growing recognition that courtship, which in the inter war years generally increased access to forms of commercial leisure such as dancing, could in fact restrict leisure access in an era when young women might earn more, or more regularly, than their male peers. Although Langhamer emphasizes continuity over the period between 1920 and 1960, close scrutiny of her evidence supports the conclusion, suggested by the evidence here, that young women were increasingly willing to 'pay their way' in leisure activities by the mid-1940s, in part to establish an economic equality that deterred their boyfriends from believing they were 'owed' sexual favours.[118] Young women workers were conscious that they were at the forefront of social change, their earnings prompting the emergence of youth as a period characterized by regular luxury consumption.[119]

Obtaining secure, relatively well-paid work in their youth was also viewed as central to the attainment of marital aspirations by an increasing number of young women. Paternal unemployment or death meant that many realized from an early age that their earnings might be necessary to them throughout adult life. Doris Knight took up dressmaking because she recognized this as a trade she could fall back on after marriage if necessary; her own mother had been deserted by Doris's father and ran a boarding house and took in washing to make ends meet.[120] By the late

117 TLSL, Manchester Studies, 1075, interview with Kathleen Holland.

118 Langhamer, *Women's Leisure*, 126–7.

119 Langhamer, *Women's Leisure*, 58–70; K. Milcoy, 'Image and Reality: Working-Class Teenage Girls' Leisure in Bermondsey during the Interwar Years', D.Phil. thesis (Sussex, 2001), 142–5.

120 D. Knight, *Millfield Memories* (London: Centreprise, 1976), 12, 34.

1930s, many women in the more prosperous regions were expanding their aspirations, but recognized that their own earnings would be central to their realization. Many young women equated marriage with buying or renting a home of their own by this stage,[121] but the finances required to afford a deposit and the rent necessitated a joint strategy between a young woman and her fiancé. As Mrs Johnson, a Coventry factory worker, recalled of her courtship, 'We had to save up for our own deposit on the house . . . which took a lot, you couldn't just meet somebody and go and get married you had to go courting a few years to save.'[122] Joint financial strategies were thus important in sustaining and developing courtship; although this was not new to our period, the significance of young women's earnings had certainly grown. Their earnings were vital for many of the purchases that changed the nature of working class life over these decades, and the desire to sustain this lifestyle, by paying the mortgage or meeting high rental costs, for example, encouraged the rise in married women's paid work in the 1950s. As Roberts highlights, one of the most significant changes in young women's marital expectations and early married life over this period was in their first marital home: whereas working class women frequently lived in their or their husband's parental home in the 1920s, by the 1950s, moving into a home of one's own was a frequent rite of passage for a newly married couple.[123]

The value placed on marrying a financially secure man continued to be high, however. The dream of retirement from full-time paid work upon marriage prevailed into the 1950s. Mass-Observation found at the end of the war that 'Even girls who have no definite prospects of marriage feel that their future is best assured by having the men in full employment.'[124] Ultimately, as Alexander has noted, a young woman's low wages could not bring her the independence and material possessions that many aspired to, heightening the economic attractions of marriage.[125] One Mass-Observation study carried out in 1949 concluded that 'many of those to whom marriage was so important seemed to be looking forward, not so much to romance, but to domesticity.'[126] Although young women increasingly viewed their wage-earning as central in defining their youth

121 J. Giles, *Women, Identity and Private Life in Britain, 1900–50* (Basingstoke: Macmillan, 1995), 62–8.

122 MRC, Coventry Women's Work Collection, MSS 266/6/4, interview with Mrs Johnson.

123 E. Roberts, *Women and Families: An Oral History, 1940–1970* (Oxford: Blackwell, 1995), 74.

124 MO-A: FR 2059, 'Do the Factory Girls Want to Stay Put or Go Home?', March 1944, 7.

125 Alexander, 'Men's Fears', 416.

126 MO-A: FR 3150, 'Teenage Girls', August 1949, 13.

as a period of leisure and affluence, full-time paid work continued to be viewed as a temporary phenomenon.

Young women's marital aspirations appear to have risen over the period. The limitation of family size was increasingly recognized as an important means of achieving the type of life that they desired. Although none of the women whose testimonies are used here mention any desire or attempt to restrict the size of their families, many do express the view that their mother had too many children, or that the large number of siblings they had increased their family's hardship. Mrs Sandys recalled that when her youngest brother was born in 1923 she was far from pleased:'we hadn't room enough and I only knew that this meant more for me, you see I was the girl, I suppose I was about ten and now that was three younger than me—all I could foresee was no more playing time again'.[127] Such sentiments are shared by Roberts's respondents, who appear to have placed increasing importance on family limitation from the 1940s onwards.[128] As Szreter suggests, young working class women's desire to enjoy a life more economically secure than that of their mothers, combined with an aspiration for greater personal freedom and independence contributed to the dramatic decline in completed family size between 1870 and 1940, which fell to 1.97 children between 1936 and 1940, and did not exceed 2.2 children prior to 1950.[129] Moreover, importantly, the age at which family size was completed also fell, aided by a declining age of first marriage, which compressed youth as a life stage. In the 1930s, women could expect to complete their family by the age of 31; by 1950 this had fallen to 28.[130] This change points to the increasing opportunities that young women had for courtship, particularly in the workplace, as chapter 5 highlighted, supporting Szreter's conclusion.[131] The rise in employment opportunities and earnings from the late 1930s made finding a 'good' man easier, and eroded the financial need for a long courtship, or to postpone starting a family. These changes point to women's assertion of their own aspirations for economic security and a greater

127 TLSL, Manchester Studies, tape 9, interview with Mrs Sandys. Unfortunately it is not known how many children Mrs Sandys herself had.

128 Roberts, *Women and Families*, 77–8.

129 S. Szreter, *Fertility, Class and Gender in Britain, 1860–1940* (Cambridge: Cambridge University Press, 1996), 576–80. See also L. Davidoff et al., *The Family Story: Blood, Contract and Intimacy 1830–1960* (London: Longman, 1999), 205. Demographic statistics are taken from D. Coleman, 'Population and Family', in A. H. Halsey with J. Webb (eds.), *Twentieth-Century British Social Trends* (Basingstoke: Macmillan, 1999), 36, Table 2.3.

130 M. Anderson, 'The Emergence of the Modern Life Cycle in Britain', *Social History*, 10/1 (1985), 73.

131 Szreter, *Fertility*, 357.

degree of social freedom, but they also demonstrate that, for most young, working class women, social aspirations continued to be centred on the establishment of the marital home.

Conclusion

Paid work structured young women's access to leisure consumption, which increased over the period, largely because of the proliferation of jobs that conformed to the industrialized working day and offered higher wages than domestic service. Trends in young women's employment were in turn shaped by this group's determination to enter employment that offered them a degree of social and financial independence. Consequently, young women became a group of particularly prominent leisure consumers, whose desire for a degree of personal freedom outside the workplace shaped the development of commercial leisure as well as popular representations of them. However, economic circumstance did not dictate this trend. Family relations, and particularly maternal aspirations for their daughters, were important in expanding young women's social and financial independence. The young women of the 1920s and 1930s became the mothers of the 1940s and 1950s; their determination that their daughters would realize the aspirations that they themselves had formed but had to give up because of lack of opportunity was part of the reason, by the late 1940s, youth was widely accepted as a period of relative affluence. Histories of youth have often emphasized generational conflict,[132] but the evidence presented here suggests a greater level of consensus existed between parents and children. Friendship groups, established in neighbourhoods and workplaces, contributed to a collective, generational identity that strengthened young women's feeling of entitlement to independence by virtue of their wage-earning, and their view of leisure as a means of enjoying a very different kind of life from that led by their mothers. Marital aspirations also changed: although finding a good provider was a priority for many young women throughout the period, preserving a degree of independence throughout courtship and sometimes into early married life was increasingly considered important. This was partly due to young women's realization of their own increasing importance as wage-earners relative to young men, and their awareness that wage-earning gave them

[132] Fowler, *First Teenagers*; Osgerby, *Youth in Britain*.

more power to participate in decision-making within the parental household and with their fiancé or husband. Their own determination to extend their social and financial independence thus significantly shaped trends in working class leisure consumption and demographic developments, as well as prompting the emergence of the 1950s 'teenager'.

Conclusion

The world of work was central to the lives of all working class people in mid-twentieth-century England, not simply to those of adult men. Whereas previous histories of women's and young people's lives during this period have focused on domestic life or leisure, this study has shown that expanding earning and employment opportunities had a tremendous impact upon the lives, relationships, aspirations, and representation of young working class women. This development was part of a longer trajectory of change; it is important not to exaggerate one's period of study as a crucial 'break with tradition', and the youthful consumer of the early 1950s can clearly be linked to the emergence of a distinct juvenile labour market in the late nineteenth century. However, young working class women's social and economic freedoms increased markedly between the end of the First World War and the beginning of the 1950s, concurrent with a significant expansion in their earning opportunities. The lifestyles and status of these young workers changed, as residential domestic service ceased to be their largest employer and increasing numbers were able to find light factory and office jobs, offering greater liberty, less arduous work, and a degree of personal affluence. This also had important political implications, with young women forming and drawing on a strong, collective identity to assert their rights as independent citizens, and to distinguish themselves and their interests from their employers as well as at times from their parents. They were not 'apathetic' workers as they have previously been portrayed, and in fact the political and social implications of their collective, assertive presence, rather than the nature of their leisure activities alone, help to explain their conspicuousness on urban streets and in the contemporary press. Clearly, strong links connected working, social, and political life that are worthy of further historical investigation.

Scrutinizing young women's lives through the prism of their employment provides valuable insights into the interaction of gender, age, and class in the formation of social and political identities and relationships among a historically neglected group and in the wider community in which they lived. Studying family relations in this context indicates that the working class family economy was far more complex, and breadwinning patterns more pluralistic and flexible, than is often assumed. Although historians widely accept that the 'male breadwinner model' was an ideal rather than a reality for working class households during this period, a continuing concentration upon the construction of this ideal means that the breadwinning strategies that were in reality employed have been greatly neglected. This book has shown that young women wage-earners were crucial to a wide range of working class households until at least the middle of the twentieth century, highlighting the persistence of poverty and indicating the insecurity of working class affluence even in the early 1950s.

As this suggests, household and family relations were shaped by economic need; however, this does not mean that they were economically determined. Relations between parents and daughters, and particularly between mothers and daughters, were a frequently complex combination of mutual economic and emotional support, affection, and obligation. An individual's financial contribution to the household had a significant impact upon their role within it and their relations with other household members, the highest earners often receiving a larger allocation of spending money, for example. However, careful examination of the mother–daughter relationship highlights that such reciprocity was not simply economic. Mutual emotional support could also be important, with maternal aspirations encouraging daughters' desire for greater social and economic freedom. The generation of young women who grew up in the interwar years have emerged as crucial in this respect. Their own aspirations, raised by employment expansion during the First World War, were frequently thwarted by the demands made upon them by household poverty, but offered them a framework of 'unfulfilled desire'[1] in which they constructed hopes and expectations for their daughters' generation, who entered a more buoyant labour market in the more affluent 1940s and 1950s, and who enjoyed a greater degree of independence than their mothers had done. Gender- and age-specific roles and identities are, then, like class, formed in material historical relationships.

In studying young women, this book has not argued for a negation of social class as an historical concept, to be replaced with a multiplicity of competing social identities, but rather for a sensitive reappraisal of gender and generational relations within the class structure. Although Davies has

[1] C. Steedman, *Landscape for a Good Woman* (London: Virago, 1986), 123.

rightly pointed out that the standard of living could differ markedly between different members of the same household, often fractured along lines of gender and age,[2] the operation of the domestic economy meant that young women's fortunes were inextricably connected to those of other sections of the working class. The material presented here challenges Griffiths's assertion that 'class, as an influence affecting the choices made, appears to have been secondary, at best'[3] and the prevailing emphasis on gender and generational divisions in working class life in current historical research. Although both gender and generation are extremely important in shaping life choices and life experience, they cannot be isolated: age, gender, and locale closely interact in the formation of social identity and the development of social relations. Youth became a distinct and increasingly homogeneous life stage within working class communities between the end of the First World War and the early 1950s, as a rising proportion of young women became wage-earners and leisure consumption occupied an increasingly significant amount of their time. Young people, female and male, experienced similar economic circumstances, because of the insecurity of a wide range of working class households across these decades, a context that also bound them to working class children and adults, primarily through the family unit, but also through the workplace and local community. Although young women's age and gender differentiated their status and their roles, their lives—and, in fact, the nature of age and gender—were shaped by this broad but crucial context. As this suggests, historians' use of age and gender as analytical categories would benefit from the critical scrutiny to which social class has recently been subjected.

The family was both a source of support and a site of socialization into a capitalist society characterized by patriarchal relations. Despite their economic importance, young women continued to be subordinate members of the family unit by virtue of their age and gender. Their attempts to extend their own independence and create a social life with their peers, escaping the supervision of family, school, and workplace, testify to their recognition of and resistance to this position. Moreover, young women's awareness of the constraints that their gender and social background placed upon their choices could fuel a desire to separate themselves from aspects of their mothers' lives, leading to resentment

[2] A. Davies, *Leisure, Gender and Poverty: Working-Class Culture in Salford and Manchester, 1900–1939* (Buckingham: Open University Press, 1992), 171.

[3] T. Griffiths, *The Lancashire Working-Classes c. 1870–1930* (Oxford: Clarendon Press, 2001), 126.

about the obligations, whether material or—more commonly by the early 1950s—emotional, that they shouldered from an early age. Young women's awareness of their social, cultural, and economic position was strengthened by the workplace, but it was learned primarily from family relations, which were particularly important in producing what Steedman has called the psychological aspects of class consciousness.[4] These facets included envy, and a wish to escape the constraints imposed by class and gender, yet also common was a desire to maintain ties to other family members, particularly to their mothers, and a positive sense of belonging to their community. Young women's desires suggest that their class identity was forged both negatively—against employers, teachers, and more affluent, middle class young women—and positively, through strong, emotional ties to their families and peers. Young working class women's identities and relationships were thus more complex than is sometimes assumed, indicative of tensions and divisions within working class families and communities that coexisted with a world view in which recognition of similarities within the working class, and difference from other classes, ultimately appears to have been dominant.

The periodization of this study argues for a redefinition of change and continuity between 1918 and 1950. The extent to which the First World War was a catalyst for fundamental social and economic changes has yet to be fully appreciated by historians who still widely cite 1939 or 1945 as more significant chronological landmarks in the terrain of twentieth-century English history. The First World War and its aftermath had a profound effect on young women's employment opportunities; the proportion in employment rose between 1911 and 1921 and many benefited from an expansion in clerical and shop work that continued during the post-war years. Its effects on their aspirations and status were even more dramatic: young women had witnessed for themselves, or through the experience of older sisters or mothers, alternatives to domestic service during wartime, while paternal absence or invalidity increased their recognition—and that of parents, employers, politicians, and the press—of their economic value.

No static 'long weekend' followed the Armistice. Many young women found their aspirations thwarted by economic depression during the 1920s and early 1930s. Domestic service, which involved leaving home at an early age, limited liberty, and deferential relations with one's employer, shaped the lives of a huge proportion of young women until the 1940s.

[4] Steedman, *Landscape for a Good Woman*, 13.

Yet even in this sector change was apparent, as young women became more aware of alternative opportunities, increasingly using domestic service as a stepping stone to a life of relative liberty in England's larger urban towns. Those who entered employment from the mid-1930s onwards benefited from a rise in job opportunities and prosperity, which enabled many to spend more of their youth residing in their parents', rather than an employer's, home. An increasing number of these homes were in newer types of houses and communities, such as the estates developing on the edges of urban conurbations. A clear generational difference is thus apparent between the lives of those who entered employment in the early 1920s and those who did so fifteen years later.

The few existing historical studies of British youth in the twentieth century have tended to terminate at the outbreak of the Second World War or commence in the mid-1950s, but no smooth progression can be traced between the relatively affluent young wage-earners of the later 1930s and the teenage consumers of twenty years later who enjoyed far greater economic and social independence.[5] As this suggests, the 1940s were a decade of profound social, economic, and cultural as well as political change. The Second World War increased young women's economic responsibilities within the household and their earnings and social freedoms. Historians' emphasis on the attraction of domesticity as safe, secure, and comfortable for women in the post-war years has failed to assess the long-term implications of the Second World War on feminine roles. Young women certainly were attracted by marriage, but the growing acceptance of youth as a distinct life stage characterized by a degree of social freedom offered women a space to articulate and pursue alternative ambitions by the early 1950s. The confinement of these aspirations to youth meant that they did not pose a direct threat to marriage or motherhood, but their articulation reflects wider uncertainties about the social, economic, cultural, and political post-war context.

By 1950 the social, economic, and cultural position of young working class women was paradoxical. Youth was increasingly compressed, because of the raising of the school-leaving age and a fall in the average age of marriage. The teenage years were increasingly a period of economic dependency on parents, because of the raising of the school-leaving age, and facilitated by the buoyancy of labour demand for adult workers that enabled parents to maintain their children for longer periods. Yet young women's social freedoms concurrently expanded with growing affluence.

[5] B. Osgerby, *Youth in Britain since 1945* (Oxford: Blackwell, 1998), 1–12.

Youth had become established as a distinct stage in the working class life cycle, a period of training for adult life by the family and the state but also of sufficient independence to challenge and test the constraints that class and gender imposed on life choices.

Our understanding of the emergence and lifestyle of the 'teenager' in the second half of the twentieth century would greatly benefit from more attention being paid to these social, economic, and demographic changes. Scrutinizing young women's lives through the prism of their wage-earning and the working class family economy over this period could offer insights into how far and how fast the post-war welfare state and the rise in married women's work reduced the economic importance of young wage-earners for their households and altered the wider experience of youth. This type of study might suggest reasons for the tenacity of gender bias in household allocation of leisure time and spending money throughout the twentieth century, enabling a fuller evaluation of the roles of economic necessity, social considerations, and custom in the development of gender and generational, as well as class, relations. It could bring a historical perspective to existing sociological examinations of the tensions implicit in youth subcultures that were grounded in capitalist consumption but were implicitly hostile to the work ethic in their pursuit of leisure. In doing so, it could offer a deeper analysis of how awareness of class and gender is transmitted to young people and experienced by them. Such a focus would illuminate how far it remained the case in the later twentieth century, as it was until the early 1950s that the lived experience of youth was shaped by surviving, adapting to, modifying, and resisting the changing demands of the labour market upon the working class household.

APPENDIX

Biographical Details of the Oral History Sample

Brief biographical records are given of the eighty-one women whose oral testimonies have been extensively used in this study. Details are given, where known, of their year and place of birth; parents' occupations (mother's occupation relates to her employment after marriage); siblings; age at which they began work; their occupations; and their year of marriage. Occupations are listed chronologically. Servants are residential domestic servants unless otherwise noted. Pseudonyms have been used here and throughout the book where this was requested.

Name	Birth year	Birth place	Parental occupations	Siblings	Age began work	Occupations	Marriage
Annie Olive	1902	Oldham	Textile workers		12	Textile worker	1922
Mrs Hughson	1904	Manchester		9	14	Factory worker, servant, cleaner, daily maid	1930
Winifred Cotterill	1905	Coventry	Father: factory worker; Mother: factory worker then invalid	None	14	Clerk, unemployed, factory worker	Never
Frances Fuller	1905	Sussex	Father: railway worker		14	Shop assistant	
Ann Smith	1905	Lancashire			13	Mill worker	
Lottie	1906	Nottingham	Father: miner; Mother: took in washing	2 sisters	13	Lace worker	1925
Olive Jones	1906	Lancashire		7	12	Weaver	
Mrs Jones	1906	Manchester	Father: soldier, transport worker	5 brothers, 2 older	16	Clerk, technical designer	1932
Katharine Kelsall	1906	Manchester	Father: carpenter; Mother: cleaner	5 sisters, 4 brothers	14	Laundry worker	1930
Lucy Lees	1906	Clitheroe	Father: butler, mill worker	1 older sister	12	Mill worker, factory worker	
Dorothy	1907	Chesterfield	Father: shopkeeper	None	15	Shopkeeper	
Janet	1907	Nottingham	Father: absent	2 younger	12	Errand-girl, lace worker, factory worker, shop worker	

Mrs Savage	1907	Manchester	Father: factory worker	8	14	Fish and chip shop worker, factory worker	1932
Eileen	1908	Nottingham	Father: skilled factory worker	2	14	Factory worker, clerk, unemployed, clerk, hairdresser, adult education tutor	1933
Mrs E. Cleary	1908	Lancashire	Father: killed in 1914	2 younger	14	Confectioner, servant	
Nellie Hilton	1908	Lancashire	Mill workers		12	Mill worker	
Mrs Mead	1908	Nottingham	Father: milkman	6	18	Factory worker	1929
Louise Pace	1908	Altrincham	Father: absent; Mother: cleaner	2	14	Servant, unemployed, servant, WREN	
Doris Addicott	1910	Coventry	Father: factory worker	1 sister	14	Factory worker	1934
Mrs Hevness	1910	Nottingham	Father: baker, unemployed; Mother: shopkeeper, street-trader	6	15	Servant, cleaner	
Elsie Lee	1910	Coventry	Father: car worker	7	14	Factory worker	1933
Mrs Mullis	1910	Coventry			14	Factory worker	
Mrs E. Johnson	1911	Coventry			14	Weaver, factory worker	1937
Bobbie Gardiner	1913	Coventry	Father: factory worker	1 older sister	14	Factory worker	1940
Mrs Halliday	1913	Teeside	Father: electrician; Mother: upholsterer		14	Laundry worker, servant	
Mrs Sandys	1913	Bury	Father: unskilled transport worker; Mother: took in washing, midwife	6, 3 older	14	Servant, cleaner, nurse, midwife	1941

Name	Birth year	Birth place	Parental occupations	Siblings	Age began work	Occupations	Marriage
Edna	1914	Nottingham	Father: absent; Mother: clothing middlewoman	2 older brothers	14	Errand-girl; clothing home-worker	
Lily	1914	Ilkeston	Father: miner	9, 7 younger	15	Servant	
Elsie Booth	1914	Lancashire		1 brother	14	Mill worker	1932
Ida Hackett	1914	Mansfield	Father: miner; Mother: took in washing		14	Co-op shop assistant	
Edith Edwards	1915	Manchester	Father: dead; Mother: charwoman	1 sister, 2 brothers	14	Servant	Never
Mrs Cottrell	1917	Reading	Father: factory manager		16	Factory worker, clerk, factory worker	
Marion Kent	1917	Derbyshire		1 brother	16	Servant	
Jean Brown	1918	Stoke			14	Clerk	1942
Mrs E. V. Ellingham	1918	Reading			15	Typist	
Peggy Blunden	1919	London	Father: clerk		17	Clerk, telegraphist	
Hilda Broughton	1919	Lancashire	Father: crane driver; Mother: mill worker	4	14	Machinist	
Helen Drinkwater	1919	Manchester	Father: carpenter		14	Textile worker, munitions worker	
Edith Hough	1919	Ordsall	Father: docker	4 brothers, 1 sister	14	Factory worker, munitions worker	

Florence Rosenblatt	1919	Liverpool			14	Shop assistant, munitions worker	1944
Margaret Sharp	1919	Clitheroe	Father: mechanic; Mother: mill worker	4	14	Mill worker, aircraft engineer, clerk	1942
Irma Smith	1919	Manchester			14	Munitions worker	1942
Mary Abbott	1920	Lancashire	Textile workers		14	Textile worker	
Lilian Airey	1920	Manchester			16	Embroidery designer	1940
Joyce Musgrove	1920	Co. Durham	Father: Post Office clerk		16	Clerk, bookkeeper	
Alice Bates	1920	Hulme	Father: coal carter; Mother: textile worker	4 older	16	Clerk, civil servant	
Elsie Beasley	1920	Manchester			14	Mill worker, factory worker	
Mabel Morrison	1920	Manchester	Father: steel worker; Mother: cleaner	1 brother 1 sister	14	Factory worker	
Kathleen Holland	1920	Manchester			14	Factory worker, munitions worker	1940
Edna Delves	1921	Manchester			14	Factory worker, transport worker	
Mrs E. C. Somerville	1921	Manchester			14	Shop assistant, waitress, clerk	
Doris Windless	1921	Sussex	Father: soldier, railway worker, bookie's runner	4 older	14	Shop assistant, servant	
Peggy	1922	Nottingham	Father: watchmaker, factory worker; Mother: factory worker, waitress	4	14	Errand-girl, factory worker, unemployed, factory worker, shop assistant	1941

Name	Birth year	Birth place	Parental occupations	Siblings	Age began work	Occupations	Marriage
Joyce Shaw	1922	Stalybridge	Father: printworker	2 younger	14	Unemployed, factory worker	1944
Joan Whitfield	1922	Sussex	Father: iron worker	4 older,	14	Servant	
Mary Collins	1923	Manchester	Father: bus driver		14	Factory worker	
Peggy Few	1923	Reading			14	Factory worker, Land Army	
Mary Gregory	1923	Lancashire			17	Munitions worker	1940
Katherine Walker	1923	Stoke			14	Laundry worker, canteen worker	
Dorothy Raby	1923	Lancaster	Father: nurse, died in 1938; Mother: nurse		14	Maid, factory worker, laundry worker, shop assistant, nurse	
Edith Jones	1923	Co. Durham			14	Daily maid, unemployed, munitions worker	
Meg Powell	1923	Co. Durham			14	Factory worker, munitions worker	
Mrs Andrews	1924	Ashton		1 younger sister	14	Shop assistant, ATS clerk	
Mrs Halten	1924	Ashton	Father: miner	2 older brothers	14	Factory worker	1942

Vera Holmes	1924	Durham	Pub owners		14	Shop assistant, munitions worker	
Kitty Burn	1924	Durham			18	Factory worker, munitions worker	1945
Annie Doherty	1924	London	Munitions workers 1940–5	1 younger brother	14	Factory worker, munitions worker, Land Army	
Elsie Bell	1925	Newcastle	Father: soldier 1940–5		14	Laundry worker, munitions worker	
Violet Braithwaite	1925	Co. Durham	Father: miner		14	Shop assistant, munitions worker	
Mrs Mayer	1925	Ordsall	Father: labourer	2 younger	14	Factory worker, Land Army	
Jean Garstang	1926	Preston	Father: police sergeant		14	Shop assistant, clerk	
Enid Henderson	1926	Newcastle			14	Servant, munitions worker	
Joan Perry	1926	Sussex	Father: owned stables	6, 2 younger	14	Shop assistant	1944
Amy Cowie	1927	Darwen	Father: absent; Mother: textile worker	3	14	Textile worker, shop assistant	
Joan Geary	1927	Manchester	Father: accountant; Mother: died in 1939		14	Warehouse packer, factory worker, shop assistant	
Mrs Howard	1927	Bath	Father: engineer		14	Shop assistant, factory machinist	
Hilda Fielding	1928	Manchester	Father: mill worker; Mother: insurance agent	2 sisters	16	Typist, teacher	

Name	Birth year	Birth place	Parental occupations	Siblings	Age began work	Occupations	Marriage
Irene Moore	1929	London			14	Servant, factory worker	1953
Joyce Shelley	1929	Liverpool			14	Shop assistant, buyer	
Mrs Midge Harris	1934	Basingstoke			14	Hotel apprentice, factory worker	
Grace Wardle	1934	Manchester			15	Baker	

Bibliography

Archival sources with abbreviations used

East Sussex Record Office (ESRO)
AMS 6416, Lewes in Living Memory collection, Archive of the University of the Third Age: Lewes and District Branch.
/1/6/13, interview with Joan Whitfield.
/1/6/19, interview with Doris Windless.
/1/7/45, interview with Frances Fuller.
/1/7/51, interview with Joan Perry.

Imperial War Museum Sound Archive (IWM)
The following recorded interviews were used:
11849, Kitty Murphy.
12832, Ivy Reaney.
12845, Nora Barlow.
14993, Anon.
19686, Anon.
19688, Anon.
19694, Anon.
19696, Anon.
19699, Anon.
19717, Anon.
19715, Anon.
19719, Anon.

Lancashire Record Office (LRO), North West Sound Archive (NWSA)
The following recorded interviews were used:
1988.0060, Marion Kent.
1992.0103, Connie Curlett.
1993.0020, Joyce Shaw.
1994.0128, Margaret Sharp.
1995.0125, Annie Olive.
1995.0125, Ann Smith.
1999.0088, Mrs Halliday.
1999.0283, Helen Drinkwater.
1999.0292, Mary Gregory.
1999.0335, Lucy Lees.

1999.0340, Nellie Hilton.
1999.0343, Olive Jones.
1999.0444, Peggy Blunden.
1999.0445, Jean Garstang.
2000.0529a, Dorothy Raby.
2000.0651, Nora Holroyd.
2000.0900, Alice Bates.
2000.1010, Ida Hackett.
2000.1174, Joyce Shelley.
2001.0722, Joan Geary.
2002.0224a, Amy Cowie.
2002.0531a, Florence Rosenblatt.

Leicestershire Record Office (Leics RO)
DE 4823, Wolsey Company records.

Mass-Observation Archive, University of Sussex (M-OA)
File Reports
FR433, 'The Human Factors in Employment Exchanges' (September 1940).
FR533, 'Women and the War Effort' (December 1940).
FR1083, 'ATS Campaign' (February 1942).
FR1157, 'What Workers Really Earn' (March 1942).
FR1353, 'The Service of Youth' (July 1942).
FR1567, 'Report on Girls between School-Leaving and Registration Age' (January 1943).
FR1780, 'Youth Questionnaire' (May 1943).
FR2059, 'Do the Factory Girls Want to Stay Put or Go Home?' (March 1944).
FR2117, 'Women at Work: The Attitudes of Working Women towards Postwar Employment and Some Related Problems' (June 1944).
FR3150, 'Teenage Girls' (August 1949).
Topic Collection, Youth 1936–43, TC51.
Box 2: Material Collected for Youth Survey 1940–1: Paddington and Bermondsey.
Box 3: Youth Clubs and Later Questionnaires and Surveys.
Worktown Project.
Boxes 28–34: Money Matters.
Box 39: Background Research of Industry; the Co-operative Movement.

Modern Records Centre, University of Warwick (MRC).
MSS 192/TGW, National Union of Tailor and Garment Workers' Archive.
MSS 243, Young Women's Christian Association (YWCA) Archive.
MSS 266, Coventry Women's Work Collection:
/3/1/2, Letter from Winifred Cotterill to J. Castle, 1983.
/6/1, interview with Doris Addicott.
/6/2, interview with Winifred Cotterill.
/6/3, interview with Bobbie Gardiner.

/6/4, interview with Mrs Johnson.
/6/5, interview with Elsie Lee and Mrs Mullis.
MSS 292, Trade Union Congress (TUC) Archive, 1920–60:
6/1, Trades Councils.
/64/1, Organisation of Women, 1930–1.
/69/1–21, Organisation of Young Persons, 1920–60.
/132, Juvenile Employment, 1919–60.
/134/1– 134.6/2, Women in Industry, 1926–63.

Nottingham Local Studies Library (NLSL)
Making Ends Meet: Earning a Living in Nottinghamshire, 1900–50.
The following recorded and transcripted interviews were used:
A14/a–b/2, Eileen.
A23/a–b/1, Mrs Mead.
A50/a, Lily.
A66/a–b/1, Peggy.
A68/a–c/1, Dorothy.
A78/a–c/1, Mrs Hevness.
A80/a–b/1, Lottie.
A85/a–c/1, Edna.
A88/a–b/1, Janet.

Reading Museum Archive (RMA)
The following recorded and partially transcripted interviews were used:
1997.127.1b, Irene Moore.
1997.127.4, Miss Peggy Few.
1997.127.5b, Mrs Midge Harris.
1997.127.26, Mrs Cottrell.
1997.127.36, Mrs E. V. Ellingham.

Tameside Local Studies Library (TLSL)
Manchester Studies tapes
The following recorded and transcripted interviews were used:
tape 9, Mrs Sandys.
26, Mrs E. Hughson.
28, Mrs E. Cleary.
36, Edith Edwards.
68, Mrs Jones.
77, L. Baker.
476, Mrs Mayer.
477, Mr and Mrs Savage.
592, Kathleen Kelsall.
638, Louise Pace.
671, Mary Abbott.
756, Elsie Booth.

1075, Lilian Airey, Elsie Beasley, Mary Collins, Edna Delves, Kathleen Holland, and Irma Smith.
1144, Lilian Airey.
1146, Mrs Somerville.
Tameside tapes collection.
The following recorded and transcripted interviews were used:
28, Grace Wardle.
60, Mrs Andrews.
71, Mrs Halten.
244, Hilda Fielding.

The National Archives (TNA)
AST 7/56, Juvenile Employment Bureaux: Administration of Unemployment Assistance through Local Education Authorities in Respect of Young Persons, 16–17 Years of Age, 1934–7.
CAB 27/202 Report and Proceedings of the Sub-Committee on Juvenile Unemployment, 1924.
ED 23/123, Lord Chelmsford's Committee on Juvenile Employment, 1921.
ED 24/1234, Report of the Executive Committee of the Juvenile Organisation Committee on Unemployed Juveniles 14–16 Years of Age, 1924.
ED 45, Local Education Authorities, 1932–8.
ED 124/46–9, 'Registration of Youth', 1941–5.
LAB 9/129, Juvenile Transference: Number Transferred and Number Returning Home, 1935.
LAB 10/164, Report of Strike at Bath Co-operative Society over Reduction of Promised Plussage of 3/- to Junior Labour and 10/- per Week to Shop Managers.
LAB 12/215, Enquiry into Present Arrangements Dealing with Juveniles at Local Offices and Juvenile Employment Bureaux, 1942–8.
LAB 18/6, Unemployment Insurance Act, 1934: Local Authorities (England and Wales) Authorised Courses for Unemployed Juveniles, 1934.
LAB 19, Youth employment: registered files, 1913–80.
LAB 23/161, Investigation into the Problems of Juvenile unemployment in the Special Areas 1937.
LAB 43, Juvenile Transference Scheme, 1937.
LAB 63, Transfer of Juveniles from Depressed Areas, 1934–9.
LAB 66, Establishment and Conduct of Courses of Instruction for Unemployed Girls and Boys. General file, 1935–6.
LAB 72, Provision of Instruction for Unemployed Juveniles, 1935–6.
LAB 76/29, Strikes and lockouts, 1939–45, E. C. Bailey.
LAB 77, Juvenile Transference Scheme: Arrangements in Special Areas, 1936–7.
LAB 93, Juvenile Transference Scheme and Co-operation with Unemployment Assistance Boards, 1934–7.
LAB 97, Notes on Schemes and Methods of Juvenile Entry into Employment in Connection with Post-war Development, 1941–2.

Trade Union Congress (TUC) Library, London Metropolitan University.
HD 5550.1, Disputes, Industrial Relations, Industrial Democracy, 1926–33.
HD 6070, Domestic Service.
HD 6137, Women's Employment, 1880–1938.
HD 6250 G7, Child labour and Youth Employment, 1921–62.
HD 6661, TUC and UK Trade Unions.

UK Data Archive, University of Essex.
SN3758, *New Survey of London* datafiles.

Parliamentary papers (PP)

Report of the Board of Education for the year:
1920–1: vii (1922), Cmd. 1718.
1926–7: ix (1928), Cmd. 3091.
1934: viii (1934–5), Cmd. 4968.
1937: x (1937–8), Cmd. 3776.
1938: x (1939), Cmd. 6013.
1947: xi (1947–8), Cmd. 7426.
1948: xiv (1948–9), Cmd. 7724.
1949: ix (1950), Cmd. 7957.
1950: xi (1950–1), Cmd. 8244.

Report of the Chief Inspector of Factories and Workshops for the Year:
1919: xvi (1920), Cmd. 941.
1920: xii (1921), Cmd. 1403.
1921: vii (1922), Cmd. 1705.
1922: xi (1923), Cmd. 1920.
1923: ix (1924), Cmd. 2165.
1924: xii (1924–5), Cmd. 2437.
1925: x (1926), Cmd. 2714.
1926: ix (1927), Cmd. 2903.
1927: x (1928), Cmd. 3144.
1928: xiii (1929–30), Cmd. 3360.
1929: xiii (1929–30), Cmd. 3633.
1930: xiii (1930–1), Cmd. 3927.
1931: ix (1931–2), Cmd. 4098.
1932: xii (1932–3), Cmd. 4377.
1933: xi (1933–4), Cmd. 4657.
1934: viii (1934–5), Cmd. 4931.
1935: x (1935–6), Cmd. 5230.
1936: x (1936–7), Cmd. 5564.
1937: x (1937–8), Cmd. 5802.
1938: xi (1938–9), Cmd. 6081.

1939: iv (1940–1), Cmd. 6251.
1940: iv (1940–1), Cmd. 6316.
1941: iv (1941–2), Cmd. 6397.
1942: iv (1942–3), Cmd. 6471.
1943: iii (1943–4), Cmd. 6563.
1944: xii (1945–6), Cmd. 6698.
1945: xi (1946–7), Cmd. 6992.
1946: xii (1947–8), Cmd. 7299.
1947: xvi (1948–9), Cmd. 7621.
1948: xvi (1948–9), Cmd. 7839.
1949: xiii (1950–1), Cmd. 8155.
1950: xii (1951–2), Cmd. 8445.

Report of the Ministry of Labour for the year:
1923–4: xiv (1924–5), Cmd. 2481.
1925: xiii (1926), Cmd. 2736.
1926: x (1927), Cmd. 2856.
1927: xi (1928), Cmd. 3090.
1928: vii (1928–9), Cmd. 3333.
1929: xv (1929–30), Cmd. 3579.
1930: xv (1930–1), Cmd. 3859.
1931: xi (1931–2), Cmd. 4044.
1932: xiii (1932–3), Cmd. 4281.
1933: xiii (1933–4), Cmd. 4543.
1934: x (1934–5), Cmd. 4861.
1935: xiii (1935–6), Cmd. 5145.
1936: xii (1936–7), Cmd. 5431.
1937: xii (1937–8), Cmd. 5717.
1938: xii (1938–9), Cmd. 6016.

Report of the Ministry of Labour and National Service for the years 1939–46: xii (1946–7), Cmd. 7225.
1947: xviii (1948–9), Cmd. 7559.
1948: xvii (1948–9), Cmd. 7822.
1949: xii (1950), Cmd. 8017.
1950: xvi (1950–1), Cmd. 8338.

Juvenile Education (Employment after the War), Interim Report, viii (1916), Cmd. 8374.
Juvenile Education (Employment after the War), Final Report, xi (1917–18), Cmd. 8512.
Report of the Women's Employment Committee, xiv (1918), Cmd. 9239.
Report of the War Cabinet Committee on Women in Industry, xxi (1919), Cmd. 135.
Report of the Women's Advisory Committee on the Domestic Service Problem, xxix (1919), Cmd. 67.

Standard Time Rates of Wages and Hours of Labour in Great Britain and Northern Ireland at 31st December 1920, xl (1921), Cmd. 1253.
First Report of the Industrial Transference Board, x (1928), Cmd. 3156.
Memorandum on the Shortage, Surplus and Redistribution of Juvenile Labour during the Years 1928 to 1937 Based on the Views of Local Juvenile Employment Committees, xvi (1928–9), Cmd. 3327.
A Study of the Factors Which Have Operated in the Past and Those Which Are Operating now to Determine the Distribution of Women in Industry, 1930, xvii (1929–30), Cmd. 3508.

Government publications

Board of Education, *Report of the Consultative Committee on the Education of the Adolescent* (London: HMSO, 1926).
—— *Report of the Consultative Committee on Secondary Education with Special Reference to Grammar Schools and Technical High Schools* (London: HMSO, 1939).
—— *The Youth Service after the War* (London: HMSO, 1943).
—— *Report on Education in England and Wales, 1939–46* (London: HMSO, 1947).
Department of Employment, *British Labour Statistics: Historical Abstract 1886–1968* (London: HMSO, 1971).
Home Department, *Report of the Departmental Committee on the Hours of Employment of Young Persons in Certain Unregulated Occupations* (London: HMSO, 1937).
Ministry of Labour, *Annual Report on the Work of the Advisory Committees for Juvenile Employment for the Year 1926* (London: HMSO, 1927).
—— *1927* (London: HMSO, 1928).
—— *1928* (London: HMSO, 1929).
—— *1929* (London: HMSO, 1930).
—— *1930* (London: HMSO, 1931).
—— *1931* (London: HMSO, 1932).
—— *1932* (London: HMSO, 1933).
Continued as *Annual Report on Juvenile Employment for the Year 1933* (London: HMSO, 1934).
—— *1934* (London: HMSO, 1935).
—— *1936* (London: HMSO, 1937).
—— *1937* (London: HMSO, 1938).
—— *1938* (London: HMSO, 1939).
—— 'Average Earnings and Hours Enquiry for October 1924', *Ministry of Labour Gazette*, 34/6 (1926)–35/9 (1927).
—— 'Average Earnings and Hours Enquiry for October 1928', *Ministry of Labour Gazette*, 37/3–37/5 (1929).

Ministry of Labour, *Annual Report on the Work of the Advisory Committees for Juvenile Employment* 'Average Earnings and Hours Enquiry for October 1931', *Ministry of Labour Gazette*, 41/1–41/3 (1933).

—— 'Average Earnings and Hours Enquiry for October 1935', *Ministry of Labour Gazette*, 45/1–45/7 (1937).

—— 'Average Earnings and Hours Enquiry for October 1938', *Ministry of Labour Gazette*, 52/2–52/7 (1944).

—— 'Average Earnings and Hours Enquiry for July 1943', *Ministry of Labour Gazette*, 52 (1944).

—— 'Average Earnings and Hours Enquiry for July 1945', 54 (1946).

—— 'Average Earnings and Hours Enquiry for October 1949', 58 (1950).

—— *Report of the Committee Appointed to Enquire into the Present Conditions as to the Supply of Female Domestic Servants* (London: HMSO, 1923).

—— *Second Interim Report of the Central Committee on Women's Training and Employment for the Period Ending Dec. 31st 1922* (London: HMSO, 1923).

—— *Inquiry into the Rates of Wages, the Hours of Employment and the Degree of Industrial Organisation in the Wholesale and Retail Grocery and Provisions Trade in England and Wales* (London: HMSO, 1926).

—— *Report upon the Results of an Investigation into the Rates of Wages, the Hours of Employment and the Degree of Industrial Organisation in the Drapery and Allied Trades* (London: HMSO, 1926).

—— *Report upon the Results of an Investigation into the Rates of Wages, the Hours of Employment and the Degree of Industrial Organisation in the Light Refreshment and Dining Room (Non-licensed) Branch of the Catering Trade* (London: HMSO, 1926).

—— *Report on an Enquiry into the Personal Circumstances and Industrial History of 3331 Boys and 2701 Girls Registered for Employment at Employment Exchanges and Juvenile Employment Bureaux in June and July 1925* (London: HMSO, 1926).

—— *Report of the Committee on Education and Industry (England and Wales), First Part* (London: HMSO, 1926).

—— *Report of the Committee on Education and Industry (England and Wales), Second Part* (London: HMSO, 1928).

—— *Report of an Enquiry into Apprenticeship and Training for the Skilled Occupations in Great Britain and Northern Ireland, 1925–26*, 8 vols. (London: HMSO, 1928).

—— *Standard Time Rates of Wages and Hours of Labour in Great Britain and Northern Ireland at 31st August, 1929* (London: HMSO, 1929).

—— *Memorandum on the Shortage, Surplus and Redistribution of Juvenile Labour in England and Wales during the Years 1930–1938* (London: HMSO, 1931).

—— *The Juvenile Transference Scheme*, leaflet (London: HMSO, 1935).

—— *The Young Worker* (London: HMSO, 1944).

—— *Report of the National Youth Employment Council on the work of the Youth Employment Service 1947–1950* (London: HMSO, 1950).

—— *Report of an Enquiry into Household Expenditure in 1953–54* (London: HMSO, 1954).

Reports of the National Advisory Council for Juvenile Employment for England and Wales (under the auspices of the Ministry of Labour):

—— *First Report* (London: HMSO, 1929).

—— *Second Report: Age of Entry into Unemployment Insurance* (London: HMSO, 1929).

—— *Third Report: Provision of Courses of Instruction for Unemployed Boys and Girls* (London: HMSO, 1930).

—— *Fourth Report: Hours of Employment of Boys and Girls in 'Unregulated Occupations'* (London: HMSO, 1932).

—— *Fifth Report: Provision of Courses of Instruction for Unemployed Boys and Girls* (London: HMSO, 1934).

—— *Sixth Report: Operation of the Scheme of Authorised Courses of Instruction for Unemployed Boys and Girls* (London: HMSO, 1937).

National Advisory Council for Juvenile Employment for England and Wales and National Advisory Council for Juvenile Employment for Scotland, *Joint Report on the Organisation and Development of the Vocational Guidance Service in Great Britain* (London: HMSO, 1934).

Reports of the Regional Advisory Committees for Juvenile Employment (England and Wales) (under the auspices of the Ministry of Labour):

Bolton and District Committee for Juvenile Employment, *Annual Report for the Year 1927* (London: HMSO, 1928).

Bristol Advisory Committee for Juvenile Employment, *Annual Report for the Year 1925* (London: HMSO, 1926).

—— *1926* (London: HMSO, 1927).

—— *1927* (London: HMSO, 1928).

—— *1928* (London: HMSO, 1929).

—— *1929* (London: HMSO, 1930).

—— *1930* (London: HMSO, 1931).

Gateshead Advisory Committee for Juvenile Employment, *Annual Report for the Year 1926* (London: HMSO, 1927).

—— *1928* (London: HMSO, 1929).

Leigh and Tyldesley Advisory Committee for Juvenile Employment, *Annual Report for the Year 1929* (London: HMSO, 1930).

Liverpool Juvenile Employment Committee, *Annual Report for the Year 1938* (London: HMSO, 1939).

London Advisory Council for Juvenile Employment, *Annual Report for 1924–1925* (London: HMSO, 1925).

—— *1925–6* (London: HMSO 1926).

—— *1926–7* (London: HMSO, 1927).

—— *1927* (London: HMSO, 1928).

—— *1928* (London: HMSO, 1929).

London Advisory Council for Juvenile Employment, *Annual Report for 1929* (London: HMSO, 1930).
—— *1930* (London: HMSO, 1931).
—— *1931* (London: HMSO, 1932).
—— *1932–3* (London: HMSO, 1934).
—— *1933–4* (London: HMSO, 1934).
—— *1934–5* (London: HMSO, 1935).
—— *A Guide to Employment for London Boys and Girls* (London: HMSO, 1928).
London Regional Advisory Council for Juvenile Employment, *Annual Report for the Year 1935* (London: HMSO, 1936).
—— *1936* (London: HMSO, 1937).
—— *1937* (London: HMSO, 1938).
—— *1938* (London: HMSO, 1939).
Manchester Juvenile Employment Bureaux, *Annual Report, 1932–33* (Manchester: Manchester Education Committee, 1933).
—— *1933–4* (Manchester: Education Committee, 1934).
—— *1934–5* (Manchester: Education Committee, 1935).
—— *1935–6* (Manchester: Education Committee, 1936).
—— *Advice to Boys and Girls about to Leave School* (Manchester: Education Committee, *c.*1933).
Oxford Advisory Committee for Juvenile Employment, *Annual Report for the Year 1929* (London: HMSO, 1930).
Sheffield Advisory Committee for Juvenile Employment, *Annual Report for the Year 1929* (London: HMSO, 1930).
South Shields Advisory Committee for Juvenile Employment, *Annual Report for the Year 1929* (London: HMSO, 1930).
Ministry of Reconstruction, 'Juvenile Employment', *Reconstruction Problems*, No. 15 (London: HMSO, 1919).
Royal Commission on the Poor Law, *Majority Report* (London: HMSO, 1909).

Census of England and Wales, 1921: County of Lancashire (London: HMSO, 1923).
Census of England and Wales, 1921: County of Northumberland (London: HMSO, 1923).
Census of England and Wales, 1921: County of Warwick (London: HMSO, 1923).
Census of England and Wales, 1921: Occupation Tables (London: HMSO, 1924).
Census of England and Wales, 1931: Occupation Tables (London: HMSO, 1934).
Census of England and Wales, 1951: Occupation Tables (London: HMSO, 1954).

Labour Party Publications

Labour Party Advisory Committee on Education, *The Juvenile Worker at the End of the War*, memorandum (London: Labour Party, 1917).
Labour Party, *What's Wrong with Domestic Service?*, leaflet (London: Labour Party, 1930).

—— *The Domestic Workers' Charter* (London: Labour Party, 1931).
—— *Women in Industry* (London: Labour Party, 1935).
—— *Women in Offices* (London: Labour Party, 1936).

Trades union congress (TUC) publications

Annual Report, 1919 (London: TUC, 1920).
—— *1920* (London: TUC, 1921).
—— *1921* (London: TUC, 1922).
—— *1922* (London: TUC, 1923).
—— *1924* (London: TUC, 1925).
—— *1925* (London: TUC, 1926).
—— *1926* (London: TUC, 1927).
—— *1927* (London: TUC, 1928).
—— *1928* (London: TUC, 1929).
—— *1929* (London: TUC, 1930).
—— *1930* (London: TUC, 1931).
—— *1931* (London: TUC, 1932).
—— *1932* (London: TUC, 1933).
—— *1933* (London: TUC, 1934).
—— *1934* (London: TUC, 1935).
—— *1935* (London: TUC, 1936).
—— *1936* (London: TUC, 1937).
—— *1937* (London: TUC, 1938).
—— *1938* (London: TUC, 1939).
—— *Methods of Organising Women*, leaflet (London: TUC, 1923).
—— *Many a Miss Mrs Marriage*, leaflet (London: TUC, *c.* 1934).
—— *Why Should You Join the Union? A Plain Talk to Women Workers*, leaflet (London: TUC, *c.*1934).
—— *Report on the Depressed Areas*, leaflet (London: TUC, 1935).
—— *Memorandum on Certain Features of the Pay of Women Civil Servants, Council of Women Civil Servants*, leaflet (London: TUC, 1936).
—— *Domestic Servants' Charter* (London: TUC, 1937).
—— *Equal Pay for Equal Work, 1914–1949*, leaflet (London: TUC, 1949).
Women's TUC Conference, *Annual Report for 1925* (London: TUC, 1926).

Trade union publications

Association of Women Clerks and Secretaries (AWCS), *The Association of Women Clerks and Secretaries: What It Is and What It Has Done* (London: AWCS, *c.* 1951).

Transport and General Workers' Union (TGWU), 'Women and Young Persons: Industrial Legislation: Industrial Health: Safety at Work: Statutory Control of Industry', published in *The Union, Its Work and Problems* (London: TGWU, 1939).

United Clothing Workers' Union (UCWU)), *Rego and Polikoff Strike Songs* 2nd edn. (London: Centreprise, 1983).

Newspapers and magazines

Bath and Wiltshire Chronicle and Herald
Daily Worker
Leicester Mercury
Manchester Evening News
Manchester Guardian
Ministry of Labour Gazette
Miss Modern
TGWU Record
Shop Assistant
The Times
Woman Clerk
Woman's Leader
Woman's Own
Woman Worker

Autobiographies and autobiographical collections

Armstrong, K., and H. Benyon (eds.), *Hello, Are You Working? Memories of the Thirties in the North East of England* (Whitley Bay: Strong Words, 1977).

Bailey, D., *Children of the Green* (London: Stepney Books, 1981).

Balderson, E., with D. Goodlad, *Backstairs Life in a Country House* (Newton Abbott: David and Charles, 1982).

Burnett, J. (ed.), *Useful Toil: Autobiographies of Working People from the 1820s to the 1920s* (Harmondsworth: Penguin, 1977).

Donaldson, F., *Child of the Twenties* (London: Weidenfeld and Nicolson, 1986).

Excell, A., *The Politics of the Production Line: Autobiography of an Oxford Car Worker* (Southampton: History Workshop, 1981).

Foakes, G., *Between High Walls: A London Childhood* (London: Shepeard-Walwyn, 1972).

Foley, W., *Child in the Forest* (London: BBC, 1974).

—— *The Forest Trilogy* (Oxford: Oxford University Press, 1992).

Gamble, R., *Chelsea Child* (London: 1979).

Gardiner, M., *The Other Side of the Counter: The Life of A Shop Girl 1925–45*, (Brighton: Queenspark Books, 1985).

Hackney People's Autobiography, *Working Lives*, 1 (London: Centreprise, 1976).
—— *The Island: The Life and Death of an East London Community 1870–1970* (London: Centreprise, 1979).
Hastings Modern History Workshop, *Hastings Voices* (Brighton: University of Sussex, 1982).
Haythorne, E., *On Earth To Make The Numbers Up* (Castleford: Yorkshire Art Circus, 1991).
Hobbs, M., *Born to Struggle* (London: Quartet Books, 1973).
Knight, D., *Millfield Memories* (London: Centreprise, 1976).
Lifetimes Group, *A Couple from Manchester* (Manchester: Manchester Polytechnic, 1975).
—— *Something in Common* (Manchester: Manchester Polytechnic, 1975).
Lowe, R., *Daddy Burtt's for Dinner: Growing Up in Hoxton between the Wars* (London: Centreprise, 1976).
Rennie, J., *Every Other Sunday* (London: A. Barker, 1955).
Roberts, R., *A Ragged Schooling: Growing up in the Classic Slum* (Manchester: Manchester University Press, 1976).
Rodaway, A., *A London Childhood* (London: Virago, 1985).
Sage, L., *Bad Blood* (London: Fourth Estate, 2001).
Scannell, D., *Mother Knew Best: An East End Childhood* (Basingstoke: Macmillan, 1974).
Thew, L. M., *The Pit Village and the Store* (London: Pluto Press, 1985).
—— *A Tune for Bears to Dance to: A Childhood* (Berwick-upon-Tweed: Bridge Studios, 1992).
Van Riel, R. (ed.), *All in a Day's Work* (Pontefract: Yorkshire Art Circus, 1985).
Weir, M., *Shoes Were for Sunday* (Bath: Chivers, 1988).
—— *Best Foot Forward* (London: Pan, 1974).

Other published books

Anthony, S., *Women's Place in Industry and the Home* (London: Routledge and Kegan Paul, 1932).
Bakke, E. W., *The Unemployed Man: A Social Study* (London: Nisbet and Co., 1932).
Beales, H. L., and R. S. Lambert (eds.), *Memoirs of the Unemployed* (London: Gollancz, 1934).
Beauchamp, J., *Women who Work* (London: Lawrence and Wishart, 1937).
—— *Working Women in Great Britain* (New York: International Publishers, 1937).
Beveridge, W. H., *Unemployment: A Problem of Industry*, 2nd edn. (London: Longman, 1930).
Blainey, J., *The Woman Worker and Protective Legislation* (London: Arrowsmith, 1928).
Bowley, A. L., *Wages and Income in the UK since 1860* (Cambridge: Cambridge University Press, 1937).

Bowley, A. L., and A. R. Barnett-Hurst, *Livelihood and Poverty* (London: Bell, 1915).

—— and M. H. Hogg, *Has Poverty Diminished?* (London: P. S. King & Son, 1925).

Brittain, V., *Women's Work in Modern England* (London: Noel Douglas, 1928).

Burns, C. D., *Leisure in the Modern World* (London: Allen and Unwin, 1932).

Butler, C. V., *Domestic Service. An Enquiry by the Women's Industrial Council*, repr. of 1916 edn. (London: Garland, 1980).

Cadbury, E., M. C. Matheson, and G. Shann, *Women's Work and Wages: A Phase of Life in an Industrial City* (London: T. Fisher Unwin, 1906).

Cameron, C., A. Lush, and G. Meara, *Disinherited Youth: A Report on the 18+ Age Group Enquiry Prepared for the Trustees of the Carnegie United Kingdom Trust* (Edinburgh: T. and A. Constable, 1943).

Caradog Jones, D., *The Social Survey of Merseyside*, 3 vols. (Liverpool: Liverpool University Press, 1934).

Carr-Saunders, A. M., P. Sargant Florence, R. Peers et al., *Consumers' Co-operation in Great Britain* (London: Allen and Unwin, 1938).

Chapman, D., *A Social Survey of Middlesbrough*, Social Survey, Report, New Series, 50 (1945).

Collier, D. J., and B. L. Hutchins, *The Girl in Industry* (London: Bell, 1918).

Dennison, S. R., *The Location of Industry and the Depressed Areas* (London: Oxford University Press, 1939).

Drake, B., *Women in the Engineering Trades* (London: Fabian Research Dept., 1917).

—— *Women in Trade Unions*, 2nd edn. (London: Virago, 1984).

Durant, R., *Watling: A Survey of Social Life on a New Housing Estate* (London: P. S. King and Son, 1939).

Elsbury, S., and D. Cohen, *The Rego Revolt: How the United Clothing Workers' Trade Union was Formed* (London: Dorrit Press, 1929).

Evans, D. E., *Women and the Civil Service: A History of the Development of the Employment of Women in the Civil Service, and a Guide to Present Day Opportunities* (London: Pitman, 1934).

Fletcher, B. A., et al., *The Welfare of Youth: A City Survey* (Bristol: University of Bristol, 1945).

Ford, P., *Work and Wealth in a Modern Port: An Economic Survey of Southampton* (London: Allen and Unwin, 1934).

Freeman, A., *Boy Life and Labour: The Manufacture of Inefficiency* (London: P. S. King and Son, 1914).

Gollan, J., *Youth in British Industry: A Survey of Labour Conditions Today* (London: Gollancz, 1937).

Graves, R., and A. Hodge, *The Long Weekend*, 2nd edn. (Harmondsworth: Penguin, 1971).

Greenwood, W., *Love on the Dole* (London: Jonathon Cape, 1931).

Hamilton, M. A., *Women at Work: A Brief Introduction to Trade Unionism for Women* (London: Routledge, 1941).

HANNINGTON, W., *The Problem of the Distressed Areas* (London: Gollancz, 1937).
HOLTBY, W., *Women and a Changing Civilization* (London: John Lane, 1934).
HUTCHINS, B. L., *Women in Modern Industry* (London: Bell, 1915).
INMAN, P., *Labour in Munitions* (London: HMSO, 1957).
JEFFERYS, J., *Retail Trading in Britain, 1850–1950* (Cambridge: Cambridge University Press, 1954).
—— *The Story of the Engineers* (London: Lawrence and Wishart, 1945).
JEPHCOTT, P., *Girls Growing Up* (London: Faber and Faber, 1942).
—— *Rising Twenty: Notes on Some Ordinary Girls* (London: Faber and Faber, 1948).
—— *Some Young People* (London: Allen and Unwin, 1954).
JEWKES, J., and S. JEWKES, *The Juvenile Labour Market* (London: Gollancz, 1938).
—— and A. WINTERBOTTOM, *Juvenile Unemployment* (London: Allen and Unwin, 1933).
KLIGENDER, F. D., *The Condition of Clerical Labour in Britain* (London: M. Lawrence, 1935).
LEWIS, E. L., *The Children of the Unskilled: An Economic and Social Study* (London: Nisbet and Co., 1924).
LLEWELLYN SMITH, H., *The New Survey of London Life and Labour*, vols. 1–8 (London: P. S. King and Son, 1931–4).
MAIS, S. P. B., *Youth after the War* (London: Macdonald and Co., 1944).
Mass-Observation, *ATS: An Investigation of the Attitudes of Women, the General Public, and ATS Personnel to the Auxiliary Territorial Service*, Social Survey, New Series, Reports, 5 (1941).
—— *People in Production* (Harmondsworth: Penguin, 1942).
—— *War Factory* (London: Gollancz, 1943).
MEARA, G., *Juvenile Unemployment in South Wales* (Cardiff: Cardiff University Press, 1936).
MORGAN, A. E., *The Needs of Youth: A Report Made to King George's Jubilee Trust* (Oxford: Oxford University Press, 1939).
ORWELL, G., *The Road to Wigan Pier*, 2nd edn. (Harmondsworth: Penguin, 1969).
OWEN, A. D. K. et al., *A Survey of Juvenile Employment and Welfare in Sheffield* (Sheffield: Sheffield Social Survey Committee, 1933).
PARKER, H. M. D., *Manpower: A Study of War-Time Policy and Administration* (London: HMSO, 1957).
Pilgrim Trust, *Men without Work* (Cambridge: Cambridge University Press, 1938).
PLUMMER, A., *New British Industries in the Twentieth Century: A Survey of Development and Structure* (London: Pitman, 1937).
Political and Economic Planning (PEP), *The Entrance to Industry* (London: PEP, 1935).
—— *Report on the Location of Industry* (London: PEP, 1939).
PRICE, J., *Organised Labour in the War* (Harmondsworth: Allen Lane, 1940).
PRIESTLEY, J. B., *English Journey* (London: Heinemann and Gollancz, 1934).
REED, B. H., et al., *Eighty Thousand Adolescents* (London: Allen and Unwin, 1950).

ROWNTREE, B. S., *Poverty, a Study of Town Life*, repr. of 1901 edn. (New York: Howard Fertig, 1971).

—— *Poverty and Progress: A Second Social Survey of York* (London: Longmans, 1941).

—— and B. LASKER, *Unemployment, a Social Study* (Basingstoke: Macmillan, 1911).

—— and G. R. LAVERS, *Poverty and the Welfare State* (London: Longmans, 1951).

—— and F. D. STUART, *The Responsibility of Women Workers for Dependants* (Clarendon Press: Oxford, 1921).

Scottish Trade Union Delegation to the Midlands, *Transfer of Scottish Girls. Report to Scottish Trades Union Congress General Council and the Organisation of Women Committee* (Glasgow: Scottish TUC, 1943).

SELLS, D., *The British Trade Boards System* (London: P. S. King and Son, 1923).

SMITH, E., *Wage-Earning Women and Their Dependants* (London: Fabian Society, 1915).

SPRING RICE, M., *Working-Class Wives: Their Health and Conditions*, 2nd edn. (London: Virago, 1981).

STRACHEY, R., *Careers and Openings for Women* (London: Faber and Faber, 1935).

THOMAS, G., *Women in Industry*, Social Survey, Reports, New Series, 104 (1949).

TOUT, H., *The Standard of Living in Bristol* (Bristol: Arrowsmith, 1938).

WILKINS, L., *The Adolescent in Britain*, Social Survey, Reports, New Series, no. 148 (1955).

YOUNG, T., *Becontree and Dagenham* (London: Samuel Sidders and Son, 1936).

YWCA, *Household Employment* (London: YWCA, *c.*1933).

ZWEIG, F., *Labour, Life and Poverty* (London: Gollancz, 1948).

—— *The British Worker* (Harmondsworth: Pelican, 1952).

Published articles

FORD, P., 'Means Tests and Responsibilities for Needy Relations', *Sociological Review*, 28 (1937).

GINSBERG, M., 'Interchange among Social Classes', *Economic Journal*, 39/156 (1929).

OWEN, A. D. K., 'The Social Consequences of Industrial Transference', *Sociological Review*, 29/4 (1937).

SEERS, D., 'The Levelling of Incomes', *Bulletin of the Oxford Institute of Statistics*, 12/10 (October 1950).

Unpublished theses

HARLEY, J. L., 'Report of an Enquiry into the Occupations, Further Education and Leisure Interests of a Number of Girl Wage-Earners from Elementary and Central Schools in the Manchester District, with Special Reference to the

Influence of School Training on Their Use of Leisure', M.Ed. diss. (Manchester, 1937).

MORGAN, O., 'A Study of the Training for Leisure Occupations Offered in a Senior Girls' School in an Industrial Area, Together with an Enquiry into the Use Made of This Training by the Girls, after Their Entry into Employment', M.Ed. diss. (Manchester, 1942).

SECONDARY SOURCES

PUBLISHED BOOKS

ALDCROFT, D. H., *The Inter-War Economy: Britain, 1919–1939* (London: B. T. Batsford, 1970).

ALEXANDER, S., *Becoming a Woman and Other Essays in 19th and 20th Century Feminist History* (London: Virago, 1994).

AMSDEN, A. (ed.), *The Economics of Women and Work* (Harmondsworth: Penguin, 1980).

ANDERSON, G. (ed.), *The White-Blouse Revolution: Female Office Workers since 1870* (Manchester: Manchester University Press, 1988).

ANDERSON, M., *Approaches to the History of the Western Family, 1500–1914* (Basingstoke: Macmillan, 1980).

——, F. BECHHOFER, and J. GERSHUNY (eds.), *The Social and Political Economy of the Household* (Oxford: Oxford University Press, 1994).

BAIN, G. S., and R. PRICE, *Profiles of Union Growth: A Comparative Statistical Portrait of Eight Countries* (Oxford: Blackwell, 1980).

BEDDOE, D., *Back to Home and Duty: Women between the Wars 1918–1939* (London: Pandora, 1989).

BENSON, J., *The Working Class in Britain, 1850–1939* (London: Longman, 1989).

BINGHAM, A., *Gender, Modernity, and the Popular Press in Inter-War Britain* (Oxford: Oxford University Press, 2004).

BOSTON, S., *Women Workers and the Trade Union Movement* (London: Davis Poynter, 1980).

BOURKE, J., *Working-Class Cultures in Britain, 1890–1960: Gender, Class and Ethnicity* (London: Routledge, 1994).

BRAVERMAN, H., *Labor and Monopoly Capital: The Degradation of Work in the Twentieth Century* (New York: Monthly Review Press, 1974).

BRAYBON, G., *Women Workers in the First World War*, 2nd edn. (London: Routledge, 1989).

BROADBERRY, S. N., *The British Economy between the Wars* (Oxford: Blackwell, 1986).

BURMAN, S. (ed.), *Fit Work for Women* (London: Croom Helm, 1979).

BURNETT, J., *Idle Hands: The Experience of Unemployment, 1790–1990* (London: Routledge, 1994).

—— *A Social History of Housing 1815–1970* (London: Methuen, 1979).

CALDER, A., *The People's War: Britain, 1939–1945* (London: Jonathan Cape, 1969).

CLARKE, J., C. CRITCHER, and R. JOHNSON (eds.), *Working Class Culture: Studies in History and Theory* (London: Hutchinson, 1979).

CLEGG, H. A., *A History of British Trade Unions since 1889, Vol. 2: 1911–1933* (Oxford: Clarendon Press, 1985).

—— *Vol. 3: 1934–1951* (Oxford: Clarendon Press, 1994).

COHEN, M., *Workshop to Office: Two Generations of Italian Women in New York City, 1900–1950* (Ithaca, NY: Cornell University Press, 1992).

COHN, S., *The Process of Occupational Sex-Typing: The Feminization of Clerical Labor in Great Britain* (Philadelphia: Temple University Press, 1985).

CROUCHER, R., *Engineers at War, 1939–1945* (London: Merlin Press, 1982).

DAVIDOFF, L. et al., *The Family Story: Blood, Contract and Intimacy, 1830–1960* (London: Longman, 1999).

DAVIES, A., *Leisure, Gender and Poverty: Working-Class Culture in Salford and Manchester, 1900–1939* (Buckingham: Open University Press, 1992).

—— and S. FIELDING (eds.), *Workers' Worlds: Cultures and Communities in Manchester and Salford, 1880–1939* (Manchester: Manchester University Press, 1992).

DAVIN, A., *Growing Up Poor: Home, School and Street in London 1870–1914* (London: Rivers Oram Press, 1996).

DEACON, A., *In Search of the Scrounger: The Administration of Unemployment Insurance in Britain 1920–31* (London: Bell, 1976).

DENNIS, N., F. HENRIQUES, and C. SLAUGHTER, *Coal is Our Life: An Analysis of a Yorkshire Mining Community*, 2nd edn. (London: Tavistock, 1969).

DYHOUSE, C., *Girls Growing Up in Late Victorian and Edwardian England* (London: Routledge and Kegan Paul, 1977).

FEINSTEIN, C. H., *National Income, Output and Expenditure of the U.K. since 1870* (Cambridge: Cambridge University Press, 1972).

FITZGERALD, R., *Rowntree and the Marketing Revolution, 1862–1969* (Cammbridge: Cambridge University Press, 1995).

FORSTER, M., *Hidden Lives: A Family Memoir* (London: Penguin, 1996).

FOWLER, D., *The First Teenagers: The Lifestyles of Young Wage-Earners in Interwar Britain* (London: Woburn Press, 1995).

GALLIE, D., C. MARSH, and C. VOGLER (eds.), *Social Change and the Experience of Unemployment* (Oxford: Oxford University Press), 1994.

GAZELEY, I., *Poverty in Britain*, 1900–1965 (London: Palgrave, 2003).

GILES, J., *Women, Identity and Private Life in Britain, 1900–1950* (Basingstoke: Macmillan, 1995).

—— *The Parlour and the Suburb: Domestic Identities, Class, Femininity and Modernity* (Oxford: Berg, 2004).

GITTINS, D., *Fair Sex: Family Size and Structure, 1900–39* (London: Hutchinson, 1982).

GLENN, S., *Daughters of the Schtetl* (Ithaca, NY: Cornell University Press, 1990).

GLUCKSMANN, M., *Women Assemble: Women Workers in the New Industries of Inter-war Britain* (London: Routledge, 1990).
—— *Cottons and Casuals: The Gendered Organisation of Labour in Time and Space* (Durham: sociologypress, 2000).
GLYNN, S., and G. OXBORROW, *Inter-war Britain: A Social and Economic History* (London: Allen and Unwin, 1976).
GOLDTHORPE, J. H., in collaboration with C. LLEWELYN and C. PAYNE, *Social Mobility and Class Structure in Modern Britain* (Oxford: Oxford University Press, 1987).
GORDON, E., and E. BREITENBACH (eds.), *The World is Ill Divided: Women's Work in Scotland in the Nineteenth and Early Twentieth Centuries* (Edinburgh: Edinburgh University Press, 1990).
GRAMSCI, A., *Selections from the Prison Notebooks*, ed. Q. Hoare and G. Newell Smith (London: Lawrence, 1971).
GRIFFITHS, T., *The Lancashire Working Classes c.1880–1930* (Oxford: Clarendon Press, 2001).
HALSEY, A. H., and J. WEBB (eds.), *Twentieth-Century British Social Trends* (Basingstoke: Macmillan, 2000).
HARRIS, J., *William Beveridge: A Biography* (Oxford: Clarendon Press, 1997).
HARRISON, R., and J. ZEITLIN (eds.), *Divisions of Labour: Skilled Workers and Technological Change in Nineteenth Century England* (Brighton: Harvester Press, 1985).
HENDRICK, H., *Images of Youth: Age, Class and the Male Youth Problem, 1880–1920* (Oxford: Clarendon Press, 1990).
HERON, L. (ed.), *Truth, Dare or Promise: Girls Growing Up in the Fifties* (London: Virago, 1985).
HOBSBAWM, E. J., *Labouring Men* (London: Weidenfeld and Nicolson, 1964).
—— *Worlds of Labour* (London: Weidenfeld and Nicolson, 1984).
HOWKINS, A., *The Death of Rural England: A Social History of the Countryside since 1900* (London: Routledge, 2003).
HUDSON, P., and W. R. LEE (eds.), *Women's Work and the Family Economy in Historical Perspective* (Manchester: Manchester University Press, 1990).
HUMPHRIES, S., *Hooligans or Rebels? An Oral History of Working-Class Childhood and Youth, 1889–1939* (Oxford: Blackwell, 1981).
—— *A Secret World of Sex: Forbidden Fruit: The British Experience, 1900–1950* (London: Sidgwick and Jackson, 1988).
JACKSON, B., *Working-Class Community* (Harmondsworth: Penguin, 1972).
JOHN, A. (ed.), *Unequal Opportunities: Women's Employment in England 1800–1918* (Oxford: Blackwell, 1986).
JOHNSON, P., *Saving and Spending: The Working-Class Economy in Britain 1870–1939* (Oxford: Clarendon Press, 1985).
JONES, G. S., *Outcast London: A Study in the Relationships between Classes in Victorian London* (Oxford: Clarendon Press, 1971).

Jones, G. S., *Languages of Class: Studies in English Working Class History 1832–1982* (Cambridge: Cambridge University Press, 1982).

Jones, S., *Workers at Play: A Social and Economic History of Leisure, 1918–1939* (London: Routledge and Kegan Paul, 1986).

Joyce, P., *Visions of the People: Industrial England and the Question of Class 1848–1914* (Cambridge: Cambridge University Press, 1991).

Kamm, J., *Hope Deferred: Girls' Education in English History* (London: Methuen, 1965).

Knowles, K. G. J. C., *Strikes: A Study in Industrial Conflict* (Oxford: Blackwell, 1952).

Lancaster, B., *The Department Store: A Social History* (Leicester: Leicester University Press), 1995.

—— and T. Mason (eds.), *Life and Labour in a Twentieth Century City: The Experience of Coventry* (Coventry: Cryfield Press, 1986).

Langhamer, C., *Women's Leisure in England 1920–60* (Manchester: Manchester University Press, 2000).

Law, C., *Suffrage and Power: The Women's Movement, 1918–1928* (London: I. B. Tauris, 1997).

Lerner, S. W., *Breakaway Unions and the Small Trade Union* (London: Ruskin House, 1961).

Lewenhak, S., *Women and Trade Unions* (London: Ernest Benn, 1977).

Lewis, J., *Women in England 1870–1950: Sexual Divisions and Social Change* (Brighton: Harvester Wheatsheaf, 1984).

Light, A., *Forever England: Feminism, Literature and Conservatism between the Wars* (London: Routledge, 1991).

Littler, C. R., *The Development of the Labour Process in Capitalist Societies* (London: Heinemann, 1982).

McKibbin, R., *The Ideologies of Class: Social Relations in Britain 1880–1950* (Oxford: Clarendon Press, 1990).

—— *Classes and Cultures: England 1918–1951* (Oxford: Oxford University Press, 1998).

Marwick, A., *Britain in the Century of Total War: War, Peace and Social Change, 1900–1967* (London: Bodley Head, 1968).

Meacham, S., *A Life Apart: The English Working Class 1890–1914* (London: Thames and Hudson, 1977).

Melman, B., *Women and the Popular Imagination in the Twenties: Flappers and Nymphs* (Macmillan: Basingstoke, 1988).

Middlemas, K., *Politics in Industrial Society* (London: Andre Deutsch, 1979).

Miles, A., *Social Mobility in Nineteenth and Early Twentieth-Century England* (Macmillan, Basingstoke, 1999).

—— and D. Vincent (eds.), *Building European Society: Occupational Change and Social Mobility in Europe 1840–1940* (Manchester: Manchester University Press, 1993).

Mowat, C. L., *Britain between the Wars 1918–1940* (London: Methuen, 1955).

Osgerby, B., *Youth in Britain since 1945* (Oxford: Blackwell, 1998).

PARKER, H. M. D., *Manpower: A Study of Wartime Policy and Administration* (London: HMSO, 1957).

PAYNE, G., and P. ABBOTT (eds.), *The Social Mobility of Women: Beyond Male Mobility Models* (London: Falmer, 1990).

POLLARD, S., *The Development of the British Economy, 1914–1990* (London: Arnold, 1992).

POLLERT, A., *Girls, Wives, Factory Lives* (London: Macmillan Press, 1981).

PUGH, M., *Women and the Women's Movement in Britain, 1914–1959* (London: Macmillan, 1992).

REID, A., *Social Classes and Social Relations in Britain, 1850–1914* (Basingstoke: Macmillan, 1992).

ROBERTS, E., *A Woman's Place: An Oral History of Working Class Women 1890–1940* (Oxford: Blackwell, 1984).

—— *Women's Work 1840–1940* (Cambridge: Cambridge University Press, 1988).

—— *Women and Families: An Oral History, 1940–1970* (Oxford: Blackwell, 1995).

ROBERTS, R., *The Classic Slum*, 2nd edn. (Harmondsworth: Penguin, 1974).

ROSE, S., *Which People's War?: National Identity and Citizenship in Britain 1939–1945* (Oxford: Oxford University Press, 2003).

ROUTH, G., *Occupation and Pay in Great Britain 1906–1979* (London: Macmillan, 1980).

ROWBOTHAM, S., *Dreams and Dilemmas* (London: Virago, 1983).

SARSBY, J., *Missuses and Mouldrunners: An Oral History of Women Pottery-Workers at Work and Home* (Milton Keynes: Open University Press, 1988).

SAVAGE, M., *The Dynamics of Working-Class Politics: The Labour Movement in Preston, 1880–1940* (Cambridge: Cambridge University Press, 1987).

—— and A. MILES, *The Remaking of the British Working Class, 1840–1940* (London: Routledge, 1994).

SAVILLE, J., *Rural Depopulation in England and Wales, 1851–1951* (London: Routledge, 1957).

SOLAND, B., *Becoming Modern: Young Women and the Reconstruction of Womanhood in the 1920s* (Princeton, NJ: Princeton University Press, 2000).

STANLEY, J., *The Autobiographical I* (Manchester: Manchester University Press, 1992).

STEEDMAN, C., *Landscape for a Good Woman* (London: Virago, 1986).

STEVENSON, J., and C. COOK, *Britain in the Depression: Society and Politics 1929–39*, 2nd edn. (London: Longman, 1994).

SUMMERFIELD, P., *Women Workers in the Second World War: Production and Patriarchy in Conflict* (London: Croom Helm, 1984).

—— *Reconstructing Women's Wartime Lives* (Manchester: Manchester University Press, 1998).

SZRETER, S., *Fertility, Class and Gender in Britain, 1860–1940* (Cambridge: Cambridge University Press, 1996).

TEBBUTT, M., *Women's Talk?: A Social History of 'Gossip' in Working-Class Neighbourhoods, 1880–1960* (Aldershot, Scolar Press, 1995).

THANE, P., *Foundations of the Welfare State* (London: Longman, 1996).
—— *Old Age in English History: Past Experiences, Present Issues* (Oxford: Oxford University Press, 2000).
THOM, D., *Nice Girls and Rude Girls: Women Workers in World War I* (London: I. B. Tauris, 2000).
THOMPSON, E. P., *The Making of the English Working Class*, 2nd edn. (Harmondsworth: Penguin, 1968).
TILLY, L., and J. SCOTT, *Women, Work and Family* (London: Methuen, 1978).
TINKLER, P., *Constructing Girlhood: Popular Magazines for Girls Growing Up in England, 1920–1950* (London: Taylor and Francis, 1995).
TOLLIDAY, S., and J. ZEITLIN (eds.), *Shop Floor Bargaining and the State: Historical and Comparative Perspectives* (Cambridge: Cambridge University Press, 1985).
WALBY, S., *Patriarchy at Work* (Cambridge: Polity Press, 1986).
WESTWOOD, S., *All Day, Every Day: Factory and Family in the Making of Women's Lives* (London: Pluto Press, 1984).
WHITE, J., *Rothschild Buildings* (London: Routledge and Kegan Paul, 1980).
—— *The Worst Street in North London: Campbell Bunk, Islington, between the Wars* (London: Routledge and Kegan Paul, 1986).
WILLIS, P., *Learning to Labour: How Working Class Kids Get Working Class Jobs*, 2nd edn. (Aldershot: Ashgate, 1993).
WOOD, S. (ed.), *The Degradation of Work?: Skill, De-skilling and the Labour Process* (London: Hutchinson, 1982).
WOOLLACOTT, A., *On Her Their Lives Depend: Munitions Workers in the Great War* (Berkeley, Calif.: University of California, 1994).
YOUNG, M., and P. WILLMOTT, *Family and Kinship in East London* (Harmondsworth: Penguin, 1962).

ESSAYS IN EDITED COLLECTIONS

BOWDEN, S., 'The new consumerism', in P. Johnson (ed.), *Twentieth Century Britain: Economic, Social and Cultural Change* (London: Longman, 1994).
DAVY, T., 'A Cissy Job for Men: A Nice Job for Girls: Women Shorthand Typists in London 1900–1939', in L. Davidoff and B. Westover (eds.), *Our Work, Our Lives, Our Words* (Basingstoke: Macmillan, 1986).
HORRELL, S., and D. OXLEY, 'Breadwinning, Family Employment and Household Resource Allocation', in C. E. Nunez (ed.), *The Microeconomic Analysis of the Household and the Labour Market, 1880–1939* (Seville: University of Seville, 1998).
MCKENDRICK, N., 'The Consumer Revolution of Eighteenth-Century England', in N. McKendrick, J. Brewer, and J. Plumb (eds.), *The Birth of a Consumer Society* (London: Hutchinson, 1983).
SMITH, H. L., 'The Effect of the War on the Status of Women', in ead. (ed.), *War and Social Change* (Manchester: Manchester University Press, 1986).
THOMAS, M., 'Labour market structure and the nature of unemployment in interwar Britain', in B. Eichengreen and T. J. Hatton (eds.), *Interwar Unemployment in International Perspective* (London: Kluwer Academic, 1988).

Tinkler, P., 'Girlhood in Transition? Preparing English Girls for Adulthood in a Reconstructed Britain', in C. Duchen and I. Bandhauer-Schoffman (eds.), *When the War Was Over: Women, War and Peace in Europe, 1940–1956* (London: Leicester University Press, 2000).

JOURNAL ARTICLES

Alexander, S., 'Men's Fears and Women's Work: Responses to Unemployment in London Between the Wars', *Gender and History*, 12/2 (2000).

Anderson, M., 'The Emergence of the Modern Life Cycle in Britain', *Social History*, 10/1 (1985).

Baines, D., and P. Johnson, 'In Search of the "Traditional" Working Class: Social Mobility and Occupational Continuity in Interwar London', *Economic History Review*, 52/4 (1999).

Beechey, V., 'Some Notes on Female Wage Labour in Capitalist Production', *Capital and Class*, 3 (1977).

Beneson, H., 'Patriarchal Constraints on Women Workers' Mobilization—The Lancashire Female Cotton Operatives 1842–1919', *British Journal of Sociology*, 44/4 (1993).

Benjamin, D. K., and L. A. Kochin, 'What Went Right with Juvenile Unemployment Policy between the Wars: A Comment', *Economic History Review*, 32/4 (1979).

Benninghaus, C., 'Mothers' Toil and Daughters' Leisure: Working-Class Girls and Time in 1920s Germany', *History Workshop Journal*, 50 (2000).

Bingham, A., ' "Stop the Flapper Vote Folly": Lord Rothermere, the Daily Mail, and the Equalization of the Franchise 1927–28', *Twentieth Century British History*, 13/1 (2002).

Blackburn, S., 'Gender, Work and Labour History: A Response to Carol Morgan', *Women's History Review*, 10/1 (2001).

Blaikie, J., 'Problems with "Strategy" in Micro-social History: Families and Narratives, Sources and Methods', *Family and Community History*, 4/2 (2001).

Bornat, J., 'Home and Work; A New Context for Trade Union History', *Oral History*, 5/2 (1977).

Bowden, S., and D. M. Higgins, ' "Productivity on the Cheap"? The "More Looms" Experiment and the Lancashire Weaving Industry during the Inter-War Years', *Business History*, 41/3 (1999).

Bruegel, I., 'Women as a Reserve Army of Labour: A Note on Recent British Experience', *Feminist Review*, 1/3 (1979).

Bruley, S., 'Gender, Class and Party: The Communist Party and the Crisis in the Cotton Industry in England between the Two World Wars', *Women's History Review*, 2/1 (1993).

Burgess, K., 'Youth Employment Policy during the 1930s', *Twentieth Century British History*, 6/1 (1995).

Childs, J., 'Quaker Employers and Industrial Relations', *Sociological Review*, 12/2 (1964).

CRAFTS, N. F. R., 'Long-Term Unemployment in Britain in the 1930s', *Economic History Review*, 40/3 (1987).

DYHOUSE, C., 'Family Patterns of Social Mobility through Higher Education in England in the 1930s', *Journal of Social History*, 26/4 (2001).

EICHENGREEN, B., 'Juvenile Unemployment in Twentieth-Century Britain: The Emergence of a Problem', *Social Research*, 54/2 (1987).

FURNHAM, A., 'The Saving and Spending Habits of Young People', *Journal of Economic Psychology*, 20/6 (1999).

GARSIDE, W. R., 'Juvenile Unemployment and Public Policy between the Wars', *Economic History Review*, 30/2 (1977).

—— 'Juvenile Unemployment between the Wars: A Rejoinder', *Economic History Review*, 32/4 (1979).

GAZELEY, I., 'Prices in Interwar Britain', *Explorations in Economic History*, 31/2 (1994).

HAKIM, C., 'Five Feminist Myths about Women's Employment', *British Journal of Sociology*, 46/3 (1995).

HATTON, T. J., and R. E. BAILEY, 'Female Labour Force Participation in Interwar Britain', *Oxford Economic Papers*, 40/4 (1988).

—— and —— 'Women's Work in Census and Survey, 1911–1931', *Economic History Review*, 54/1 (2001).

—— and —— 'Unemployment Incidence in Interwar London', *Economica*, 69/276 (2002).

HEIM, C. E., 'Industrial Organization and Regional Development in Interwar Britain', *Journal of Economic History*, 43/4 (1983).

—— 'Structural Transformation and the Demand for New Labor in Advanced Economies: Interwar Britain', *Journal of Economic History*, 44/2 (1984).

HIGGS, E., 'Women, Occupations and Work in the Nineteenth-Century Censuses', *History Workshop Journal*, 23 (1986).

HILL, B., 'Rural–Urban Migration of Women and Their Employment in Towns', *Rural History*, 5 (1994).

HILTON, M., 'The Fable of the Sheep, or, Private Virtues, Public Vices: The Consumer Revolution of the Twentieth Century', *Past and Present*, 176/1 (2002).

HORRELL, S., and J. HUMPHRIES, 'The Origins and Expansion of the Male Breadwinner Family: The Case of Nineteenth-Century Britain', *International Review of Social History*, 42/supplement, (1997).

—— and D. OXLEY, 'Crust or Crumb?: Intrahousehold Resource Allocation and Male Breadwinning in Late Victorian Britain', *Economic History Review*, 52/3 (1999).

HOULBROOK, M., ' "Lady Austin's Camp Boys": Constituting the Queer Subject in 1930s London', *Gender and History*, 14/1 (2002).

HUGHES, A., 'Representations and Counter Representations of Domestic Violence on Clydeside between the Two World Wars', *Labour History Review*, 69/2 (2004).

HUMPHRIES, J., 'Class Struggle and the Persistence of the Working Class Family', *Cambridge Journal of Economics*, 1/3 (1977).

—— 'The "Emancipation" of Women in the 1970s and 1980s: From the Latent to the Floating', *Capital and Class*, 20/6 (1983).

LAWRENCE, J., 'The British Sense of Class', *Journal of Contemporary History*, 35/2 (2000).

MOEHLING, C. M., 'Women's Work and Men's Unemployment', *Journal of Economic History*, 61/4 (2001).

MORGAN, C., 'Gender Constructions and Gender Relations in Cotton and Chain-Making in England', *Women's History Review*, 6/3 (1997).

—— 'Women's Work, Artisanal Discourse, and Community: A Response to Sheila Blackburn', *Women's History Review*, 10/1 (2001).

OLIVER, L., ' "No Hard-Brimmed Hats or Hat-Pins Please", Bolton Women Cotton Workers and the Game of Rounders, 1911–39', *Oral History*, 25/1 (1997).

POLLERT, A., 'Gender and Class Revisited; or, the Poverty of Patriarchy', *Sociology*, 30/4 (1996).

POPE, R. ' "Dole Schools": The North-East Lancashire Experience, 1930–39', *Journal of Educational Administration and History*, 9/2 (1977).

—— 'Education and the Young Unemployed: A Pre-War Experiment', *Journal of Further and Higher Education*, Vol. 2, No. 2, 1978.

ROSE, S. O., 'Gender Antagonism and Class Conflict: Exclusionary Strategies of Male Trade Unionists in Nineteenth Century Britain, *Social History*, 13/2 (1988).

—— 'Gender and Labor History: The Nineteenth-Century Legacy', *International Review of Social History*, 38/1 (1993).

—— 'Sex, Citizenship and the Nation in World War II Britain', *American Historical Review*, 103/4 (1998).

ROSS, E., 'Survival Networks: Women's Neighbourhood Sharing in London before World War I', *History Workshop Journal*, 15 (1983).

SAVAGE, M., 'Trade Unionism, Sex Segregation, and the State: Women's Employment in "New Industries" in Inter-war Britain', *Social History* 13/2 (1988).

SCOTT, P., 'The State, Internal Migration, and the Growth of New Industrial Communities in Interwar Britain', *English Historical Review*, 115/461 (2000).

—— 'Women, Other "Fresh" Workers, and the New Manufacturing Workforce of Interwar Britain', *International Review of Social History*, 45/3 (2000).

THANE, P., 'The Working-Class and State Welfare in Britain 1880–1914', *Historical Journal*, 27/4 (1984).

TOLLIDAY, S., 'Militancy and Organisation, Women Workers and Trade Unions in the Motor Trades in the 1930s', *Oral History*, 11/2 (1983).

VAN DER LINDEN, M., 'Connecting Household History and Labour History', *International Review of Social History*, 38/1 (1993).

VERDON, N., 'The Rural Labour Market in the Early Nineteenth Century: Women's and Children's Employment, Family Income, and the 1834 Poor Law Report', *Economic History Review*, 55/2 (2002).

WEBSTER, C., 'Healthy or Hungry Thirties?', *History Workshop Journal*, 13 (1982).

WHITESIDE, N., 'Counting the Cost: Sickness and Disability among Working People in an Era of Industrial Recession, 1920–39', *Economic History Review*, 40/2 (1987).

WHITSTON, K., 'Worker Resistance and Taylorism in Britain', *International Review of Social History*, 42/1 (1997).

ZIMMICK, M., 'Strategies and Strategems for the employment of women in the British Civil Service, 1919–1939', *Historical Journal*, 27/4 (1984).

PUBLISHED RESEARCH PAPERS

HAKIM, C., *Occupational Segregation: A Comparative Study of the Degree and Pattern of the Differentiation between Men and Women's Work in Britain, the United States and Other Countries*, Research Paper 9 (London: Department of Employment, 1979).

UNPUBLISHED DISSERTATIONS AND THESES

DARCY, G., 'Changes and Problems in Women's Work in England and Wales 1918–1939', Ph.D. thesis (London, 1984).

JONES, B., 'Social Life and the Built Environment: Council Housing in Brighton 1918–1940', MA dissertation (Sussex, 2003).

HIGGINS, N., 'The Changing Expectations and Realities of Marriage in the English Working Class, 1920–1960', Ph.D. thesis (Cambridge, 2003).

INNES, S., 'Love and Work: Feminism, Family and Ideas of Equality and Citizenship, Britain, 1900–39', Ph.D. thesis (Edinburgh, 1998).

LEWENHAK, S., 'Trade Union Membership among Women and Girls in the United Kingdom, 1920–1965', Ph.D. thesis (London, 1972).

MILCOY, K., 'Image and Reality: Working-Class Teenage Girls' Leisure in Bermondsey during the Interwar Years', D.Phil. thesis (Sussex, 2001).

TODD, S., 'Young Women, Employment, and the Family in Interwar England', D.Phil. thesis (Sussex, 2003).

WHITWORTH, L., 'Men, Women, Shops and "Little Shiny Homes": The Consuming of Coventry, 1930–1939', Ph.D. thesis (Warwick, 1997).

Index

Lightning Source UK Ltd.
Milton Keynes UK
UKHW04n1147260918
329479UK00007B/374/P

9 780199 282753